D1443586

UNC A to Z

UNC A to Z

What Every Tar Heel Needs to Know about the First State University

Nicholas Graham & Cecelia Moore

THE UNIVERSITY OF NORTH CAROLINA PRESS

Chapel Hill

Designed by Jamison Cockerham
Set in Scala, Scala Sans, and Quire Sans Fat
by Tseng Information Systems, Inc.

Cover illustration by Kristen Solecki

Manufactured in the United States of America

The University of North Carolina Press has been a member
of the Green Press Initiative since 2003.

LIBRARY OF CONGRESS CATALOGING-IN-PUBLICATION DATA
Names: Graham, Nicholas, (Nicholas M.), author. | Moore, Cecelia, author.
Title: UNC A to Z : what every Tar Heel needs to know about the
first state university / Nicholas Graham and Cecelia Moore.
Other titles: University of North Carolina A to Z
Description: Chapel Hill : The University of North Carolina Press,
2020. | Includes bibliographical references and index.
Identifiers: LCCN 2019046671 | ISBN 9781469655833
(cloth) | ISBN 9781469655840 (ebook)
Subjects: LCSH: University of North Carolina at Chapel Hill—
History—Dictionaries. | University of North Carolina at Chapel
Hill—Miscellanea—Dictionaries. | University of North Carolina
at Chapel Hill—Students—Social life and customs.
Classification: LCC LD3943 .G73 2020 | DDC 378.756/565—dc23
LC record available at https://lccn.loc.gov/2019046671

Contents

Introduction   *vii*

UNC A to Z   *1*

Acknowledgments   *241*

Sources   *243*

Index   *249*

Introduction

UNC A to Z is a book that we have wanted for a long time. Through our many years of work at Carolina, we have spent a great deal of time working on research projects with students, faculty, administrators, community members, and visiting scholars. Their questions ranged widely across subject matter and time, touching many aspects of UNC–Chapel Hill's more than 225-year history.

Whenever we work on state history, we rely extensively on William S. Powell's *North Carolina Gazetteer, Dictionary of North Carolina Biography,* and *Encyclopedia of North Carolina*. Researching North Carolina history without those books is unfathomable. Powell's reference books and the example he set as a thorough and accessible scholar were inspirations.

Just as we were deeply appreciative of the North Carolina reference trilogy, we were equally frustrated when it came to sources about UNC–Chapel Hill history. The same questions kept coming up: What are the origins of building names, significant firsts and anniversaries, and student traditions? and Who are the notable faculty, alumni, and administrators who had been at UNC–Chapel Hill in the past two centuries? We had no single source to turn to. Instead, we combed through published histories, vertical files, newspaper clippings, websites, and official documents. Since we had the resources of the Wilson Library collections at our disposal, we were usually able to get to the answers, but often it was not easy or accomplished quickly. Guided by Bill Powell's examples, and in response to the need for a book like this, a need that we see almost every day in our work on campus, we finally decided to write *UNC A to Z*.

UNC A to Z is a reference book. It was not our intention to introduce a bold, new interpretation of UNC–Chapel Hill history; nor was it our goal to produce a work that you would sit down and read cover to cover.

Though our research has involved extensive use of existing histories and primary sources, this book is not intended to replace the currently available narrative histories of UNC. The book we envisioned would be useful, educational, and fun for anyone who cares for or is curious about Carolina. It is a reference book that readers will be able to open to any page and find interesting, informative stories and facts about UNC–Chapel Hill history.

Selecting topics to include was one of the hardest parts of this process. We set out to produce a work that was comprehensive but that did not attempt to be exhaustive. All of the major buildings on campus are included, as are many significant groups, events, and traditions. There is a greater representation of recent history in the book because we believe the book will be more useful to today's readers if it addresses the origins and histories behind the university we know today.

Some readers might be surprised to find only a cursory treatment of two significant topics: academics and athletics. In discussing academics, we have included entries for the College of Arts and Sciences and for all of the professional schools. We chose not to include entries for each of UNC–Chapel Hill's many (and often notable) academic departments. The academic work in these departments, spanning decades and in some cases centuries, resists easy summarization. We felt that writing short entries for most academic units would oversimplify their work and leave out too many important people and movements. We refer readers instead to the many published histories of the university's academic departments and programs. The few programs we do include are those with notable origins or stories that we felt were especially significant in the greater history of the university.

While many different sports and venues are included in *UNC A to Z*, most are not discussed at length. This is certainly not due to a lack of interest or documentation. Even more so than academic programs, UNC–Chapel Hill sports are widely covered in a great deal of readily available published information, including histories of the football, basketball, and soccer teams. This also includes a wealth of information shared by the UNC–Chapel Hill Department of Athletics (the media guides alone are must-reads for anyone interested in Carolina sports history). We decided to focus more of our time on buildings and traditions that are not as well known or as well represented in existing histories.

Following the example of William S. Powell's *Encyclopedia of North Carolina*, we made the difficult decision not to include separate entries about people. A book that attempted to include entries on every prominent faculty member, administrator, athlete, and alumnus would end up being little more than a "Who's Who" of Carolina history and would be outdated as soon as it was published. We also found that, even without separate biographical entries, many of the most prominent figures in UNC–Chapel Hill history would still be represented in the book in the entries about buildings, programs, and campus traditions. So while there are no entries specifically about people, important figures like Frank Porter Graham, Wilson Caldwell, Sonja Haynes Stone, and Dean Smith are well represented in *UNC A to Z*.

Throughout the book, we refer to the University of North Carolina at Chapel Hill using the familiar, shortened terms "UNC–Chapel Hill," "Carolina," or simply "the university." In acknowledgment of the university's name change in 1963, when "at Chapel Hill" was added, references in this book to "UNC" refer to the university primarily during the period before the creation of the consolidated state university system.

As we were writing the entries for this book, university history was being studied, debated, and contested all around us. We began work on the encyclopedia shortly after Saunders Hall was renamed and continued amid ongoing protests and discussions about the Confederate Monument, building names, and Kenan Stadium. All of these events reaffirmed what we already knew: that the UNC–Chapel Hill community is passionate about campus history and that this history is unquestionably relevant to the university today. What has been surprising over the past few years is that, even with the dozens of books on UNC–Chapel Hill history that have already been published, so many topics still need further research. This is especially true about some of the topics that are most relevant to current discussions, including the history and legacy of slavery at the university, memorialization on campus, and the university's resistance to admitting women and African American students.

We hope that *UNC A to Z* will be a helpful and reliable foundation for learning about and understanding campus history but will also spark further research and writing. Rather than being the last word on UNC–Chapel Hill history, we envision this book as a launching pad for new projects, inspiring other researchers, writers, and especially students to explore and interpret Carolina history on their own.

UNC A to Z

Harmonyx, the a cappella group of UNC's Black Student Movement, performing at a concert in August 2018. Photo by Jon Gardiner, UNC–Chapel Hill.

Abernethy Hall. Located on South Columbia Street across from Fraternity Court, Abernethy Hall was originally built as a campus infirmary. Completed in 1907, the building was expanded in the 1930s to house additional beds and serve as a teaching facility for students in the medical school. Known for decades as the Infirmary, the name was changed to Abernethy Hall in 1945 in honor of alumnus Dr. Eric Abernethy, who served as the university physician from 1919 to 1933. The campus infirmary moved to a new building in 1946, and Abernethy has since housed a variety of different departments and offices, including the Evening College, the North Carolina High School Athletic Association, and the Playmakers Theatre ticket office. The Department of Public Policy later moved into the building. The American Indian Center was located in Abernethy Hall for many years. In 2019 Abernethy became the home for the newly established UNC Latinx Center.

A cappella. The tradition of campus groups singing without accompaniment goes back at least to the 1920s, when a group of students and local residents formed an a cappella choir, which performed traditional songs. A new breed of a cappella groups, inspired by barbershop quartet–style singing, began at UNC–Chapel Hill in 1978 with the founding of the Clef Hangers, an all-male vocal group that quickly became popular on campus. Many other groups followed, including the Loreleis, an all-women group formed in 1981, and Harmonyx, founded in 1995 as a subgroup of UNC's Black Student Movement. By the 1980s a cappella concerts were common on campus, and they have remained popular with students. The Clef Hangers' annual "Old Well Sing" performance on the last day of classes each spring has become a university tradition. In 2009 Clef Hangers member Anoop Desai received national attention when he appeared on the popular TV competition *American Idol*. In 2015 the Clef Hangers brought UNC–Chapel Hill a cappella to the White House, performing a song for President Barack Obama.

Ackland Art Museum. The Ackland Art Museum has one of the most complicated origin stories of any building on campus. When William Hayes Ackland, a lawyer and art collector from Tennessee, died in 1940, he left his estate to establish an art museum at a southern university. Ackland was an heir through his mother to the vast fortune of Isaac Franklin, a plantation owner and partner in Franklin and Armfield, the largest slave-trading operation in the United States. Ackland's mother inherited six Louisiana plantations, among other assets, that eventually became the site for the Louisiana State Penitentiary known as Angola. Duke University was Ackland's first choice for the museum; Duke ultimately decided to decline the gift. Though not stated publicly, it was thought that Duke was reluctant to accept Ackland's condition that his body be placed in a sarcophagus in the museum in his name. This decision left the gift without a clear home and led to nine years of legal battles, culminating in a decision by the U.S. Supreme Court. In 1949 the estate (and Ackland's body) was awarded to UNC. After several construction delays, the museum was finally dedicated in 1958.

UNC–Chapel Hill was in need of an art museum. The university's growing art collection was managed by the art department, and exhibits were often held in Person Hall. With the Ackland, the university had a professional museum staff and a teaching museum that could be used for the benefit of students as well as visitors to campus. The initial focus on the museum collection was European and American art; in the 1980s the collecting focus expanded to include more Asian art, which became a significant collecting area.

Activism. UNC–Chapel Hill students have often worked together to advocate for issues or push for change. Early in the university's history, students collectively petitioned the administration, for example, to complain about food on campus. In 1861 a group of students wrote to the university administration to ask that classes be canceled so that they could leave to join the Confederate army; the president and board denied their petition.

One of the earliest examples of students working together to protest national issues came in the 1930s, when students joined national anti-

UNC–Chapel Hill students march past Wilson Library in 1987 in support of efforts to urge the university to divest from companies that did business in South Africa. Durham Herald Co. Newspaper Photograph Collection, North Carolina Collection Photo Archives, Wilson Library.

war efforts and held rallies in Memorial Hall, some attracting hundreds of people. Student activists engaged in a statewide debate in the early 1960s in protest of North Carolina's Speaker Ban Law. Their challenge to the law eventually led to its being overturned.

Student activism was at its peak in Chapel Hill, and around the country, in the late 1960s and early 1970s. The founding of the Black Student Movement at UNC–Chapel Hill in 1967 led to increased advocacy for African American students and workers, including participation in strikes by cafeteria workers in 1969. However, the issue that galvanized students more than any other was opposition to the Vietnam War. Student activists held regular vigils on Franklin Street and joined other students across the country in teach-ins and walkouts. In 1970 an estimated 11,000 UNC–Chapel Hill students (well over half of the student body) left class as part of a nationwide effort to protest the war.

Although the numbers were not as great, UNC–Chapel Hill students remained politically active beyond the 1970s. In the 1980s students pushed the university to divest from companies in South Africa in protest of that country's apartheid government, in the 1990s students were instrumental in getting the university to agree to build a free-standing black cultural center (now the Stone Center), and in the 2010s student activists led the push to rename Saunders Hall and were at the forefront of efforts to remove the Confederate Monument from campus.

Adams School of Dentistry. The idea of dental education at UNC was discussed as early as 1921. Medical professionals around the state continued to advocate for a school of dentistry, successfully lobbying university administrators, who agreed to add the new program to the campus at Chapel Hill. In 1949 the North Carolina state legislature voted unanimously to establish and fund a school of dentistry at UNC. John Brauer, dean of the dental school at the University of Southern California, was hired to start the new program at Carolina. He worked quickly: hired in January, he developed a curriculum and hired faculty, and the School of Dentistry began admitting students by the fall 1950 term. The first classes were held in temporary Quonset huts on campus while a permanent home was being built (it would be completed in 1952).

Two early decisions have helped ensure the long-term success of UNC's dental school. Having faculty work as practicing dentists began early in the school's history. This decision was made in part to help attract talented practitioners to teach in the school but was also used to help supplement faculty salaries. The Dental Foundation of North Carolina was also established early in the history of the school. This privately supported endowment is used to fund scholarships, research, and faculty support.

The School of Dentistry grew rapidly, both in size and in reputation. It expanded with a research center in 1967 and dedicated a new building (now named Brauer Hall) in 1969. By 1973 one survey named the UNC–Chapel Hill School of Dentistry the top program in the country. The school added a Ph.D. program in 1995 and expanded facilities for research, teaching, and patient care, with the addition of Tarrson Hall in 2007 and the Koury Oral Health Sciences Building in 2002. In 2019, following a major gift from the estate of former Durham dentist Claude Adams III, the name of the school was formally changed to the Claude A. Adams Jr. and Grace Phillips Adams School of Dentistry in honor of Dr. Adams's parents.

One of the most tragic events in campus history occurred in 2015 when UNC–Chapel Hill dental students Deah Shaddy Barakat and Yusor Mohammed Abu-Salha were murdered in their off-campus apartment. (North Carolina State University student Razan Mohammad Abu-Salha was also killed.) To celebrate the lives of these students and honor their commitment to service, students in the School of Dentistry organized an annual day of community service called DEAH DAY (Directing Efforts and Honoring Deah and Yusor).

African, African American, and Diaspora Studies, Department of. This department has its roots in the 1960s-era activism of African American students at predominantly white universities. Still within the first decade of integration, such institutions faced increasing criticism from students about admissions policies, campus life, and academic programs. In December 1968, UNC's Black Student Movement presented a list of twenty-three demands to the chancellor that included a call for a department of African and Afro-American studies. In 1969 the faculty council endorsed such a curriculum and approved a major in 1970. With tracks in African studies and Afro-American studies, the curriculum had codirectors for its first fourteen years. It was made a department in 1997, twenty-two years after it was first proposed, becoming the Department of African Studies and Afro-American Studies.

The department adopted its current name in 2013. The change better reflected the department's research and teaching focus. The department offers a bachelor of arts degree with a major in African, African American, and diaspora studies, and a concentration in either African studies or African American and diaspora studies. At first housed in Alumni Hall, the department now resides in Battle Hall.

Alderman Residence Hall. Located on Raleigh Street behind the university president's house, Alderman was completed in 1937 as a dormitory for women, providing much-needed on-campus housing for the rapidly expanding population of female students. At first known simply as the Graduate Women's Dormitory, the dorm was named for former university president Edwin Anderson Alderman in 1941, probably in recognition of the role he played in arguing for the admission of the first women students at Carolina in 1897. A native of Goldsboro, North Carolina, and lifelong advocate of public education, Alderman joined the university faculty as a history professor in 1893. He was elected president in 1896 but served in that role for only a few years before leaving in 1900 to become president of Tulane University. Alderman was named president of the University of Virginia in 1904 and remained in that role until his death in 1931.

Alexander Residence Hall. Completed in 1939, Alexander was one of three new dormitories for men built using Public Works Administration funds. The building is named for Eben Alexander, a faculty member who taught Greek at Carolina in the late nineteenth and early twentieth centuries. He served for several years as U.S. ambassador to Greece, Serbia, and Romania under President Grover Cleveland. Alexander was in Greece for the revival of the modern Olympic games in 1896 and was instrumental in getting American athletes to participate.

Alma mater ("Hark the Sound"). UNC–Chapel Hill's school song was performed for the first time by the campus Glee Club at the graduation ceremony on June 2, 1897. The lyrics, written by student Walter Starr Myers, were a little different from those we know today. The song began, "Hark the sound of loyal voices / ringing sweet and true, / Telling Carolina's glories / Singing NCU." After that initial concert, the song was apparently not performed for several years. When it was revived in the early 1900s, it had the familiar first line, "Hark the sound of Tar Heel voices / Ringing clear and true." When it was sung at the 1904 University Day celebration, the *Tar Heel* reported that the song "was never sung so well before." By that point the lyrics were fixed and the song was a part of Carolina tradition. While the lyrics are unique to UNC–Chapel Hill, the melody is not. It is based on the old Italian tune "Amici," which has been adapted by many schools for their alma maters. It is believed to have been used first by Cornell students and was soon picked up by others. Both the University of Alabama and the University of Georgia use the tune from "Amici" for their school songs. The Carolina alma mater is usually followed immediately by the song "Tar Heels Born and Tar Heels Bred," which appears to have been adopted around the same time. It was first reported sung at a baseball game in 1903. The full lyrics for both songs follow.

Hark the Sound

> 1. *Hark the sound of Tar Heel voices*
> *Ringing clear and true*
> *Singing Carolina's praises*
> *Shouting N.C.U.*

Hail to the brightest Star of all
Clear its radiance shine
Carolina priceless gem,
Receive all praises thine.

2. *'Neath the oaks the sons true hearted*
Homage pay to thee
Time worn walls give back their echo
Hail to U.N.C.

3. *Though the storms of life assail us*
Still our hearts beat true
Naught can break the friendships formed at
Dear old N.C.U.

Tar Heels Born and Tar Heels Bred

I'm a Tar Heel born,
I'm a Tar Heel bred,
And when I die
I'm a Tar Heel dead.
So it's RAH, RAH, *Car'lina 'lina*
RAH, RAH, *Car'lina 'lina*
RAH, RAH, *Car'lina*
RAH! RAH! RAH!

All Carolina graduates know that the proper last line of the fight song is either "Go to Hell Duke!" or "Go to Hell State!," depending on which was the more heated rivalry when they were in school.

Alumni Association. The UNC Alumni Association (now the General Alumni Association) was formed in May 1843 with thirty-one members, the oldest from the class of 1801. Its first president was North Carolina governor John Motley Morehead (1796–1866), UNC class of 1817. The alumni often gathered at commencement and participated in the ceremonies. One of the earliest projects of the association was the erection of a memorial to former UNC president Joseph Caldwell in 1847. Alumni also played an active role in lobbying for the reopening of the university in 1875 and in the celebration of UNC's centennial in 1889.

In 1922 the Alumni Association opened an office on campus and hired its first staff. One of the initial efforts of the new employees was the creation of an alumni directory, a major project listing every known graduate of the university. As the number of alumni increased, so too did the work and impact of the Alumni Association. The association began publishing the *Alumni Review* in 1912 and began to take a more prominent role in raising money for and promoting the university. After working from different locations around campus over the years, the association dedicated the George Watts Hill Alumni Center in 1993.

The work of the Alumni Association is visible around campus in Alumni Hall (dedicated in 1901) and in Alumni Distinguished Professorships (first available in 1960).

Alumni Hall. Located on McCorkle Place, Alumni Hall was a gift from Carolina alumni. The Alumni Association launched a campaign for the building in 1895, the centennial of Carolina's first entering class 100 years earlier. When completed in 1901, the building, designed by architect Frank Wilburn and modeled on the neoclassical Boston Public Library, housed the offices of the president, other university officials, and the Alumni Association, as well as lecture rooms and laboratories. For many years, Commencement Day and University Day processions began at Alumni Hall before processing to Memorial Hall.

During the 1920s construction of Polk Place and buildings around it, the general contractor, T. C. Thompson and Brothers of Charlotte, as well as architects and other construction officials, including the resident architect, Arthur C. Nash, were housed in Alumni Hall. In the late 1920s university administrators moved to a renovated South Building. A half story was added to Alumni Hall in 1939. It has at various times housed the University of North Carolina Press; the Departments of Physics, Sociology, City and Regional Planning, and Anthropology; and the Research Laboratories of Archaeology.

American Indian Center. The American Indian Center was established in 2006 to promote and support American Indian scholarship and scholars and to incorporate Native American issues into the intellectual life of the university. The state of North Carolina has the largest American Indian population east of the Mississippi River, and Carolina committed itself to expanding its research, educational, and service efforts in this area. The center is a campus home for scholars and students, hosting programs such as the annual Michael D. Green Lecture in

The Area Health Education Center airplanes were an important way for UNC doctors to reach communities around the state. In the foreground is an AHEC plane at the Horace Williams Airport, ca. 1980s. News Services Photo Collection, University Archives, Wilson Library.

American Indian Studies and Elder-in-Residence program. Student engagement is supported through scholastic awards and an ambassadors program, among other initiatives. In addition, the center serves Native communities in North Carolina through a variety of initiatives and programs. Based in Abernethy Hall for many years, the center moved to Wilson Street in 2019.

Anderson Stadium. Opened in 2002 to serve as a home for the UNC women's softball team, Anderson Stadium is located off of Raleigh Road near the UNC System office. The stadium and its field (Williams Field) are named in honor of donors Eugene A. Anderson and Ken and Cheryl Williams.

Area Health Education Centers. In 1972 the UNC School of Medicine received federal funding to open Area Health Education Centers (AHEC) as part of an effort to improve health care across North Carolina by providing training and access to information for health care providers in rural areas. In 1974 the program was expanded with support from the North Carolina General Assembly. AHEC doctors and staff have been able to reach all parts of the state quickly through the university's Medical Air Service, which operated out of the Horace Williams Airport. The flight service moved to Raleigh-Durham International Airport in 2007.

The program also includes librarians at UNC's Health Sciences Library who provide support for health professionals seeking information and access to the latest medical research and information.

Argyle. In 1993 UNC–Chapel Hill basketball coach Dean Smith called on fashion designer Alexander Julian to help redesign the team's uniforms—Smith had liked what Julian did with the Charlotte Hornets uniforms. Julian came up with a variety of different design possibilities. Uncertain which way to go, he and Smith consulted Michael Jordan, who helped make the decision to select the uniforms that incorporated argyle elements. Julian later said that he saw the argyle as timeless and classy, the personification of "Carolina cool." It quickly caught on— after Carolina won the 1993 basketball national championship, *Sports Illustrated* published a commemorative issue with argyle stripes on the cover, demonstrating that the design was already an established part of the basketball team's visual identity. In 2015 the university embraced the design even further: with help from Nike, the department announced that elements of the signature argyle would be incorporated into the uniforms of all UNC–Chapel Hill athletic teams.

Asian American Students Association. Founded in 1989 as the Asian Students Association, the student group is a social and advocacy organization dedicated to promoting the interests and needs of UNC–Chapel Hill's Asian and Asian American students. The group was formed during a period when the university's Asian and Asian American student population was increasing rapidly. Early activities of the group included social gatherings and promotion of Asian culture on campus. Since the 2010s the Asian Students Association has been active in advocacy for an Asian American studies program at Carolina. In 2018 the organization adopted its current name.

Astronaut training. In 1959 the university welcomed a different type of student to campus when a group of astronauts arrived to learn celestial navigation at the Morehead Planetarium. The state-of-the-art planetarium was used to teach future astronauts to find their way using the stars, in case of equipment failure (which they needed for the *Apollo 12* and *Apollo 13* missions). Nearly every American astronaut between 1959 and 1975—including John Glenn and Neil Armstrong—trained at the planetarium.

Astronauts Edward Higgins White II (*left*) and James Alton McDivitt preparing for a Gemini mission, ca. 1965. UNC Image Collection, North Carolina Collection Photo Archives, Wilson Library.

Astronomy. Education in astronomy was on the minds of the university's founders even before the first brick was laid on the campus. In his 1792 "Plan of Education" for the newly established university, Samuel McCorkle wrote of the need for "the procurement of apparatus for Experimental Philosophy and Astronomy." It would take a few decades for his suggestion to be heeded. Joseph Caldwell, the first president of UNC, was also interested in astronomy and persuaded the trustees to appropriate money for new, state-of-the-art astronomical equipment, which Caldwell traveled to Europe in 1824 to purchase. The equipment was used by faculty, including Elisha Mitchell, whose arrival in Chapel Hill in 1818 is often marked as the beginning of serious scientific education at the UNC. The university had a professor of natural philosophy and astronomy as early as the 1830s.

Astronomical research at Carolina took a significant step forward in the 1940s when alumnus John Motley Morehead decided to provide a major gift to the university. He consulted Harvard astronomer Harlow Shapley, who declared North Carolinians to be "the most astronomically ignorant people in all America." Morehead decided to build a planetarium. The Morehead Planetarium opened in 1949 and has been an important education and research facility for UNC–Chapel Hill faculty and students ever since. Recognizing the growing importance of astronomy in teaching and research at Carolina, in 1973 the Department of Physics was reorganized as the Department of Physics and Astronomy.

Athletics. According to historian Kemp Plummer Battle, early students in Chapel Hill had little interest in athletics, choosing to spend their free time taking walks and carriage rides, hunting, and playing music. In cooler weather some students played a game called "bandy," a sort of predecessor to field hockey. By the mid-nineteenth century there was enough interest in sports that the university set aside a dedicated athletic field, located roughly in the area now occupied by Hamilton and Manning Halls. The university's first organized athletic team was the "University Club of Chapel Hill," a baseball team that played a few games in 1866 and 1867. Following the university's reopening in 1875 there was renewed interest in organized sports, and Battle reports that students were playing baseball and football in the 1880s. They organized a varsity football team, which played its first intercollegiate game in 1888. Intercollegiate baseball began on campus in 1891, while basketball was not organized as a varsity sport until 1910. Other early-twentieth-century varsity sports included tennis, track and field, wrestling, and golf. Swimming and diving became varsity sports in 1939, and soccer and lacrosse were added after World War II. Fencing is the most recent varsity sport at UNC–Chapel Hill, added in 1967.

Women students in Chapel Hill formed the Women's Athletic Association in 1934 to encourage exercise and intramural sports. Women students were increasingly active in club intramurals in the 1950s and began competing against other schools in sports, including basketball and field hockey. Women's athletics at UNC–Chapel Hill and nationwide were transformed in the early 1970s with the creation of the Association for Intercollegiate Athletics for Women (UNC–Chapel Hill was a charter member) and passage of Title IX of the Educational Amendments Act of 1972. Multiple women's varsity sports began during this period, including basketball, tennis, gymnastics, golf, field hockey, volleyball, swimming, and fencing.

Like many of its peer institutions, UNC–Chapel Hill has often struggled with the balance between athletics and academics. The university has faced multiple scandals involving athletics, including the Dixie Classic gambling allegations in the 1960s and accusations of academic irregularities benefiting athletes in the early 2010s. In the 1930s university president Frank Porter Graham issued a proposal that was intended to prevent an overemphasis on intercollegiate sports at the university. The Graham Plan would limit recruiting, abolish scholarships and postseason play, and place athletics under the control of the faculty. Although the plan was supported by administrators at other schools, it never came close to being adopted—athletics were already too popular with students and alumni. Graham was not the last UNC leader to push for athletic reform. William C. Friday, longtime president of the UNC System, was one of the cofounders in 1989 of the Knight Commission on Intercollegiate Athletics. While helping raise awareness of issues faced by student athletes, its efforts had little effect on curbing the growth and popularity of athletics at UNC and elsewhere.

In the early 2010s the athletic program was at the center of a long-running academic scandal. While the university did not receive major sanctions from the NCAA, the accusations and investigations lasted for many years and brought significant negative attention to the university and its teams.

From the late twentieth century through the present, UNC–Chapel Hill has consistently had one of the most successful university athletic programs in the country. While men's basketball and women's soccer often receive the most attention for their multiple national championships, they are hardly the only championship programs at the school. UNC has also won team NCAA championships in women's basketball, field hockey, men's and women's lacrosse, men's soccer, and men's and women's tennis. Tar Heel athletes have won individual championships in tennis, fencing, golf, gymnastics, swimming, cross-country, track and field, and wrestling. In 1994 UNC–Chapel Hill won the Sears Cup, which honored success across all collegiate athletic programs.

Atlantic Coast Conference. UNC–Chapel Hill was one of the charter members of the Atlantic Coast Conference, formed in 1953 along with six other former Southern Conference members frustrated with that conference's ban on postseason football. (The others were Clemson, Duke, Maryland, N.C. State, South Carolina, and Wake Forest.)

By 2018 the university fielded teams in thirteen men's and fourteen women's varsity sports in the ACC and had won more than 250 conference championships, the most of any of the member schools.

Avery Residence Hall. Opened in the fall of 1958, Avery was built at the same time as Parker and Teague Residence Halls. Avery, located at the end of Stadium Drive, was a first step in expanding campus housing toward South Campus. The building is named for William Waightstill Avery, a Burke County native who graduated from Carolina in 1837. Avery was a lawyer, an occupation that led to trouble in 1851 when he was attacked by a man involved in one of his cases. A week later Avery shot the man in a courtroom, killing him instantly. He was acquitted on the grounds of "provocation" and temporary insanity. During the Civil War Avery represented North Carolina in the Confederate Congress before joining the army. He died from wounds received in battle. It is not clear why the UNC Board of Trustees decided in the 1950s to name a campus dorm for Avery.

Aycock Family Medicine Center. Located on Manning Drive adjacent to Fordham Boulevard, the center is home to the Department of Family Medicine and its clinics. UNC–Chapel Hill has one of the top-ranked programs in the country for training family physicians. The state legislature funded the building, which was named in honor of William Brantley Aycock, alumnus, long-time faculty member, law school dean, and chancellor from 1957 to 1964. As chancellor, Aycock presided over a landmark expansion period, bringing significant growth in the numbers of students, buildings, medical facilities, and research programs. He brought the men's basketball program through a bribery scandal and NCAA sanctions and hired a young Dean Smith with the goal of restoring integrity to athletics. He took over just two years after the first African American undergraduates enrolled at the university and led a campus that was slowly (and often reluctantly) adapting to a fully integrated student body. After retiring as chancellor, Aycock returned to the law school faculty, where he argued for the importance of academic freedom against North Carolina's Speaker Ban Law.

Aycock Residence Hall. Completed in 1924, Aycock was one of three new dorms built on the east side of campus (Graham and Lewis are the others). It was named in 1928 for Charles Brantley Aycock. At the time

Aycock was one of the most revered men in the state. A member of the UNC class of 1880, Aycock was a successful lawyer and served as North Carolina governor from 1901 to 1905. He was known as the education governor for his work to expand public schools for white students in North Carolina. Aycock was also known as a skilled speaker. He traveled the state during the 1898 "white supremacy" campaign, helping spread fear and resentment of African Americans among white voters. His efforts were successful, and he was rewarded by Democratic Party leaders, who nominated him for governor a few years later. As governor, Aycock helped pass new laws that effectively disenfranchised African American voters and established a system of racial segregation and discrimination that would take more than a half century to dismantle. In recognition of Aycock's undeniably racist speeches and actions, three North Carolina universities have chosen to remove Aycock's name from buildings on their campuses: East Carolina University and Duke University renamed residence halls in 2015 and UNC-Greensboro renamed its Aycock Auditorium in 2016.

B

Baity Hill Graduate and Family Housing. This housing complex, completed in 2005, sits on land once owned by Herman G. and Elizabeth Chesley Baity. Their family home now serves as the student center there. Over a number of years the Baitys sold more than fifty acres to the university, including the areas now occupied by the Dean Smith Center, Koury Natatorium, and part of the Kenan-Flagler Business School. The university purchased the home and surrounding nine acres in 1991. The complex was designed to replace Odum Village, Carolina's first purpose-built family housing complex.

Herman G. Baity, UNC class of 1917, was a prominent faculty member who earned the first ever doctor of science degree in sanitary engineering from Harvard University. At Carolina he was dean of engineering until that program was transferred to North Carolina State College of Agriculture and Engineering in Raleigh (now North Carolina State University). Baity convinced university leaders that clean water was a public health issue and succeeded in keeping his program at the university within what is now the Gillings School of Global Public Health. In the 1950s he was director of the environmental division of the World Health Organization, helping eradicate malaria. His work was honored with the naming of the Herman G. Baity Environmental Laboratory, dedicated in 1990, adjacent to McGavran-Greenberg Hall.

Elizabeth Chesley Baity, UNC class of 1929, taught anthropology at Carolina. She also wrote poetry and children's books, including *Man Is a Weaver* (1942) and *Americans before Columbus* (1951).

Baseball was one of the earliest sports in which UNC played against other schools. In December 1866, as baseball was catching on across the Southeast following the Civil War, a group from Carolina known as the

UNC baseball team on McCorkle Place, ca. 1890s. UNC Image Collection, North Carolina Collection Photo Archives, Wilson Library.

University Club of Chapel Hill defeated the Pioneer Team in Raleigh. The university team played again, against another Raleigh club, in early 1867. This early interest in baseball appears to have faded as the student population dwindled prior to the university's closing in 1870. Baseball came back to Carolina in 1891 when a varsity team was formed and intercollegiate competition began. The baseball team soon found itself overshadowed by the rising popularity of other sports. In 1916 members of the Carolina team wrote a letter to the *Tar Heel* complaining of inferior treatment compared to the football and basketball teams. Nonetheless, the baseball team did well, winning the Southern Conference several times in the 1930s and 1940s under Coach Bunn Hearn.

The early 2000s saw the most successful run in UNC–Chapel Hill baseball history: the team made it to the College World Series six times in seven seasons, going all the way to the final round in 2006 and 2007 before falling to Oregon State both times. Several UNC baseball alums have gone on to play Major League Baseball, including Walt Weiss, B. J. Surhoff, Brian Roberts, and Andrew Miller. One of the best-known baseball players from the university is probably Archibald "Moonlight" Graham, brother of Frank Porter Graham, who graduated in 1901. After several years in the minor leagues, Graham was called up to the New York Giants. He played only one inning in the major leagues and never got a chance to bat. His story caught the attention of author W. P. Kinsella, who made Graham a character in his novel *Shoeless Joe*. Graham's story got even more attention when the novel was made into the 1989 movie *Field of Dreams*.

Carolina baseball has an interesting connection with George Steinbrenner, former owner of the New York Yankees. Steinbrenner's daughter and son-in-law are Carolina alums. In 1977, 1979, and 1981 the Yankees played exhibition games against the Tar Heels in Chapel Hill. In 2006 Steinbrenner gave $1 million toward the renovation of Boshamer Stadium. The area outside of the renovated stadium was named the Steinbrenner Family Courtyard.

Basketball was first organized as a varsity sport at the university in late 1910, with the team playing its first game on January 27, 1911, a victory over Virginia Christian College. The team played its home games in Bynum Gymnasium. Though basketball initially was not as popular as football and baseball, the university developed a successful basketball program in the 1920s, winning the Southern Conference several times and completing an undefeated season in 1924. It was during this era that a sportswriter, commenting on the fast play and white uniforms of the team, gave them the unofficial nickname "White Phantoms," which would continue to be used through the 1950s.

Even amid growing concerns on campus in the 1930s about the role of athletics in the university, the basketball team continued to have success. The games moved into a larger space in the new Woollen Gym in 1938. UNC–Chapel Hill was one of the founding members of the Atlantic Coast Conference in 1953 and built intense and lasting rivalries with Duke and N.C. State. The program rose to national prominence in 1957 when a team of players primarily from New York won the national championship in a thrilling triple overtime victory over Kansas.

The basketball program faced a series of challenges in the early 1960s, including NCAA investigations, the departure of coach Frank McGuire for the NBA, and a gambling scandal at the popular Dixie Classic tournament. With increased scrutiny on college sports in general and especially basketball, university administrators decided not to go after another high-profile coach and instead simply promoted a young assistant coach named Dean Smith.

Despite some challenging years early in his tenure—students hanged Smith in effigy after a particularly bad loss in 1965—Smith would go on to become one of the most revered coaches in basketball history, leading the Tar Heels for thirty-one seasons. He led the team to multiple ACC championships and NCAA Final Four games and won national championships in 1982 and 1993. His national reputation was evident in his selection as coach for the 1976 Olympic basketball team. When UNC–Chapel Hill opened a new, much larger basketball arena in 1986, it was named for Smith.

Smith was instrumental in recruiting African American players to the basketball team for the first time. Willie Cooper, who played on the freshman team in 1964, was the first African American basketball player at UNC. He was followed a few years later by Charles Scott, who became the first African American varsity basketball player at Carolina and had a very successful career at UNC.

Carolina basketball entered a new era in 2003 with the hiring of Roy Williams, an alumnus and former assistant coach under Dean Smith. Tar Heel teams led by Williams won national championships in 2005, 2009, and 2017.

The number of retired and honored jerseys hanging from the Dean Smith Center rafters is evidence of the many great Carolina basketball players over the years. Some of UNC–Chapel Hill's most honored players include player-of-the-year award winners Lennie Rosenbluth, Phil Ford, Antawn Jamison, and Tyler Hansborough. Many former Tar Heel stars, including James Worthy, Vince Carter, and Danny Green, have gone on to long and successful NBA careers. But the university's best-known player (and almost certainly its most recognizable alumnus) is Michael Jordan, who played at Carolina from 1981 to 1984. Beginning with his championship-winning shot as a freshman and continuing through an outstanding NBA career, Jordan became one of the most popular athletes in the world. Even decades after his playing career, Jordan remained popular at Carolina, with fans wearing #23 jerseys to games and his "Jumpman" silhouette appearing on the team's uniforms.

UNC women students first organized a basketball team in 1930. Called the Tar Heelettes by the *Daily Tar Heel*, they played other local club teams. The first women's intercollegiate game was played a few years later. Women's basketball was established as a varsity sport in 1971. The team won its first ACC championship in 1984. In 1986 Sylvia

Michael Jordan going up for a dunk in a game
against the University of Virginia in 1983.
Photo by Hugh Morton. Hugh Morton Photo Collection,
North Carolina Collection Photo Archives, Wilson Library.

Hatchell was hired as head coach. Hatchell would become one of the most successful women's basketball coaches of all time, leading the Tar Heels to a national championship in 1994 and multiple ACC championships. She was inducted into the Naismith Memorial Basketball Hall of Fame in 2013.

Battle Hall. Built in 1912 as a dormitory, Battle Hall was one of the three buildings on the northwest corner of McCorkle Place on Franklin Street (Vance and Pettigrew Halls are attached). Converted to office space in the late 1960s, Battle Hall housed the university's personnel department for many years. It is one of only a few examples of a building named for a living person. Kemp Plummer Battle, who served as university president from 1876 to 1891, was still on the faculty when the building opened. An 1849 graduate of Carolina, Battle was active in the campaign to reopen the university in 1875. After he left the college presidency he was appointed Alumni Professor of History, a position he held until his death in 1919. Battle helped begin graduate study in history at UNC and worked to build the library's collections of historic artifacts and manuscripts. His two-volume *History of the University of North Carolina* (1907–12) is still considered an essential source for understanding the early history of the university.

Battle Park is the wooded area on the east side of campus extending from the Forest Theatre and encompassing the Order of the Gimghoul's Hippol Castle. The park is named for former university president Kemp Plummer Battle, who was fond of walking in the woods and who forged many of the trails that are still used today. Battle named many of the notable trees and overlooks in the park. Names like Trysting Poplar and Flirtation Knoll hint at the use of the park by students for romantic encounters.

The park has passed through several owners over the years. Part of the initial acquisition of land by the university in the 1790s, much of the park land was sold in the 1870s to pay off debts incurred during and after the Civil War. It was purchased by alumnus Paul Cameron and later passed into the hands of faculty member Horace Williams, who explored the idea of building a housing development on the property. The land was eventually purchased by the Order of the Gimghoul, who used part of it as the site of their castle. The order deeded several large tracts of land back to the university on the condition that it be used as a park. In 1971 the park, along with the adjacent residential areas in the Chapel Hill Historic District, was placed on the National Register of Historic Places. Since 2004 Battle Park has been under the management of the North Carolina Botanical Garden.

Beard Hall has been the home of the School of Pharmacy since its dedication in 1960. The *Daily Tar Heel* reported that approximately 1,000 people attended the dedication, including a large number of pharmacists. The building is named for John Grover Beard, a native of Kernersville who came to Chapel Hill as an undergraduate and never left. He earned a degree in pharmacy in 1909 and was hired as an assistant instructor right after graduation. He was a full professor by 1919 and served as dean from 1931 until his death in 1946. In 2015 the School of Pharmacy began renovations in Beard Hall to enable students and faculty to better incorporate technology in their teaching and research.

Beat Dook Parade. The practice of misspelling the name of UNC–Chapel Hill's rival as "Dook" probably began in the 1930s, when "Beat Dook" banners were common at pep rallies. The annual Beat Dook Parade, sponsored by Pi Kappa Alpha fraternity, began in 1948 with a procession of twenty-eight cars and floats. The parade, held on the weekend of the UNC-Duke football game, traveled down the main block of Franklin Street. The number of floats grew steadily, as did the number of spectators, with thousands turning out to watch the parade each year. The 1962 parade was an especially rowdy one, drawing the criticism of Chapel Hill officials and university administrators. Several floats were said to be offensive and in bad taste—examples included floats with a large screw ("Screw Dook") and an outhouse ("Dump on Dook"). The sponsoring fraternities were reprimanded, and campus administrators threatened to cancel the parade. The fraternities worked out an arrangement where their floats would be submitted for official review prior to entering the parade. With increased scrutiny and caution, the parade continued through the mid-1990s.

Bell tower. The university's iconic bell tower was dedicated on November 26, 1931. The official name—Morehead-Patterson Bell Tower—recognizes the families of the two men who donated the funds to build it in the heart of campus. John Motley Morehead, UNC class of 1891,

Float from
the 1973 Beat
Dook Parade.
Yackety Yack,
1974, North
Carolina
Collection,
Wilson Library.

and his cousin Rufus Lenoir Patterson II first tried to place a bell tower on top of South Building but were turned down. They then suggested the center of Polk Place, where the flagpole now stands, but the architectural plan for the quad called for it to remain open space. In 1930 they asked the university to include it in the plan for the new Memorial Hall but were eventually persuaded to accept the site south of Wilson Library.

Located at the north end of Kenan Stadium, the bell tower rises 172 feet. Its belfry originally contained a carillon of twelve manually operated bells. Two additional bells were added in the 1980s and the system was mechanized. The bells chime the hour and quarter-hours and play songs on special occasions. In a letter to John Motley Morehead a few weeks after the tower dedication, university president Frank Porter Graham wrote that the "chimes are becoming part of the atmosphere and the spirit of the place."

Interior of the Morehead-Patterson Bell Tower, ca. 1965, showing
a student manually ringing the bells. UNC Photo Lab Collection,
North Carolina Collection Photo Archives, Wilson Library.

A student serves as master bell ringer, an honor that comes with a
key to the door and the chance to play "Carolina Victory" on home football game days. It is a campus tradition for seniors to climb the narrow
spiral staircase to the top at the end of the year. Many of their signatures
fill the inside walls.

Benefactors. Even though the University of North Carolina has always
been a public university, state financial support has varied greatly over
time. At the beginning the state provided no direct support. Instead, it
authorized the university to charge tuition and to collect on the state's
unpaid debts and escheats, the estates of people who died without legal
heirs. The legislature did make a loan of $10,000 toward construction
of the first building, Old East, which they eventually agreed to turn into
a gift. There was no direct appropriation until 1881, and not until the
1920s did the university began to receive regular appropriations to operate the institution.

What has been consistent throughout its history is that tuition and
public funds have not been sufficient to meet the need. Therefore, the

university has always relied on benefactors—those people or entities that make gifts of one form or another. The practice began with eight Orange County landowners who donated some 700 acres to serve as the site for the campus and town of Chapel Hill. At the same time, donations by Benjamin Smith and Charles Gerrard of land claims received in payment for their service in the Revolutionary War eventually funded the construction of Smith Hall (now historic Playmakers Theatre) and Gerrard Hall.

The first significant cash gift was from Thomas Person, who gave Carolina 1,050 silver dollars in 1796 to complete construction of the building that now bears his name. While throughout the nineteenth century the university president and trustees traveled throughout the state to solicit donations, campus leaders did not start a formal fund-raising program until the mid-twentieth century.

Some benefactors gave in an involuntary way. The Smith lands, for example, were not university property until the United States expropriated the area from the Chickasaws through treaties in the early 1800s. Gifts that enriched the university from antebellum donors originated largely from the profits of enslaved labor, while funds from the sale of enslaved people in escheats also provided significant income before the Civil War. Others intentionally provided for the university in their wills, some of which made a significant difference in the ability of university leaders to strengthen academic programs. Two noteworthy bequests were from Mary Ruffin Smith, who bequeathed a family plantation in Chatham County to the university to support scholarships for indigent students, and Mary Lily Kenan Flagler Bingham, whose will established the Kenan Professorships.

In the early twentieth century Carolina began to build a modern re-search university. Leaders sought support from northern philanthro-pists, including Andrew Carnegie, George Peabody, and the Rockefeller family. In North Carolina a generation of industrialists made significant investments in the university, including the Hill family of Durham, the Hanes family of Winston-Salem, the Kenans, and the Moreheads. As the university expanded its medical school and health care programs in the 1950s and 1960s, families like the Linebergers and the Loves contributed to the facilities. Their gifts augmented the major investments that the people of North Carolina made through state appropriations. Some names are virtually unknown because they do not appear on the landscape. Joseph Ezekiel Pogue, an alumnus who made his fortune in petroleum exploration, left his $11 million estate to Carolina as an unrestricted endowment. It has been used in many ways over the years, including for library acquisitions, scholarships, and research.

Berryhill Hall opened in 1971 to provide much-needed classroom and laboratory space for the growing School of Medicine. It was named in 1973 for W. Reece Berryhill, longtime dean of the school. Berryhill, from Charlotte, graduated from UNC in 1921. He practiced medicine for several years before returning to Chapel Hill as director of student health. He served as dean of the School of Medicine from 1941 to 1964, a period that saw the school grow from a two-year to a four-year program and expand its statewide outreach. In 2017, citing the need for a building that would provide more flexibility and an improved technical infrastructure, the university announced a plan to replace the aging Berryhill Hall.

Bingham Hall was completed in 1929 for use by the School of Commerce. It shared the same architectural style as nearby Murphey and Saunders Halls. Bingham housed the Department of English from the 1950s through the early 1970s, followed by the Department of Speech (now the Department of Communication). The building is named for Robert Hall Bingham, an 1857 graduate of UNC. Bingham was a Civil War veteran and an educator, serving as headmaster of the Bingham School in Hillsborough, which was founded by his grandfather. Bingham was known as an especially enthusiastic alumnus. He was a prolific speaker and writer on education, race, and the Civil War. His article "An Ex-Slave Holder's View of the Negro Question in the South," published in *Harper's* in 1900, outlined his beliefs in white supremacy and racial purity and argued against African American suffrage.

Black Student Movement. Formed in 1967 by a group of around forty African American students, the Black Student Movement (BSM) has grown into one of the largest student organizations at UNC–Chapel Hill. The group was founded by students frustrated with the campus chapter of the NAACP and by lack of representation in student government. Led by Preston Dobbins, one of the founders of the BSM and its first president, and cofounder Reggie Hawkins, the group was an outspoken advocate for African American students and workers on campus. In December 1968 the BSM presented Chancellor J. Carlyle Sitter-

Black Student Movement members.
Yackety Yack, 1976, North Carolina Collection, Wilson Library.

son with a list of twenty-three demands for improved access, resources, and support for African American students, campus workers, and local African Americans, drawing a point-by-point response from the university administration. The BSM was especially active in the spring 1969 cafeteria workers' strike, supporting the workers as they advocated for improved wages and working conditions.

In 1969 the BSM began publishing *Black Ink*, a monthly newspaper dedicated to coverage of African American students, culture, and issues on campus. The BSM remained active in protests and organized advocacy throughout the years, with members participating in anti-apartheid demonstrations on campus in the 1980s and leading an ultimately successful campaign in the 1990s for a freestanding black cultural center on campus. In celebration of the organization's thirtieth anniversary in 1997, the BSM presented Chancellor Michael Hooker with a revised list of demands.

As the BSM grew along with the number of African American students on campus, it remained an active voice for student and community needs but also began to serve as a parent organization for student performing arts and cultural groups, including the UNC Gospel Choir, Opeyo! Dance Company, Ebony Readers/Onyx Theatre, and the a cappella group Harmonyx. The BSM celebrated its fiftieth anniversary in

2017 with a celebration, symposium, fund-raising campaign, and a renewed commitment to advocate for African American students at UNC.

Blood on the Old Well is the title of a book by Sarah Watson Emery. Published in 1963, the book contains a series of scandalous accusations against the university. Writing about "the forces of moral and spiritual disintegration on display" at the university, Emery accused faculty of anti-Christian and anti-American teaching and alleged that there were a number of mysterious deaths on the campus. Emery was a resident of Chapel Hill for over a decade while her husband taught in the philosophy department. *Blood on the Old Well* contains extreme examples of the kinds of accusations that were often directed at UNC during the 1950s and 1960s, when the university was perceived as being too liberal and said by some to be subjecting its students to Communist influences.

Blue Jeans Day. In the 1980s and early 1990s, as part of Gay Awareness Week on campus, the Carolina Gay and Lesbian Association announced "Blue Jeans Day." On that day all gay and lesbian students and their allies were encouraged to wear jeans. In response, according to a 1983 *Daily Tar Heel* editorial, large numbers of straight students consciously wore khakis or corduroys on that day. The event was an attempt to encourage all students to consider how simple daily choices could subject them to discrimination and stereotyping.

Board of trustees. Each constituent institution of the UNC System has a board of trustees that advises the chancellor on the management and development of the university. UNC–Chapel Hill's board of trustees has thirteen persons: eight are elected by the UNC Board of Governors, four members are appointed by the North Carolina General Assembly, and the remaining member is the president of the student government, ex officio. The board chair is elected by board members for a two-year appointment. The appointed members serve four-year terms and are allowed to serve two consecutive terms.

The university has had a board of trustees since it was chartered in 1789, but its structure and responsibilities have changed over time. The 1789 charter provided for a forty-member board selected by the North Carolina General Assembly, with the governor as board president. The board's responsibilities included financial and capital management. This structure remained roughly in place until 1932, although some aspects changed. Board members had life memberships until 1868, when a new state constitution provided for eight-year terms and membership from each county, which eventually made the board 100 members. From 1868 to 1873 the State Board of Education selected members; thereafter, selection returned to the General Assembly. Under consolidation in 1932 the board of trustees assumed oversight of three institutions: the University of North Carolina, North Carolina State College of Agriculture and Engineering (North Carolina State University), and the North Carolina College for Women (now UNC-Greensboro). It continued to have 100 members, but 10 seats were reserved for women. The reorganization of 1971 into the UNC System replaced that board with the UNC System Board of Governors.

Bondurant Hall was known for several decades as the Medical Sciences Research Building. Completed in 1962, it was the first building at the School of Medicine devoted primarily to research. In 2003 the building closed for extensive renovations. It was rededicated in 2006 and named for Dr. Stuart Bondurant, who served as dean of the School of Medicine from 1979 to 1994. Bondurant Hall contains classrooms and administrative offices. With a new facade modeled after the School of Medicine's first building, MacNider Hall, it now serves as the "front door" to UNC–Chapel Hill's medical and health education programs.

Book Exchange. The Book Exchange was a university-operated campus store that opened in 1915 after students and faculty complained about textbook prices in local stores. Housed in the Campus Y building, the store focused primarily on textbooks but also sold school supplies. Store offerings and services changed over the years. In the 1930s the Book Exchange offered typewriter cleaning and repair services. The fact that the store was run by the university appeared to do little to alleviate complaints over prices. Stories and editorials frequently appeared in the *Daily Tar Heel* complaining about prices and overcrowding at the "Book-Ex." The bookstore was located in the basement of Steele Building in the 1950s and 1960s before moving to much more spacious quarters in the new Daniels Building when it opened in 1968.

Boshamer Stadium is the home of the Carolina baseball team. Opened in 1972, Boshamer replaced Emerson Field, the longtime home of Tar Heel baseball and other sports. The stadium is named for Cary C. Boshamer, an alumnus and former football player who had a successful career in the textile industry in Gastonia, North Carolina. He was an active supporter of the university, funding an endowed professorship in his name and a scholarship. The UNC baseball team moved to the site of Boshamer Stadium in 1966, playing games at the new field in front of a few fans on temporary stands. When the new stadium opened in time for the 1972 season, it included seats for more than 2,000 fans. The stadium underwent a significant renovation following the 2007 season, expanding seating to 4,100 and adding modern amenities. When it re-opened in 2009 the playing field was named for supporter and former player Vaughn Bryson and his wife, Nancy, and the expanded courtyard area was named for the family of New York Yankees owner George Steinbrenner, who donated money to support the renovation.

Bowman Gray Memorial Pool. Carolina students were excited when the Bowman Gray Memorial Pool opened on April 15, 1938. There had been no pool on campus since the closing of the pool in Bynum Gymnasium in 1924. The new pool was built as part of Woollen Gym. When it opened, the *Daily Tar Heel* proclaimed it to be the "largest indoor swimming pool south of Philadelphia." While primarily built for recreational swimming, the pool was also used by the UNC swimming teams. While the U.S. Navy pre-flight school was on campus during World War II, it was used for training exercises by navy cadets. The pool was one of many contested sites on campus when the first African American students enrolled in 1951. Harvey Beech, who entered the UNC School of Law that year, recalled receiving a swimming card when he first enrolled, only to have it taken away, told that it was given to him "by mistake."

The pool is named for alumnus Bowman Gray Sr., who had a successful career at R. J. Reynolds Tobacco Company. After Gray's death in 1935 his family gave money for the construction of the university pool and supported multiple institutions in Winston-Salem, especially Wake Forest University.

Boxing was a popular varsity and intramural sport for a few decades in the early twentieth century. It began informally in 1924 with a match between UNC student boxers and soldiers from Fort Bragg. The university hired a boxing coach the following year, and it was soon established as a varsity sport. By the 1940s campus administrators began to consider dropping varsity boxing. Attendance was waning, there were continued concerns about student safety, and UNC was having a hard time scheduling matches because few nearby schools had boxing teams. Varsity boxing was discontinued in 1948.

Brauer Hall has been the home of the School of Dentistry since it opened in 1969. Originally known simply as the Dental Education Building, it was renamed in 1972 for John C. Brauer, the founding dean of the School of Dentistry. Brauer was dean of the dental school at the University of Southern California when he was hired in 1950 to start the program at UNC. He designed the curriculum, hired staff, and welcomed the first students within a year. Brauer was an innovator in dental education. His plan to have faculty also serve as practicing dentists has inspired similar programs around the country. He also helped further dental education in the state by installing closed-circuit television, enabling far-flung dentists to observe complicated procedures at the school. Anticipating the need for private support for the school, he helped start the Dental Foundation of North Carolina, which now provides more than $2 million a year to fund scholarships, research, and faculty support. When Brauer retired in 1966, the School of Dentistry was recognized as one of the top dental schools in the country.

Bricks. Throughout the nineteenth and early twentieth centuries all of the walkways on campus were covered in gravel (or, to be more precise, Chapel Hill grit). In the mid-1940s, inspired by the brick walkways at Colonial Williamsburg, the university announced a plan to create Williamsburg-style brick walks. While some alums lamented the loss of the old, dusty paths, the plan was recognized as an improvement over the unpaved walkways, which frequently covered shoes in dust or mud, depending on the weather. The bricks brought a new challenge in the regular maintenance they required. Stray tree roots and construction projects result in frequent repairs to the paths, as do souvenir-seeking students—a 2015 *Daily Tar Heel* article described the common practice of removing bricks as mementos of the campus. A facilities staff member estimated that in an average week more than 100 bricks had to be replaced.

Brinkhous-Bullitt Building. The towering Brinkhous-Bullitt Building was completed in 1973 to house research facilities for the School of Medicine. Originally known as the Preclinical Education Building, it

UNC Facilities staff members Clifton Jones (*left*) and Claiborne Baker
work on repairing the brick walkways around the Old Well, 2009.
News Services Photo Collection, University Archives, Wilson Library.

received its current name in 1983 in honor of two former faculty members and chairs of the Department of Pathology: James B. Bullitt and his successor, Kenneth M. Brinkhous. For many years, the Caduceus, the health sciences bookstore, was located in Brinkhous-Bullitt.

Brooks Computer Science Building. The Frederick P. Brooks Jr. Computer Science Building was dedicated in 2008. It adjoins Sitterson Hall and is home to UNC–Chapel Hill's Department of Computer Science. Brooks, a North Carolina native, was working at IBM in 1963 when he came to campus to deliver a lecture on computer science. He caught the attention of campus administrators, who hired Brooks the following year to begin a computer science department at the university, only the second in the country. Already renowned for his software development at IBM, Brooks was an influential writer, teacher, and administrator. His book *The Mythical Man-Month: Essays on Software Engineering* (1975) is an important contribution to the teaching of software project management. Brooks led collaborations with academic departments and with other universities, helping develop real-world applications for the research at Carolina. Brooks's recent personal research explores 3D graphics and virtual reality.

Brooks Hall. The home of the University of North Carolina Press since 1980, Brooks Hall is a two-story building at the corner of Boundary Street and Hooper Lane. The building is named for North Carolina attorney, politician, and author Aubrey Lee Brooks and his sons Thornton H. Brooks and James T. Brooks. The elder Brooks, an 1893 graduate of the UNC School of Law, established the Brooks Scholarship Fund at Carolina and an endowment for UNC Press.

UNC–Chapel Hill first proposed this building site in 1977, a controversial choice given its location in a historic neighborhood and the necessity to demolish three vacant houses that had been part of the university's 1920s-era faculty row. The town's historic district committee denied the university's request. After months of debate among the university, neighbors, the Chapel Hill Preservation Society, and the town, the North Carolina legislature passed a law that exempted state and university lands from local historic district oversight, thus clearing the way for construction. A grant from the W. K. Kresge Foundation and other gifts funded the building, along with a warehouse for the press off of Airport Road.

In 1990 an electrical fire destroyed most of Brooks Hall. While the sole occupant of the building at the time escaped injury, the fire demolished the archival copy of each of the more than 4,000 books published by UNC Press, along with manuscripts and most of its office records. Using insurance funds, the university rebuilt and expanded the building, which reopened in 1993.

Building names. Most campus buildings, along with some schools, units, and physical spaces, have a namesake. While the mechanism for selecting people to honor in this way has changed over time, the reasons for doing so remain much the same. In general, the university has honored donors, past presidents and chancellors, deans, faculty members, and other employees who are considered important to the life of the institution. In another category are buildings named for governors and illustrious alumni.

Naming buildings for donors was an early practice. The first was the second building to be constructed in the 1790s, Person Hall, named to recognize Thomas Person's financial gift that enabled the first trustees to finish construction of Old East and Person. The only other antebellum building to be named for a donor was Smith Hall, now historic Playmakers Theatre. Benjamin Smith, who like Person was a trustee, donated 20,000 acres of land in Tennessee that he received for service in the Revolutionary War.

Examples of buildings named for governors, trustees, and other notable alumni are the first set of classroom buildings completed in 1922, Manning, Murphey, and Saunders (now Carolina Hall), and the 1924-era upper quad of dormitories, Mangum, Manly, Grimes and Ruffin. In this case, a committee of the trustees selected the namesakes. In 1928 the trustees adopted a policy to name academic buildings for influential professors and dormitories for important figures in the state.

Today's campus reflects this mix of donor appreciation and historical commemoration. Approximately 38 percent of campus names reflect a donation, while 62 percent derive from some mix of faculty and trustee designation for remembrance. Of note are more recent namings that reflect the community's desire to recognize those left out of such commemorations. In 1967 trustees chose to name a new residence hall for Hinton James, the university's first student. In 1998 UNC–Chapel Hill recognized campus employees by renaming the University Laundry for Kennon Cheek and Rebecca Clark, both of whom worked for better conditions for staff. In 2007 another residence hall was named for George Moses Horton, an enslaved poet who worked on campus and sold his poetry to students.

Bull's Head Bookshop. In 1927 English professor Howard Mumford Jones set up the Bull's Head Bookshop in his office in Murphey Hall. Jones wanted to bring a different kind of bookstore to campus: one with modern books and comfortable chairs that could serve as a sort of informal gathering place for reading and discussion. While it sounds a lot like a contemporary bookstore (though without a coffee shop), there was nothing else like it on campus or in Chapel Hill at the time. The bookstore was popular, quickly outgrowing Jones's office and moving to the Campus Y and then to the ground floor of Wilson Library. In addition to selling new books, the Bull's Head hosted readings and lectures and ran a book rental service. When the new Daniels Building was completed in 1968, the Bull's Head moved into a much larger space on the main floor, remaining separate in function and philosophy from the textbook department.

Burnett-Womack Clinical Sciences Building. Opened in 1975 to house administrative and research space for the Departments of Medicine,

Bull's Head Bookshop, ca. 1950s, when it was located on the ground floor of Wilson Library. UNC Image Collection, North Carolina Collection Photo Archives, Wilson Library.

Surgery, Pediatrics, Dermatology, Ophthalmology, Neurology, and Anesthesiology, the building is nine stories tall. It accommodated the medical school's principal clinical research labs and an animal facility. In 2006 the building had a complete renovation to accommodate growth and new technology and to relocate the animal facility elsewhere. It now houses the Department of Surgery and the Divisions of Cardiology, Endocrinology, and Nephrology for the Department of Medicine, the Carolina Vaccine Institute, clinical skills assessment facilities, a base for clinical trials, and a center for training in radiological science. The original construction was funded by the North Carolina legislature and a grant from the National Institutes of Health. The renovation was part of the 2000 higher education bond referendum.

The building is named in honor of Dr. Charles H. Burnett (1913–1967) and Dr. Nathan A. Womack, first chairs of the Departments of Medicine and Surgery, respectively. Burnett, a native of Colorado, came to Chapel Hill when the Department of Medicine expanded to a four-year school. He resigned in 1965 due to illness. Womack, a North Carolinian who attended UNC–Chapel Hill for his first two years of medical study, returned in 1951 to lead the Department of Surgery. After stepping down as chair in 1966 he continued to be active in the department. In 1969 his colleagues founded the Womack Surgical Society to honor him and provide a forum for networking, and later a scholarship fund for surgical residents. The society's activities continue as part of the surgery department's annual Research Day.

Bynum Hall was originally built as a gymnasium. It was completed in 1905 and named in honor of William Preston Bynum Jr., a student in the 1890s who died of typhoid fever after his sophomore year. Bynum's grandfather provided the funding for the building. It is one of only two on campus named for students solely in honor of their experiences as students (Hinton James Residence Hall is the other). The gym was fully equipped with early-twentieth-century fitness equipment. The *Tar Heel* reported that the medicine balls and punching bags were especially popular. One of the more interesting features of the gym was a second-floor balcony track. The basement held a swimming pool (the only indoor pool in Chapel Hill at the time) and locker rooms, including showers, which were popular in an era when many dorms did not have them. Bynum served as the primary gym on campus until the opening of Woollen Gym in 1938. A 1947 *Alumni Review* article fondly remembered the old gym, especially "that 'gymnasium smell,' which provides an olfaction unfamiliar to students now accustomed to the air-blown dressing rooms of Woollen Gym."

The old gym space was converted to offices and housed the School of Journalism and the University of North Carolina Press. Student services, including the university cashier, were housed in Bynum for many years.

C

Cafeteria workers' strikes. In the fall of 1968, dining hall workers at UNC–Chapel Hill presented Chancellor J. Carlyle Sitterson with a list of suggestions for improved working conditions. They lobbied for pay raises, shorter workdays, and better treatment from supervisors. Their cause was soon joined by members of the Black Student Movement, who listed improved treatment for African American staff at the university in their list of twenty-three demands to the chancellor in December 1968. In February 1969, still waiting for a response from campus administration, the cafeteria workers went on strike. They were supported by some students and faculty who joined the picket lines and helped set up an alternative food stand in Manning Hall. Black Student Movement members helped emphasize the demands of the workers by slowing down dining hall service and overturning tables in Lenoir Hall, actions that drew the attention of Governor Robert Scott. The governor first ordered students to be arrested if they disrupted campus services or facilities and then sent North Carolina Highway Patrol officers to campus to ensure that the dining hall could open and operate without incident. In March 1969 the campus administration agreed to meet several of the workers' demands, including a small raise, extra pay for overtime work, and back pay. However, a few months later the university outsourced its dining services to Saga Corporation, a private food service company. The cafeteria workers, now unionized, continued to complain of poor treatment and pay and went on another strike in late 1969, but campus administrators argued that their issues were now with Saga, not the university.

Cake Race. In the 1920s students began an annual tradition of running a cross-country race around the campus, with the winners receiving a

Cafeteria workers on the picket line during the second cafeteria workers strike in late 1969. *Yackety Yack*, 1970, North Carolina Collection, Wilson Library.

cake. There were apparently many participants and many opportunities to win: for the 1923 race, the "ladies of Chapel Hill" prepared 100 cakes for the runners. Cake races were common at many universities, and the tradition continues at Davidson College. The Cake Race was popular in the 1920s and 1930s and then was revived and run a few more times in the 1950s and 1960s.

Caldwell Hall. Dedicated in 1912, Caldwell was built to house the UNC School of Medicine. It is named for Joseph Caldwell, the university's first president. Designed as a state-of-the-art medical facility, it included laboratories and classrooms. In the basement it also contained pens for animals, including dogs, rabbits, guinea pigs, and mice, that students used for experiments. Known informally as Carolina's Zoo, the animal pens were a source of controversy. Students in nearby dorms complained about the noise, and the facilities hastened the tragic end of the first two Rameses mascots. Rameses I, the first live ram mascot at UNC, was purchased in the fall of 1924. He died in Caldwell Hall the following summer, believed to have been overheated in the closed facilities. In 1926 Rameses II died after medical students drew blood from him.

By the late 1930s the School of Medicine had outgrown the facilities in Caldwell Hall, and the building was converted to be used for classrooms. During World War II it served as the headquarters of the U.S. Navy pre-flight school. Renovated and expanded in the 1970s and 1980s, Caldwell now serves as the home of the Departments of Philosophy and Women's Studies.

Joseph Caldwell (1773–1835) came to UNC in 1796 to teach mathematics. He was a graduate of Princeton, where he also qualified for the ministry. He became UNC's first president in 1804 and served to 1812 but afterward remained on the faculty. The trustees asked him to take on the presidency again in 1817, and he served until his death in 1835. Caldwell not only labored to build academic programs, using his own funds to purchase books and astronomical equipment, but also was tireless in raising money and support for the new university. During his tenures UNC completed South Building, added a floor to Old East, and constructed Old West and Person Hall.

Caldwell monuments. The Joseph Caldwell Monument is an obelisk that sits in the middle of McCorkle Place. It is dedicated to Joseph Caldwell, UNC's first president from 1804 to 1812 and again from 1817 to 1835. Caldwell and his family are interred beneath this monument. There is another, similar-looking obelisk in the Old Chapel Hill Cemetery. It marks the grave of Wilson Caldwell, a university employee born into slavery on campus, who was an educator and became one of the first African Americans elected to town government.

Joseph Caldwell was first buried in the cemetery and then reburied in 1846 with his second wife, Helen Hooper Caldwell, at a monument located near the present site of New West. This first monument, a sandstone obelisk, did not weather well. In 1858 the alumni association erected a new monument to the president in its current location. The graves remained near New West. In 1876 Mrs. Caldwell's son, William Hooper, who had been a member of the faculty, died and was buried next to his mother and stepfather. Their remains were reinterred at the current location in 1904. At the same time, the alumni of the class of 1891 asked that the old obelisk be erected in the cemetery in memory

Wilson Swain
Caldwell,
ca. 1890s.
Portrait
Collection,
North Carolina
Collection
Photo Archives,
Wilson Library.

of Wilson Caldwell and other African American men who had served
the university while enslaved and later as free men. This finally took
place in 1922.

Cameron Avenue. Built on an old carriage path that led west from the
campus, the street now known as Cameron Avenue was originally called
College Avenue. In the early 1880s it was named for Paul Cameron,
in appreciation his many contributions to the university as a trustee
and donor, and for the sugar maple trees he donated to plant along the
road. Cameron, born into a wealthy family in Orange County, attended
UNC briefly in the 1820s before being expelled for fighting. He eventually graduated from nearby Trinity College. He was a supporter of
higher education throughout his life. He provided funds to help reopen
Carolina in the 1870s and to build the original Memorial Hall in the
1880s. Cameron was also a member of the UNC Board of Trustees. The

The YMCA Building, shown here with signs for student government elections in April 1942, was the center of UNC student life for decades. Photo by Hugh Morton. Hugh Morton Photo Collection, North Carolina Collection Photo Archives, Wilson Library.

Camerons were one of the wealthiest families in the South. They owned property throughout North Carolina, including what is now the historic Stagville plantation in Durham, as well as plantations in Alabama and Mississippi. By the late 1850s Paul Cameron and his siblings enslaved more than 1,000 people.

Campus Y. The campus chapter of the Young Men's Christian Association was founded in 1859 as a religious organization for students and was initially housed in South Building. The Y was a popular gathering place and by the late nineteenth century began to administer nonreligious programs. Many student services were run through the Y, including the campus bookstore. For a brief period the Y even ran student athletics. The YMCA Building, designed by Frank Milburn, opened in 1907 and quickly earned a place at the heart of student life. The YMCA published a student handbook, organized a freshman orientation program, offered career services, and hosted a popular soda fountain. A campus chapter of the Young Women's Christian Association (YWCA) was founded in 1936 to support the growing population of women at UNC. The two organizations worked closely together and merged in 1964.

In the 1920s the Y began to look beyond the campus, sponsoring the Institute on Human Relations (later renamed the Symposium on Public Affairs), bringing prominent speakers to campus to discuss national and international issues. The outward-facing role of the Y grew as other campus organizations began to take responsibility for student services and as religion played a less prominent role in student life. The Y's active role in community life increased under the leadership of Anne Queen, who came to Carolina in 1956 to lead the YWCA and later served as the director of the combined Campus Y from 1964 to 1975. During this period of great change and protest, Queen was a mentor to student activists and placed the Campus Y at the center of the struggle for social justice at UNC–Chapel Hill. Students affiliated with the Campus Y were active in protests against the Vietnam War and in support of civil rights and racial justice. Ending its formal affiliation with the YMCA in 1978, the Campus Y, now administered by UNC Student Affairs, hosts programs and provides services for student groups working on community engagement and social justice.

Cardboard Club. In 1948 home football games got a lot more colorful when cheerleader Norm Sper founded the Cardboard Club. The club made creative displays out of squares of painted cardboard that students held up during football games to make composite pictures. Requiring careful organization and coordination, the sometimes elaborate displays were a highlight of football games in the 1950s and 1960s. The displays contained pictures and sayings, the most popular of which was "GO TO HELL STATE." By the late 1960s there were frequent threats to suspend the card stunts when some students started throwing their cards. Faculty in particular complained of this as their seats were below the student section. The card stunts returned in the early 1980s, aided by students who employed computers to design the patterns, but were canceled after a few years when students started throwing cards again.

Carmichael Arena. With basketball growing in popularity following the 1957 national championship, UNC decided in the early 1960s to build a new arena. Completed in 1965, Carmichael Auditorium, as it was then named, was the home of the Tar Heel basketball team for more than twenty years. Originally seating 8,000 fans (later expanded to more than 10,000), the notoriously loud venue played host to many of Coach Dean Smith's greatest teams, including the 1981–82 national champions. Built along South Road next to Woollen Gym—the previous location of home basketball games—Carmichael was completed in time for the October 12, 1965, University Day celebrations. Lectures and concerts were also held there, including a performance by the Supremes just a month after it opened. In the fall of 1982 Carmichael hosted a week of lectures by evangelist Billy Graham.

The first men's basketball game in Carmichael was played on December 4, 1965, a UNC victory over William and Mary. By the 1980s the men's basketball team was in need of an even larger venue and moved to the Dean Smith Center once it was completed. Carmichael underwent an extensive renovation in 2010 and was renamed Carmichael Arena when it reopened. Carmichael currently hosts Tar Heel volleyball, gymnastics, wrestling, and women's basketball.

The building is named for William D. Carmichael Jr., a university administrator in the 1940s and 1950s. A native of Durham, Carmichael graduated from UNC in 1921 and was a captain of the basketball team. He had a successful career on Wall Street before returning to Chapel Hill in 1939 to serve as controller for the UNC System (coincidentally, he succeeded Charles T. Woollen, namesake of the building Carmichael Auditorium was built to replace). Carmichael, a successful fund-raiser, was named acting head of the university after Frank Porter Graham left in 1949 and was considered a possible successor to Graham. He was later named vice president and finance officer of the UNC System, serving in that role until his death in 1961.

Carmichael Residence Hall. When Carmichael Residence Hall opened for the fall 1986 semester, it was the first new dorm on campus since the 1960s. More important for students, it was the first dorm with air conditioning. The coed dorm also included four new "living-learning" programs, giving students from the same major the opportunity to live together. Carmichael now houses students with similar academic interests, as well as a makerspace, a design and fabrication facility operated as part of UNC–Chapel Hill's Innovate Carolina program.

The building is named for Katherine Kennedy Carmichael (1912–1982). A legendary figure both feared and loved by students, Carmichael served as dean of women from 1946 until 1972. The position of dean of women oversaw the academic and social lives of the growing population of women enrolling at Carolina. While men on campus could largely come and go as they pleased, dress how they liked, and socialize wherever and whenever they chose, female students were subject to a strict set of rules, including mandatory study halls and curfews, a ban on drinking, and a dress code. All of these were overseen by Dean Carmichael, whose *Women's Handbook* was required reading. Raised in Birmingham, Alabama, Carmichael was known for her proper dress and manners and expected the same from her students. At first seen as practical and necessary, the "women's rules," and Carmichael's strict interpretation of them, were challenged by students in the 1960s, leading to gradual changes throughout the late 1960s and early 1970s, until finally women at Carolina were subject to the same rules and restrictions as men. When that happened, the university abolished the position of dean of women, and Carmichael served as an associate dean of UNC Student Affairs. Although she no longer oversaw women students, she continued to advocate for the advancement of women at Carolina.

Carolina blue. The university's distinctive school color originated only a few years after the university opened. Not long after the first students arrived, they organized two debating groups: the Dialectic and Philanthropic Societies. The "Di" and "Phi" societies played a large role in campus academic and social life. Early students were required to join one or the other. They proclaimed their membership by wearing ribbons in their society's color. The Phi's color was white, and the Di's color was light blue. The ribbons were also used on diplomas awarded by the society. Examples of these from the early 1800s survive today in Wilson Library.

When UNC began competing in intercollegiate sports in the late 1880s, the students followed the lead of other universities in adopting school colors. There does not appear to have been any debate: the Tar Heel athletic teams used the colors long associated with the debating societies. The light blue soon became a signature color for the university. By the 1930s newspapers were referring to it as "Carolina blue." Used in official publications and on clothing, it was embraced by students and administrators. By the end of the twentieth century the color was an inseparable part of campus life, but there were questions about the "true" Carolina blue. Printers and manufacturers used different versions of the color. The men's basketball uniforms used a darker version that was supposed to look better on television, but campus publications had a much lighter shade.

Alumnus and fashion designer Alexander Julian was particularly offended by the color of the graduate gowns he saw on students walking past his store on Franklin Street. After lobbying for several years to "improve the true blueness" of the robes, Julian was given the job of redesigning the gowns in 2010. Julian's new, "true blue" robes were worn at graduations starting in the spring of 2011. To eliminate further confusion about the proper shade of the color, the university worked with Nike in 2015 to standardize the school's athletic uniforms. In the process, the university established Pantone 542 as the official version of Carolina blue.

Carolina Buccaneer. First published in 1924, the *Buccaneer* was a popular humor magazine on campus. There had been earlier, short-lived humor magazines, but the *Buccaneer* was one of the longest-lasting ones, published for more than a decade. With its glossy pages and colorful cover illustrations, the *Buccaneer* had the appearance of a professional magazine. Its content, however, was very much the work of undergraduates. The issues are filled with in-jokes and attempts at bawdy humor. The magazine was known for testing the limits of what could be published on campus. In 1928, as the *Buccaneer* was preparing a "Girls' Issue," the *Tar Heel* wrote that the content was so scandalous that it would have to be printed on asbestos paper. In 1939 the editors finally pushed too far. The *Buccaneer* "Sex Issue," which featured a drawing of a scantily clad woman on the cover, was immediately banned from campus. The student body president said that it would "seriously and permanently damage the reputation and lessen the prestige of the university in general." The *Buccaneer* didn't survive long after the scandal, publishing its last issue in 1940.

Carolina Center for Public Service was established in 1999 to help connect the university's students, faculty, and staff with communities through teaching, research, and service. The idea came from an earlier Public Service Roundtable, a grassroots group of faculty and staff leaders who were interested in building on the university's tradition of public service. The center has programs for students, faculty, and staff to learn more about engagement, to learn new skills, and to connect academic endeavors with communities throughout North Carolina. One of the center's most successful projects was the Tar Heel Bus Tour, created in 1997 to introduce new faculty, staff, and administrators to the state of North Carolina. The weeklong tour traveled around the state to businesses, to historic and cultural sites, and to UNC faculty and students working in the field. The center also houses the APPLES Service-Learning program, Buckley Public Service Scholars, and the Thorp Faculty Engaged Scholars. The center is located at 207 Wilson Street.

Carolina Coffee Shop is the oldest continuously operating business in Chapel Hill, operating at 138 East Franklin Street since 1922. It opened as a soda fountain called the Carolina Confectionary. It later added full meals and "Coffee Shop" to the name. By the mid-1930s it was known simply as the Carolina Coffee Shop. The restaurant has long been known for its booths (described as "cozy alcoves" in a 1937 ad), dark wood interior, and classical music.

Carolina Hall. The building now known as Carolina Hall was named Saunders Hall from 1922 to 2015. Completed as part of the campus expansion in the early 1920s, Saunders was built as a classroom building, originally housing the Departments of History, Economics, and Commerce. It was named for William L. Saunders, an 1854 graduate of UNC who served in the Confederate army during the Civil War. After the war he worked as a newspaper editor, North Carolina secretary of state, and historian, compiling the ten-volume *Colonial Records of North Carolina* (1886–90). He was a member of the UNC Board of Trustees from 1878 until his death in 1891. When he was selected as the namesake for the new building on campus, he was called an "ardent friend of the University and one of the master minds of North Carolina." He also led the Ku Klux Klan in North Carolina.

In the late 1860s Saunders and other conservative leaders in North Carolina were angered by the multiracial coalition that had elected a Republican government and approved a new state constitution that, for the first time, gave every man, regardless of race, the right to vote. Saunders helped organize Ku Klux Klan groups throughout the state to intimidate, threaten, and in some cases murder opposing politicians and supporters. Saunders and his allies forced the impeachment of Governor William Holden in 1871 after the governor tried to suppress Klan violence in the state. Saunders's leadership of the Ku Klux Klan was cited by the board of trustees when the building was named in his honor.

By the late twentieth century students at UNC–Chapel Hill were frequently calling for Saunders's role in the Klan to be acknowledged by the university and the building renamed. In 2014 a coalition of students

"Hurston Hall" banner hung by student activists
calling for the renaming of Saunders Hall, April 2015.
Photograph by Stephanie Lamm from the *Daily Tar Heel*.

from the Real Silent Sam Coalition, the Black Student Movement, the Campus Y, and other organizations organized the largest protests yet around Saunders Hall. Students and faculty from the Department of Geography, which was housed in the building, were especially active. The students called for the building to be renamed Hurston Hall in honor of author Zora Neale Hurston, who visited UNC in the late 1930s as a guest of playwright Paul Green.

In a rare acknowledgment of poor judgment by their predecessors, the UNC–Chapel Hill Board of Trustees voted in 2015 to remove Saunders's name from the building. Instead of following the students' requests to name the building for Hurston, the trustees selected Carolina Hall as the new name. Student activists were further frustrated when the trustees immediately followed the action by declaring a sixteen-year moratorium on renaming buildings on campus. In 2016 the university installed an exhibit in the lobby of Carolina Hall that examines the history of Saunders and his allies in the late nineteenth-century white supremacy campaigns in North Carolina.

Carolina Indian Circle was founded in 1974, when there were only ten Native American students on campus. The circle provides academic and social support for Native American students, helps with recruitment, and sponsors ways for the campus community to learn more about Native American cultures. The group has hosted the annual Carolina Indian Circle Powwow since 1987, the largest powwow held on at any university on the East Coast. The organization also sponsors Unheard Voices, an a cappella group, and hosts Indigenous Peoples Day in October. The First Nations Graduate Circle, founded in 2000, is the graduate and professional student counterpart to the Carolina Indian Circle. It has hosted a Native Leaders Symposium, a day-long program on leadership for Native leaders and academics.

Carolina Inn. In 1921, following an uncomfortable night at a dilapidated Franklin Street boarding house, alumnus John Sprunt Hill decided to build a proper hotel near the university. Hill, already a frequent donor, initially tried to raise money from alumni. When those efforts fell short, he decided to pay for the whole thing himself. Built on land Hill owned near campus, the Carolina Inn opened in late 1924. It was designed by Arthur Nash, the architect responsible for many of the buildings built on campus during the 1920s expansion.

The Carolina Inn quickly became a fixture of campus life, hosting visiting alumni and serving as the de facto site for formal dinners and receptions by campus groups. In 1935 Hill formally transferred ownership to the university with the stipulation that any profits would go to the University Library, in particular the collections devoted to North Carolina (now known as the North Carolina Collection).

While the university began to admit African American students in the 1950s, the Carolina Inn was slower to act. The inn cultivated an "Old South" atmosphere, exemplified by a brochure in use for decades showing on its cover a smiling African American porter ready to open the front door. One of the earliest African Americans to attend a public event at the inn was Martin Luther King Jr., who was a guest at a dinner there during a campus visit in 1960.

Facing growing demand, the inn had significant renovations and additions in the 1940s and 1970s. But it remained a financial headache for the university. By the early 1990s, with the inn losing money, the university decided to lease management to a private company. Another renovation followed, this one bringing the loss of the inn's cafeteria,

Carolina Inn in the snow, ca. 1960. UNC Photo Lab Collection, North Carolina Collection Photo Archives, Wilson Library.

long a favorite lunchtime spot for local residents and university employees. Even under private management, the inn remained, as UNC System president William C. Friday called it, the "University's living room."

Carolina Magazine. The *Carolina Magazine* was an important part of campus life at Carolina for more than a century. First published in 1844 as a biographical and historical review, the magazine included essays from faculty and local residents. By the 1880s the magazine expanded into a general literary publication, with creative writing by students. Many prominent alumni authors published in the *Carolina Magazine* as students, including Thomas Wolfe, Paul Green, Walker Percy, and Joseph Mitchell. In the 1920s the magazine occasionally began publishing the work of African American authors. In May 1927 the magazine published its first "Negro Number," which contained creative works by African American authors, including Langston Hughes and Countee Cullen. This special edition was an annual tradition for a few years, and while the issues were usually preceded by condescending commentaries about African American writing, they provided an outlet for African American authors and enabled them to reach new audiences in North Carolina. By the mid-1940s interest in the *Carolina Magazine* began to wane. The student body was growing, and students were focusing their creative efforts on other publications, including a variety of humor publications such as *Tarnation* and the *Carolina Buccaneer*. The last issue of the magazine ran in 1948.

Carolina North is a planned research and mixed-use academic campus on 250 acres on land the university owns that includes the Horace Williams Airport. The satellite campus has been discussed for more than twenty years and is modeled in part on similar expansions at other schools, such as the Centennial Campus at North Carolina State University. In 2009 the university completed a development agreement with the town of Chapel Hill that will guide development of the site and began plans for a new law school building there. The economic recession of 2009–10 delayed building construction indefinitely. The university continues to work on infrastructure projects and maintain the forest and trails for recreational use.

Carolina Playmakers. The Carolina Playmakers was the name for the drama program and the faculty, staff, students, and community members who staged plays at the university. The Playmakers started in 1918 with the arrival of Frederick Henry Koch, a professor from the University of North Dakota. Koch had developed a type of playwriting he called "folk drama" that focused on local themes and ordinary people. The Carolina Playmakers staged original plays on campus and on tour, traveling as far as New York and visiting the White House. The Playmakers published four books of student folk plays in the 1920s, as well as a theater journal, the *Carolina Play-Book*, from 1922 to 1944.

A number of well-known North Carolina writers and theater artists came from the Carolina Playmakers, including Bernice Kelly Harris, Thomas Wolfe, Paul Green, his wife Elizabeth Lay Green, Andy Griffith, and Louise Fletcher. Smith Hall was renamed Playmakers Theatre in the 1920s when it became the new home for the program, and in the 1970s PlayMakers Repertory Company adopted a variation of the name as a tribute to the earlier group.

Carolina Political Union. Organized in 1936 by students in E. J. Woodhouse's political science class, the Carolina Political Union sought to

The Carolina Playmakers about to embark on a statewide tour in 1925.
Department of Dramatic Art Photos, North Carolina
Collection Photo Archives, Wilson Library.

share information and promote debate about current affairs. The group
invited speakers to campus and succeeded in bringing many prominent
politicians to Chapel Hill, including President Franklin D. Roosevelt
(1938), Speaker of the House Sam Rayburn (1941), and Congressman
John F. Kennedy (1947). The group also invited controversial speakers
to campus, most notably Ku Klux Klan leader Hiram Wesley Evans
(1937) and Communist Party leader Earl Browder (1938). The club was
discontinued in the mid-1950s and then revived for a few years in the
late 1960s.

Carolina Population Center. With a worldwide population boom in the
decades following World War II, UNC, along with other universities,
was interested in starting a program to study population growth and
change. With support from the Ford Foundation and federal grants,
the Carolina Population Center was established in 1966. The research
projects and programs offered by the center involved organizations
and communities in North Carolina and around the world and have in-

cluded such topics as family planning, adolescent sexual behavior, and health and nutrition. The research efforts of the center are led by faculty fellows from a variety of UNC–Chapel Hill schools and departments.

Carolina Quarterly. Established in 1948 as the successor to the *Carolina Magazine*, the *Carolina Quarterly* is a student-run literary journal. Originally limited to the work of students, the journal soon opened its pages to other writers, becoming a publication of national significance in the process. Renowned authors such as Don DeLillo, Annie Dillard, and Joyce Carol Oates have been published in the *Carolina Quarterly*. In an interview in 2008, novelist Robert Morgan, who had edited the *Quarterly* as a student at UNC in the 1960s, referred to it as a "venerable institution" at Carolina, putting the university on the map in the world of creative writing.

Carolina Women's Center. Established in 1997, the Women's Center is the home for information and programs related to women and gender equity at Carolina. Center staff work with the campus and community to educate and advocate for gender equity and women's empowerment. The proposal for such a center came from a recommendation made by a student organization called the Women's Issues Network, which was further supported by a Task Force on Women at Carolina, convened in 1995. Regular programs sponsored by the Women's Center include HAVEN (Helping Advocates for Violence Ending Now) workshops to train allies for survivors of sexual assault and relationship violence, an informational program for expectant mothers called What to Expect When You're Expecting @ UNC, and Women's/Gender Week. The center is currently housed in the Stone Center and serves students, faculty, and staff.

Carr Building. Opened in 1900 as a dormitory, the Carr Building was funded in its entirety by Julian Shakespeare Carr, an alumnus and frequent donor to the university. The dorm was built with all the modern (for 1900) conveniences, including electricity and indoor plumbing. It housed students through the 1970s and was converted to office space in the 1980s. It currently serves as the home of several departments, including faculty governance and student affairs.

Carr, who attended the university in the 1860s, made his fortune in the tobacco industry with W. T. Blackwell in Durham, the company that made the famous Bull Durham tobacco. Carr was also involved in banking, railroads, and the textile industry. After purchasing the majority of the mills in the town adjacent to Chapel Hill, then known as Venable, he asked that it be renamed to Carrboro.

Carr, a Confederate veteran, was active in politics, campaigning on behalf of the Democratic Party and championing the cause of white supremacy. He spoke out against allowing African Americans to vote and endorsed racial violence when it served his political goals. In his retirement, Carr helped organize and lead reunions of Confederate veterans throughout the country. He frequently spoke at these and other events, his speeches often featuring racist depictions of African Americans and a defense of the Confederacy. In a widely quoted speech at the dedication of UNC–Chapel Hill's Confederate Monument in 1913, Carr spoke of the period after the Civil War when Confederate veterans "saved the very life of the Anglo Saxon race in the South."

Carrington Hall is home to the School of Nursing, located on Columbia Street and Medical Drive. Before it was completed in 1969, nursing programs were housed in parts of the medical school that have since been demolished. An eight-story addition in 2005 doubled the building's size, adding new classrooms, laboratories, and research spaces, including a human patient simulator laboratory. The addition was the first campus structure to earn LEED (Leadership in Energy and Environmental Design) certification by the U.S. Green Building Council.

The building is named in memory of Elizabeth Scott Carrington, to honor her efforts to establish a four-year school of nursing at Carolina and her work to improve the quality of nursing education in North Carolina. Born in Alamance County, Elizabeth Scott became a nurse, and along with her husband, a physician, she supported the state's Good Health Plan of the 1940s, a campaign to expand medical education and health services. Put in charge of the committee to promote the university's new four-year program, she worked to recruit students, raise funds, and secure scholarships. She persuaded alumnus James M. Johnston to designate part of his bequest to the university for nursing student scholarships. In 1983 UNC–Chapel Hill awarded an honorary degree to Carrington in recognition of her extraordinary public service.

Carroll Hall opened in the spring of 1953, one of three new buildings to house the university's growing School of Business Administration (along with Hanes and Gardner). The building was named for Dudley Dewitt Carroll, the dean of the school; he took over as dean in 1919, when it was known as the School of Commerce, and stayed in the position for thirty-one years. The building was expanded in 1970, but it wasn't long before the business school began looking for a larger home, eventually moving to a new building on South Campus in 1997. The building was renovated and then occupied by the School of Journalism and Mass Communication in 1999.

Caudill Labs opened in 2007 next to Wilson Library to provide expanded and improved space for the study of chemistry at UNC–Chapel Hill. The building was part of an effort in the 2000s to build new physical science facilities to replace the long-outdated Venable Hall. The building is named for alums and donors W. Lowry and Susan S. Caudill.

Cellar Door is the long-running undergraduate art and literary journal at UNC–Chapel Hill. Published continuously since 1974, *Cellar Door* contains short stories and poetry, as well as student art and photography. Notable writers who published in *Cellar Door* as undergraduates include poet and creative writing faculty member Michael McFee, novelist Jill McCorkle, and singer-songwriter Tift Merritt.

Chancellors. The chancellor is the administrative and executive head of each institution within the UNC System. The president is the leader of the UNC System. This structure came about in 1971, when the North Carolina General Assembly established a single sixteen-university system, with a chancellor and a board of trustees for each institution, and a board of governors for the system. The first step toward this idea came in 1931, when the General Assembly decided to consolidate administrative operations of three public campuses—the University of North Carolina in Chapel Hill, North Carolina College for Women (now UNC-Greensboro), and North Carolina State College of Agriculture and Engineering (now North Carolina State University). Frank Porter Graham, then UNC's president, became president of the newly dubbed Consolidated University. The leader of each institution at first had the title of dean of administration, changed to chancellor in 1945.

Since 1932 there have been eleven chancellors of UNC–Chapel Hill:

Robert Burton House (dean of administration, 1934–45; chancellor, 1945–57)
William B. Aycock: 1957–64
Paul F. Sharp: 1964–66
J. Carlyle Sitterson: 1966–72
Nelson Ferebee Taylor: 1972–80
Christopher C. Fordham III: 1980–88
Paul Hardin: 1988–95
Michael Hooker: 1995–99
William O. McCoy (acting and interim): 1999–2000
James Moeser: 2000–2008
H. Holden Thorp: 2008–13
Carol L. Folt: 2013–19
Kevin Guskiewicz: 2019–

Chancellor's residence. Quail Hill, the current official residence of the university chancellor, is located adjacent to campus, off Raleigh Road. It was built by George Watts Hill (class of 1922), a Durham banker and philanthropist who served on the UNC Board of Trustees and later on the UNC System Board of Governors. The university purchased Quail Hill in 1993 from his widow, Anne Gibson Hill. Before 1993, the chancellor's residence was a house on Country Club Road.

Hill was interested in architecture and oversaw the design and construction of Quail Hill. His architectural influence is also evident on campus. He managed construction of the Carolina Inn, which was built by his father, John Sprunt Hill (class of 1889), in 1924. He also contributed funds and architectural direction for the George Watts Hill Alumni Center, which opened in 1993.

There have been discussions over the years about whether the chancellor and the system president should switch official residences. The President's House, on Franklin Street, is much closer to the campus, while Quail Hill is adjacent to the UNC System offices on Raleigh Road.

Chapel Hill. In 1792, when trustees selected this site for the university, locals called the area New Hope Chapel hill, for a deserted Anglican chapel that had once stood on a high ridge near a crossroads. In 1793, when university trustees sold lots to create a town, its name became Chapel Hill. It was a small village in its early years and began to grow only in the early 1900s, along with the university. A typical college town that, along with Raleigh and Durham, is also one of the points of the Research Triangle, Chapel Hill has a reputation for being a progressive and liberal outpost in a conservative South.

Despite its reputation, the town was not all it might seem to be. In 1960, when African American high school students challenged segregation laws with sit-ins and picket lines, Chapel Hill business owners resisted change, and the community watched in dismay as their town, too, became the site of violent altercations between citizens. Yet in 1969 residents elected Howard Lee as mayor, the first African American mayor since Reconstruction in any majority-white city in the South.

In the 1990s Chapel Hill was the center of an emerging independent music scene, anchored by groups such as Superchunk, Squirrel Nut Zippers, Ben Folds Five, and the recording company Merge Records. Local musicians have also helped revive traditional music, including the Red Clay Ramblers, Ayr Mountaineers, and the Carolina Chocolate Drops.

Chapel Hill grit is the reddish-brown gravel seen throughout the university campus and downtown, including the pathways in the Coker Arboretum and on some of the sidewalks on Rosemary Street. Composed of decomposed granite, the sand-like gravel is unique to the area. Before the majority of the pathways were covered in brick, students often complained about the dust from the gravel walkways covering their shoes. But there were some who looked back on it fondly as a distinctive part of their Carolina experience. Chancellor Robert B. House, in a memoir about his early days as a student at Carolina, wrote, "I think the miracle of falling in love with Chapel Hill comes when you get one of its red grits in your shoe. Chapel Hill then enters your soul to stay."

Chapman Hall. Dedicated in 2006, Chapman was built as part of the Carolina Physical Science Complex, one of the largest construction projects in the university's history. When it opened, Chapman Hall included classroom and laboratory space for several departments, including physics, astronomy, math, and marine sciences. It also included a rooftop observatory and control room for telescopes operated by UNC–Chapel Hill in Chile and South Africa. The building is named for Max C. Chapman Jr., a 1966 graduate of Carolina who went on to a successful career on Wall Street and who donated $5 million in support of its construction.

Chase Hall, ca. 1965. UNC Image Collection, North
Carolina Collection Photo Archives, Wilson Library.

Chase Hall opened in fall 1965 to serve as a dining hall for the growing
population of students on South Campus. With a modern design and
bright furnishings, the building was impressive, but the cafeteria service was plagued with problems from the start. Despite plans to serve
up to 5,000 students per meal, customers complained of long lines and
food that was inadequate in both quality and quantity. After the cafeteria received a "C" sanitation rating in 1967, students formed Project
RETCH (Refuse to Eat Trash in Chase Hall) to lobby for better food and
service. Yet problems persisted—a 2001 *Alumni Review* article called
Chase "a metaphor for nearly everything students dislike about campus food." The original Chase was torn down in 2005 to make room
for two new campus buildings. The Chase Hall name moved to Ram's
Head Plaza.

The building was named for former UNC president Harry Woodburn Chase. Serving as president from 1919 to 1930, Chase, a native of
Massachusetts, presided over a period of significant growth and change
at the university. Building on plans started by his predecessor, Edward
Kidder Graham, Chase helped develop Carolina into a modern research
university. Under his leadership the university expanded graduate education, more than doubled the size of the faculty, and launched an extensive building campaign that would include new dorms, classrooms
on Polk Place, and major new buildings, such as Kenan Stadium and

Wilson Library. Chase also stood up for the university in the mid-1920s when the North Carolina legislature proposed a bill that would limit the teaching of evolution in state-supported schools. Using language that would inspire university responses to future ideological battles, Chase wrote to the legislature about the importance of academic freedom and the necessity of faculty being able to teach without interference from the state. Chase left Carolina in 1930 to take over as president of the University of Illinois, staying there for just a few years before going to New York University, where he spent a long tenure as president to finish his career.

Cheek/Clark Building (University Laundry). Located on West Cameron Avenue next to the chiller plant, this building currently houses offices and meeting rooms for Carolina's grounds, housekeeping, and building services operations. Employees in these units maintain and operate Carolina's 300-plus academic buildings, research facilities, and residence halls, more than 700 acres of campus grounds and landscapes, and 4,000 total acres throughout Orange County.

The building's original purpose is illustrated by the name that still adorns the front entrance: University Laundry. The university opened the building in 1925 to operate laundry service for campus and town and hired African American employees to staff it. Carolina offered laundry services—a revenue stream—from 1925 until some time in the late 1970s, when all of the residence halls contained coin-operated machines, and transferred other laundry and dry-cleaning services to outside vendors. Over time the building served as a headquarters for Carolina employees who cared for buildings and grounds and was a center for employee activism over the years, as various people lobbied for better working conditions for the university's lowest-paid workers.

The building was rededicated in September 1998 as the Kennon Cheek/Rebecca Clark Building. The renaming recognized Kennon Cheek and Rebecca Clark, two people who advocated for better working conditions for Carolina's lowest-paid employees and who were also important figures in the Chapel Hill community.

Kennon Cheek was born in Chatham County and came to work at Carolina in 1917. In 1930 he cofounded the Janitors Association to lobby the administration for better working conditions for all of its African American employees. During the early years of the Janitors Association, janitors not only provided cleaning services but also painted, did

Cheek/Clark Building, 2018. Photo by Jon Gardiner, UNC–Chapel Hill.

repair work and carpentry, ran errands, and delivered campus mail. In the Chapel Hill community, Cheek helped move Hackney's Educational and Industrial School from its location on South Merritt Mill Road to the Northside neighborhood west of campus, and helped raise funds for the rebuilding of St. Joseph CME Church on West Rosemary Street after the church burned down.

Rebecca Clark, also from Chatham County, began work at the university as a maid at the Carolina Inn in 1937 and later worked in the laundry building. Clark returned to the university in 1953 as a nurse's aide and became the first licensed practical nurse to work in the campus infirmary. During her time in the university laundry, Clark began to work on labor issues. She met with then-president Frank Porter Graham to appeal for better working conditions in the laundry. In 1942 she took over as the shop steward for the State, County, and Municipal Workers of America, a subgroup of the Congress of Industrial Organizations that advocated for the rights of low-wage public workers. Building on the relationships created between the Janitors Association and Graham's administration, Clark was able to win wage increases for the laundry workers, in addition to safer work spaces and more reasonable work schedules.

Cheerleading. Organized cheering was a part of the game day experience since the earliest days of UNC sports. Students in the stands, led by an elected "chief cheerer," chanted or sang from a variety of prepared cheers. The cheerleaders left the stands in the 1920s, led by Vic Huggins. An enthusiastic supporter of university athletics, Huggins is credited with bringing the first group of uniformed cheerleaders to Carolina. One of the most influential cheerleaders in campus history was Norm Sper, who came to Carolina in the late 1940s and helped establish lasting traditions, including the Beat Dook Parade, the Victory Bell, and the Cardboard Club. Some notable alums have served as cheerleaders at UNC, including future president Frank Porter Graham, who was elected chief cheerer in 1909, and bandleader Kay Kyser, who organized a large group of students called the Carolina Cheerios, known for their matching outfits and coordinated cheers. By the 1940s women joined the cheerleading squad and the cheerleaders followed other schools in developing a more modern style of cheerleading, with colorful uniforms, organized cheers, and gymnastic stunts.

Cheers. When UNC began participating in intercollegiate sports in the 1890s, students developed a series of school cheers for the games and pep rallies. Unlike the alma mater and other school songs, the "university yells" were not set to music. Among the most popular was the "Yackety Yack," from which the college yearbook took its name, and variations on a cheer involving spelling the word "Carolina." The cheers published in the 1902 handbook were typical of those used early in the twentieth century:

> *Hackie, Hackie, Hackie,*
> *Sis Boom Bah,*
> *Carolina, Carolina,*
> *Rah Rah Rah.*

> *Boom Ray Ray*
> *Boom Ray Ray*
> *Carolina Varsity*
> *S-s-s- Boom Tar Heel.*

> *Yackety Yack Hooray Hooray*
> *Yackety Yack Hooray Hooray*
> *Carolina Varsity*
> *Boom Rah Boom Rah*
> *Car-o-li-na.*

Songs and Yells

HARK THE SOUND (Tune: "Amici")

Hark the sound of Tar Heel voices,
Ringing clear and true,
Singing Carolina's praises,
Shouting "N. C. U."

Chorus

Hail to the brightest star of all!
Clear in its radiance shine!
Carolina, priceless gem,
Receive all praises thine.

Refrain

I'm a Tar Heel born,
I'm a Tar Heel bred,
And when I die
I'm a Tar Heel dead.
So it's—
Rah, Rah, Carolina-lina
Rah, Rah, Carolina-lina
Rah, Rah, Carolina!
Rah, Rah, Rah!

LESTER
OSTROW
Cheerleader

CAROLINA LOCOMOTIVE

C-c-c-c————A!
R-r-r-r————O!
L-l-l-l ———— I!
N-n-n-n————A!
Carolina!
Team! Team! Team!

SPLIT CAROLINA

C-aro————————Li-na!
C-aro————————Li-na!
C-aro—Li-na! C-aro—Li-na!
Carolina!
Team! Team! Team!

LET'S GO CAROLINA

Let's go Carolina!
Let's go Carolina! (louder)
Let's go Carolina! (louder still)
(4-second pause)
Hit 'em!

BLUE AND WHITE

Blue——And——White!
Fight! Fight! Fight!
White——And——Blue!
N. C. U.!
(Whistle) Boom!
Tar Heels! Tar Heels! Tar Heels!

YACKETY YACK

Yackety Yack, Ray! Ray!
Yackety Yack, Ray! Ray!
Carolina Varsity!
Boom Rah! Boom Ray!
Carolina!
Team! Team! Team!

SPELL CAROLINA

C—A—R—O—L—I—N—A!
Carolina!
Team! Team! Team!

This page of "Songs and Yells" is from the 1935–36 student handbook.
North Carolina Collection, Wilson Library.

School cheers continued to appear in student handbooks for several decades. It appears that by the 1960s they were no longer in regular use.

Chemistry, Department of. Part of the College of Arts and Sciences, the chemistry department is one of the oldest on campus and has produced a number of academic leaders and major donors to the university in addition to distinguished graduates in the discipline. Chemistry dates its founding to 1818, when UNC hired Denison Olmsted (1791–1859) from Yale to teach the subject. A formal department was organized around 1890 under Francis P. Venable (1856–1934), first department chair and the university's first faculty member to hold an earned Ph.D. He led the department, and the university as president from 1900 to 1914, as both developed more rigorous academic and research programs.

An earlier chemistry professor was at the center of a major controversy. Benjamin S. Hedrick, an alumnus and professor of agricultural chemistry, supported the Republican Party antislavery candidate in the 1856 presidential election. In a university comprising mostly slave-owning students, faculty, and trustees, Hedrick was attacked on campus and in the press for this position. He was fired for engaging in political conflicts.

Chemistry has had various homes over the years. It was first housed in South Building from the early 1820s until the 1850s. With the need for a laboratory space to conduct experiments, the department took over basement space in Smith Hall (now Playmakers Theatre) in the 1850s. When the university reopened in 1875, chemistry moved into Person Hall, where it stayed until 1906. That year, the legislature made the first ever appropriation for a university building—for chemistry, which was later named Howell Hall. In 1925 the department moved into Venable Hall. In 1971 and 1985, respectively, the department added Kenan and Morehead Laboratories. They are named for two chemistry graduates, John Motley Morehead and William Rand Kenan Jr., who would become two of the university's most consistent and generous donors. The old Venable Hall was replaced in 2010 by the new Venable and Murray Halls.

Cherry trees. A feature of McCorkle Place that is especially evident in early spring is the cherry trees that line the east and west sides of the quad. The original trees were the senior gift of the class of 1929. A sandstone tablet set into the stone wall on Franklin Street recognizes that fact. Because the average lifespan of flowering cherry trees is only about twenty to thirty years, none of the original trees is still there. But because students, alumni, and visitors love seeing the cherry blossoms in the spring, the university's grounds staff continues to replace the trees as they die. An endowed fund, given in memory of alumnus and former dean Martha Decker Deberry, helps continue this practice. A stone marker beneath a cherry tree near Franklin Street and Graham Memorial Hall recognizes this gift.

Interior of the Circus Room showing *Circus Parade* carving, ca. 1960s.
Durwood Barbour Postcard Collection, North Carolina
Collection Photo Archives, Wilson Library.

Circus Room. Located in the Monogram Club building (now Jackson Hall), the Circus Room was a popular soda fountain and snack bar. The Circus Room opened following World War II. It was decorated with dark wood paneling and a twenty-five-foot-long wooden carving of circus animals. The *Circus Parade* was carved by hand by university employee Carl Boettcher, based on drawings by illustrator William Meade Prince. After renovations in the 1970s the *Circus Parade* moved to the Carolina Inn cafeteria. It now hangs in the George Watts Hill Alumni Center. The Circus Room remained open as a snack bar and convenience store and was popular with students for decades: when the Office of Undergraduate Admissions was planning an expansion in the 1980s, students circulated a petition asking that the Circus Room not be closed. It remained in place until the mid-2000s.

Civil War. When North Carolina joined other southern states and seceded from the United States in May 1861, university president David Lowry Swain kept the school open. Students circulated a petition calling for a temporary closure until fall term, reasoning that the conflict would be short. Swain and the board instead argued for the need to protect students from the war and their own inexperience. Most students and faculty did leave, however. As the war continued, Swain success-fully argued for an exemption from the Confederate government's con-scription order for younger students, maintaining that the small num-ber would do little for the army and wreak permanent damage to the institution. Carolina managed to remain open throughout the conflict, despite dwindling numbers of faculty and students and fierce political criticism.

In the closing days of the war in spring 1865, Chapel Hill found itself in the middle of the action. Confederate forces moved through the town on their flight from General William Sherman's Union troops, who entered the village the next day. President Swain was part of a team sent by the governor to negotiate a surrender and protection for Raleigh and the university. Sherman agreed to the terms and thus spared both the capital and the university buildings. Swain's role in this earned him further political enmity, only intensified months later by his daughter's marriage to the leader of the Union brigade that occupied Chapel Hill.

Approximately 1,000 alumni and students (about 40 percent) served in the Confederate forces, and 287 died in service. Of the fourteen fac-ulty at UNC in 1861, six also joined the war. Three of them died in ser-vice, as did four of the five university tutors. At least five alumni served the Union.

Class gifts. Senior class gifts are a long-standing tradition at UNC–Chapel Hill and other colleges and universities. The outgoing class typi-cally selects a project and raises money from class members and others. The statues of Venus de Milo, Minerva, and Apollo in Murphey Hall were gifts from the classes of 1900, 1901, and 1902. As electricity came to the campus, the class of 1903 purchased electric lights for Gerrard Hall. The class of 1988 raised money to create Fordham Court, the foun-tain and seating area between Carr Building, Bynum Hall, and historic Playmakers Theatre. The class of 2001 may be unique in that its gift in-cluded living creatures—the aquarium in the Graham Student Union. The class of 2002 provided funding for the Unsung Founders Memorial on McCorkle Place. Perhaps the most notorious class gift to date was the *Student Body* sculpture from the class of 1985. Other classes have donated benches, bronze plaques, campus gateways, trees, and more.

A class gift may also be a fund. Classes have given to the library, for teaching awards and other faculty recognition, and for scholarships and student support. The class of 1969 may have been the first to endow a student scholarship, and some subsequent classes have chosen to add their gift to the fund. Since the early 2000s senior classes have encouraged its members to pledge an annual gift to any university need. Stone markers at the base of the bell tower recognize each class's total participation.

Coates Building. The Coates Building, located on Franklin Street across from McCorkle Place, was built to house the Institute of Government in 1939. After the institute moved to a new building on the other side of campus, the space was used for academic offices and centers, including the Center for International Studies and the Department of Geography. In 1997 it was renamed in honor of Albert and Gladys Coates. Albert Coates was the founder and first director of the Institute of Government. He and his wife, Gladys Coates, were active in university life for more than a half century. Both wrote about university history, including a book they coauthored on the history of student government at the university.

Cobb Residence Hall. When it opened in 1952, Cobb was the university's largest dorm, constructed at a cost of nearly $1 million and housing more than 400 students. The building is named for Collier Cobb, professor of geology for more than forty years. Cobb joined the faculty in 1892 and taught until shortly before his death in the 1934. When the building was named, Cobb's son, Collier Cobb Jr., was on the Board of Trustees Building Committee.

Coker Arboretum. In 1903 William C. Coker, a professor of botany at the university, proposed turning a large area on the east edge of campus into an arboretum. The five-acre space once housed university president David Lowry Swain's cattle. By the time Coker started work, it was described as an "uninviting crayfish bog." Coker supervised the draining of the area, the laying of walkways, and the planting of hundreds of different species. Some of the plants in the arboretum had a practical use early in its history. Working with a former student, Coker developed a "drug garden" that contained plants used for medicinal purposes. Intended to serve as a sort of outdoor classroom for the study of native plants, Coker later added many East Asian trees and shrubs. Housing more than 400 different plants, it is known for its ornamental trees and flowers and a large wisteria arbor that runs along Cameron Avenue.

One of the more notable events in the history of the arboretum came in the 1930s when a student named Kemp Nye, inspired by the popular Tarzan movies then in the theaters, bet another student that he could cross the entire arboretum by swinging on trees. As onlookers watched, Nye succeeded in making it all the way across without touching the ground. The narrow, unlit walkways and secluded gardens in the arboretum were often rumored as the sites of romantic liaisons between students, but for many the arboretum was a place to be avoided. In 1965 a UNC–Chapel Hill student was murdered in the middle of the day in the arboretum. In the 1970s, after several sexual assaults were reported, the perception that the arboretum was unsafe was reinforced and students were told to avoid the area after dark. Some students and administrators urged that lights be added to the arboretum walkways, but they remain unlit. The arboretum is currently managed by the North Carolina Botanical Garden.

Coker Hall opened in 1963 as classroom and laboratory space for the Department of Botany. After the Departments of Botany and Zoology combined to create the new Department of Biology, Coker Hall was the departmental home. It is named for William C. Coker, professor of botany at the university for more than four decades. A South Carolina native, Coker came to Chapel Hill to teach in 1902 and remained until his retirement in 1945. He was a prolific author and a popular teacher, known for the frequent field trips he led so that students could study plant specimens in their natural environments. Coker's most lasting legacy at UNC–Chapel Hill is the Coker Arboretum, also named in his honor, making him one of only a few people to have been the namesake for multiple places on campus.

College of Arts and Sciences. The heart of the academic experience and home to most of UNC–Chapel Hill's students, the College of Arts and Sciences is where all undergraduates begin their Carolina education. The current unit structure was created in 1935 with the merger of the College of Liberal Arts and the School of Applied Science. The General College, which is the program for the first-year and second-year students, was a separate entity until 1961, when it was merged in the College of Arts and Sciences. In addition to the 16,000 plus undergraduates, the college has the largest group of graduate students—more than 2,500—on campus. Within the college are forty-three departments, divided among fine arts and humanities, natural sciences and mathematics, social sciences, and global programs. In addition, it has multiple research institutes, centers, and interdisciplinary programs. It also houses Honors Carolina, undergraduate research, first-year seminars, academic advising, the Writing Center, and other offices that support undergraduate education.

Colors. The university's school colors come from the two debating societies that were prominent in early campus life: the Philanthropic Society's color was white, and the Dialectic Society's color was light blue. Students wore ribbons in their society's color to important school events, and the ribbons also were used on diplomas awarded by the societies. In the late 1880s, when UNC began competing in intercollegiate athletics, the teams adopted white and light blue as the school colors. Early coverage of Carolina football games in the *Tar Heel* sometimes referred to the team as "the white and blue." In 1894 students started a short-lived newspaper called the *White and Blue* to serve as a competitor to the *Tar Heel*. The school colors also featured prominently in a song written by W. S. Myers in 1897:

> *Only a bow of ribbon,*
> *A ribbon of white and blue,*
> *Faded, soiled, and crumpled,*
> *A token so true.*
> *Only a bow of ribbon,*
> *Of ribbon white and blue,*
> *The emblem of departed days,*
> *The colors of N.C.U.*

Though performed a few times by the UNC Glee Club, "Only a Bow of Ribbon" has not had the staying power of Myers's other composition, "Hark the Sound."

Commons Hall. In 1885 students were eager to have a new ballroom to host dances. When the university was unable to provide one, a group of students formed a private association and had one built on campus on the current site of Phillips Hall. When it wasn't used for dances, the building was leased to the university for use as a gymnasium. In 1898, following the opening of Bynum Gymnasium, the building was converted into a dining hall. It served as the main dining facility for students until Swain Hall opened in 1914, often offering cheaper meals than other boarding houses located off campus. However, the fare was not always popular with the students. A 1911 *Tar Heel* article described a student deciding to become a vegetarian after attempting to eat a Commons Hall steak. In 1915 the building was given to the university. During World War I students used the facility for military training. It was later demolished.

Communism. Having weathered complaints of excessively liberal bias since the leadership of Frank Porter Graham in the 1930s, the university faced new accusations, beginning in the 1950s, of being a training ground for Communists. The claims were frequent enough that consolidated university president Gordon Gray addressed them in his 1950 inaugural address, stating that "Communists are not welcome" at Carolina or the other two system schools. The accusations were heightened a few years later when UNC alumnus Junius Scales, who was then working as an organizer for the U.S. Communist Party, began distributing publications on campus. The continued claims of Communist influence were a major factor in the passage of North Carolina's Speaker Ban Law by the state legislature in 1963, which prohibited known Communists from speaking at any of North Carolina's state-supported schools. UNC administrators, especially system president William C. Friday, had to balance their continued resistance to claims of Communist influence with a defense of academic freedom. The university's resistance to the speaker ban only further supported the views of some North Carolinians that Chapel Hill was a haven for Communist sympathizers.

Computers. The university entered the computer age in 1959 when a nineteen-ton, $2.4 million UNIVAC 1105 arrived on campus. The newly established Computation Center, housed in Phillips Annex, drew national attention. The Census Bureau and the National Science Foundation were early partners, placing the university among national leaders in computer research. In 1962 Frederick P. Brooks Jr., then working at IBM, gave a presentation on campus titled "Ten Research Problems in Computer Science." The presentation was a factor in inspiring campus administrators to create a new academic department. The Department of Computer Science (originally called the Department of Information Science) was established in 1964, and Brooks was hired to lead it. At the time, only one other American university (Purdue) had a separate aca-

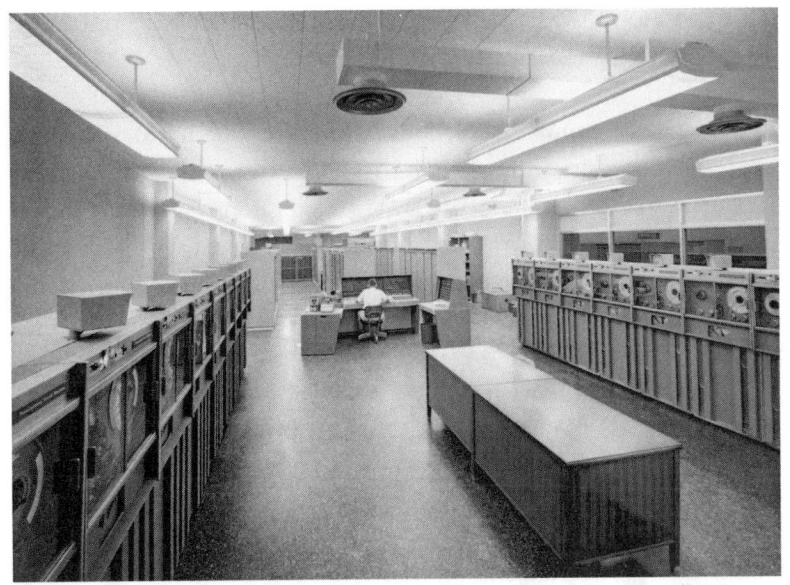

The UNIVAC computer in the UNC Computation Center, ca. 1959. UNC Photo Lab Collection, North Carolina Collection Photo Archives, Wilson Library.

demic department dedicated to computer science. In 1968 presidential candidate Richard Nixon made a brief visit to campus to view the university's computer center. By the 1980s the increasing availability of personal computers began to transform teaching and learning across campus. Computers were used throughout the undergraduate curriculum, and the university responded to the growing need by building several computer labs in libraries and dorms. In the late 1990s the Carolina Computing Initiative was established as part of a program that required all incoming undergraduates to have laptop computers by the fall of 2000.

Cone-Kenfield Tennis Center. Located near the Friday Center and Finley Golf Course, the Cone-Kenfield Tennis Center opened in 1992 to serve as a home for the UNC–Chapel Hill men's and women's tennis teams. It is named for Ceasar Cone II, a tennis player at Carolina in the 1920s and son of a prominent textile industry leader. The Cone family contributed significantly toward the construction of the facility. The name also honors John Kenfield, Carolina's first tennis coach and one of the most successful in its history. Kenfield coached tennis at UNC from 1928 to 1955. He came to Carolina when the tennis program was fairly new and created one of the leading programs in the country, winning multiple national championships.

Confederate Monument ("Silent Sam"). In 1908 the board of trustees approved a request from the North Carolina division of the United Daughters of the Confederacy (UDC) to build a Confederate monument on campus. University president Francis Venable was actively involved in planning and fund-raising for the monument and committed university funds to the effort when money from the UDC and alumni fell short. The university and the UDC chose Boston sculptor John Wilson to create the monument. It was dedicated in June 1913 to the university men who had fought for the Confederacy. The dedication ceremony included speeches by UDC and UNC leaders, North Carolina governor Locke Craig, and alumnus Julian S. Carr. Carr's speech has attracted the most attention. In it, he praised the Confederate army for "sav[ing] the very life of the Anglo Saxon race in the South" and recalled "horse-whipp[ing] a negro wench until her skirts hung in shreds" for insulting a white woman.

During its first decades on campus, the monument was either viewed as a war memorial or simply ignored by students. By the mid-twentieth century, students were calling it "Silent Sam," a nickname attributed both to the impassive look on the soldier's face and to his lack of ammunition. An enduring joke among undergraduates was that the soldier's rifle goes off whenever a virgin walks by.

The first public calls to remove the statue came in the mid-1960s and intensified in the late 1960s amid civil rights protests. Students and others have argued for decades that the statue is a monument to racism and white supremacy, claims supported by historians who place the monument within the context of early twentieth-century efforts to disenfranchise African American voters, establish the Jim Crow system of racial segregation, and rewrite the history of the Civil War.

The focus on the statue intensified in the mid-2010s in the midst of a national conversation about Confederate monuments in public spaces and following the decision by several cities and universities to remove monuments. In 2018, after a rally off campus, a group of protesters pulled the statue down from its base. In 2019 Chancellor Carol L. Folt ordered the remaining parts of the monument to be removed in the same message in which she announced her resignation. The toppling of the statue and subsequent debates about what to do with it have kept

UNC housekeeper Elaine Massey holds a sign under the Confederate Monument, protesting institutional racism during a Martin Luther King Day protest in 1999. Photo by John Kenyon Chapman. John Kenyon Chapman Papers, Southern Historical Collection, Wilson Library.

UNC at the center of national discussions about white supremacy and Confederate memorialization. In its end-of-the-year review issue, the *Daily Tar Heel* called 2018 the Year of Sam.

Connor Residence Hall was one of three new dorms opened in 1948 to accommodate the expanding student population entering the university following World War II. The other two built at the same time are Winston and Alexander, now known collectively as the Connor Community. The lawn framed by the dorms, known as "Connor Beach," was home to the popular Springfest music festival in the 1980s, and its successor, Connorstock, which began in the 2000s.

Known informally as B Dorm when it opened, the dorm was later named for archivist and historian Robert Digges Wimberly Connor.

A native of Wilson, North Carolina, Connor graduated from UNC in 1899. After graduation he was a school teacher and helped establish the State Archives of North Carolina, which he led for several years. Connor joined the UNC Board of Trustees in 1913 and the faculty in 1921 when he was named a Kenan Professor of History. He left the university in 1934 when he was appointed by President Franklin D. Roosevelt as the first Archivist of the United States. He returned to Carolina in 1941, teaching and writing until his death in 1950.

Consolidation. From its founding in 1789 until 1932, the University of North Carolina was a single campus in Chapel Hill. During the Great Depression, the Brookings Institution recommended several cost-saving measures for the state government, which included consolidating the operations of the North Carolina College for Women in Greensboro (now UNC-Greensboro) and the North Carolina State College of Agriculture and Engineering in Raleigh (now North Carolina State University) with UNC in Chapel Hill. Under consolidation, the university operated with one board of trustees that oversaw all three campuses, along with a system leader initially designated chancellor but eventually changed to president. The leader of each campus was designated vice president at first, which changed to dean of administration, and eventually to chancellor.

Part of the consolidation plan included the elimination of duplicate programs. The most notorious decision was to eliminate UNC's engineering program in favor of North Carolina State's program. However, Carolina managed to retain its sanitary engineering courses, which eventually became the Department of Environmental Sciences and Engineering in the Gillings School of Global Public Health.

Contempo. Published for only a few years in the early 1930s, the Chapel Hill literary magazine *Contempo* managed to attract national attention. Former UNC students Milton Abernethy and Anthony Buttitta founded the magazine and began to solicit contributions from well-known authors. They published works by William Faulkner, Ezra Pound, and William Carlos Williams, among many others. The magazine's December 1931 issue drew controversy for including Langston Hughes's poem "Christ in Alabama." The publication coincided with Hughes's visit to campus for a talk in Memorial Hall.

Craige North Residence Hall opened in the fall of 2002, one of four new dorms completed at the same time (Hardin, Horton, and Koury are the others). The new dorms were built near existing high-rise dorms and given temporary names borrowing from the names of the older dorms. Craige North's temporary name has lasted longer than any of the others. The new dorms were in high demand when they opened, with students camping out to reserve a space. They also began a new experiment in bringing academic and residential life closer together by including classrooms in the dorms.

Craige Residence Hall. One of the new high-rise dorms built on South Campus in the 1960s, Craige was completed in 1962. The six-story building was designed to house around 700 students—all men when it first opened. Nicknamed "Maverick House" by early residents, Craige was home to the "Victory Gong," which was apparently given to the dorm by a former marine who got it in Japan. In 1965 the gong was stolen by students from Morrison dorm, an event that attracted significant coverage in the *Daily Tar Heel* and led to many years' worth of animosity between the two dorms.

Craige is named for Francis Burton Craige, an 1829 graduate of the university. Craige was a lawyer and politician, serving in both the state legislature and U.S. Congress. As the Civil War approached, Craige was an outspoken advocate for secession. He was a member of the state secession convention in 1861 and introduced the ordinance that led to North Carolina's joining the Confederacy. He later served in the Confederate Congress.

Creative writing. Carolina students were writing and publishing creative works long before creative writing became part of the curriculum. Beginning in the late nineteenth century with the *Carolina Magazine*, students published poetry and short stories in campus publications. Dramatic writing became a focal point at Carolina when Frederick Koch started the Carolina Playmakers in 1918 and his students—including future novelist Thomas Wolfe—wrote original "folk plays." In the 1940s Jessie Rehder, a faculty member in the English department, taught creative writing. Her classes were popular enough that by 1966 a creative writing program was established within the English department. Novelist Max Steele was the first director of the program and led it for more than twenty years. Many well-known authors have since taught in the department, including Doris Betts, Jill McCorkle, Bland Simpson, Randall Kenan, and Daniel Wallace.

The Cube, a large wooden display located between the Pit and the Graham Student Union, is used as a space for students to announce campus programs and events. The colorful, hand-painted box was first built in the early 1970s and became known as the graffiti cube. While it has grown and been rebuilt many times since it first appeared, the Cube has been a consistent part of the campus landscape ever since. The public display has occasionally been the site of controversy and debate. In 1979 an announcement by the Navy ROTC was defaced and covered with "Imperialists Off Campus."

In 1990 an announcement on the Cube for National Coming Out Day, posted by the Carolina Gay and Lesbian Association, was scratched out and covered with hate speech.

Cyprett's Bridge. After the University of North Carolina received its charter, the board of trustees had to find a location for the university. Wanting a site near the center of the state, they considered several locations before settling on an area within a fifteen-mile radius of Cyprett's Bridge in northern Chatham County, a few miles south of Chapel Hill. Cyprett's Bridge crossed New Hope Creek and was located on the road between Raleigh and Pittsboro. The location of Cyprett's Bridge is now believed to be underneath Jordan Lake, near the area where Highway 64 crosses the lake.

D

Daily Tar Heel. First published in 1893 as the *Tar Heel*, the *Daily Tar Heel* has been a vital part of the Carolina student experience for more than a century. It was first published by the Athletic Association, a fact that drew criticism and an early competitor, the *White and Blue*. The *White and Blue* did not last long, and the *Tar Heel* expanded its coverage on other aspects of student and university life. In 1923 the paper separated from the Athletic Association and became an official student publication, which included accepting money from student fees. By 1929 it was thriving, and began publishing six days a week, changing its name to the *Daily Tar Heel*. Though it has never been formally associated with the journalism school, the paper has drawn heavily from journalism students for its staff.

In the 1940s and 1950s the *Daily Tar Heel* was at the center of the anti-Communist furor that swirled around the campus. The university had been accused of being too liberal since the leadership of Frank Porter Graham in the 1930s. The claim of liberal bias was soon applied to the student paper. It ran a few columns from a student who was a Communist Party member, and it drew the attention of the FBI in 1954 by publishing an April Fool's Day issue called the *Daily Witch Hunt*, which featured a photo of J. Edgar Hoover examining the rear end of a horse. The accusations of favoring left-leaning stories and opinions would continue to follow the paper into the 1960s as it covered the North Carolina Speaker Ban Law and student involvement in civil rights protests. The *Daily Tar Heel* increased its coverage of national issues during this period, even sending reporters to cover protests in Mississippi and Alabama.

The continuing criticism of the paper's coverage by conservative students and state residents often focused on the paper's acceptance

Two over breezy

Fair and partly cloudy today with light winds. High, low 60s. Low, mid 40s.

The Daily Tar Heel

All-blue wardrobe

Having trouble getting Carolina blue paint out of your clothes? Good luck, say local cleaners. See story on page 3.

Serving the students and the University community since 1893

Volume 90, Issue ~~20~~ 117 | Tuesday, March 30, 1982 | Chapel Hill, North Carolina

Damn we're good—NCAA champs

Fans turn Franklin into blue bedlam

From Staff Reports

"*This is awesome!*" said one fan. "Awesome, awesome, awesome," that was the mood of the more than 25,000 Tar Heel basketball fans who rushed onto Franklin Street immediately following the University of North Carolina's NCAA championship victory over the Georgetown Hoyas.

"Finally, after all these years we get to see them win," said Chapel Hill policeman Sonny Austin. "We'll probably be out here till daybreak."

In true Carolina fashion, the revelers celebrated the first UNC national basketball championship in 25 years with large amounts of beer drinking, light-blue paint pouring, and dancing and cheering up and down Franklin Street.

"It's the greatest thing that ever happened to this city, to win one for Dean (Smith)," said Aiah Gbakima, who insisted that the love for the Heels stretched farther than the bounds of the campus. "Even in West Africa there are Tar Heel fans. Even though they're sleeping in Africa, they know we won it for Dean."

On Franklin Street, toilet paper was hurled through the air. Men, women, children and police officers exchanged high-five handshakes and celebrants tried to turn over cars and vans while the nearly 100 police officers tried to maintain order.

"This is the greatest party in America!" shouted Rich Synderman. "There is no basketball team like them," said sophomore Sissy Twiggs.

"I think this is the greatest thing to ever happen to Carolina," said Tasker Flemming, Jr.

"What the hell is a Hoya?" asked Jean Larrabee.

On campus, students reported phone calls from Indiana University, whose basketball team knocked off the Tar Heels for the title last year.

As the party wore on there were reports of injuries from broken glass and firecrackers. "They have had several emergency calls for ambulances," said a town policeman.

The majority of the crowd, however, maintained its calm as Franklin Street celebrated. And as expected, many of the rowdy students committed themselves to skipping class today.

"This is just a real important event that hasn't happened in 25 years and I think we ought to celebrate it by not having to go to class," said Tish McCown. "One professor even postponed an exam until next week because of the basketball finals."

Those Tar Heel fans who do attend class faithfully tomorrow can make up for lost celebration at 2:30 p.m. in Kenan Stadium. Homecoming reception has been organized by Carolina Athletic Association, Student Government and the UNC administration.

Written by Alan Chapple. Compiled by John Conway, Charlotte Holmes, Alan Marks, Sarah Raper and Jim Wrinn.

After 25 years . . . we did it again!

Dean Smith cuts his first NCAA championship net after the Tar Heels 63-62 victory over the Hoyas. Above, even young and old UNC fans rank the Tar Heels No. 1. For another, left, Carolina blue paint captured the excitement of those celebrating on Franklin Street.

NC rocks Hoyas, grab 63-62 win for Smith's first

By CLIFTON BARNES
Staff Writer

NEW ORELANS — And on the seventh try, Dean created national champions.

UNC coach Dean Smith, after six previous trips to the Final Four, finally came away with the big one — the NCAA collegiate basketball title as the North Carolina Tar Heels beat the Georgetown Hoyas 63-62.

"I thought it was really just another game, but now that you talk to me after it's over it's not," coach Smith said. "I've very grateful to my players."

Maybe he ought to be especially grateful to James Worthy, who scored 28 points and was named the tournament's outstanding player.

But it took a 15-foot shot by Michael Jordan with 13 seconds left to give North Carolina the lead and the game.

"I didn't see it go in," Jordan said. "I was just praying it would go. I never did look at the ball."

Worthy showed his worth when he took the ball with seven seconds left on an attempted pass from Georgetown's Fred Brown to Eric Smith.

The 6-foot-9 junior, who will now consider going pro, dashed in front of the pass and dribbled it downcourt until he was fouled with two seconds left.

He missed both free throws but it didn't matter; North Carolina was the national champion.

"Champions, not finalists," Assistant Coach Eddie Fogler shouted. "We're champions."

But it was never easy as the Hoyas pressured the Heels the whole game defensively.

"We exchanged baskets and it could have gone either way," said UNC sophomore Sam Perkins. "They made us hustle and work for it. They made us work for everything."

The Hoyas' pressure defense gave North Carolina trouble at the start and Georgetown opened it up with a six-point lead at 12-6, seven minutes into the game.

But James Worthy scored 10 straight points, including a dunk off a missed shot by Matt Doherty, to tie the score for the first time at 20-20.

The Tar Heels took the lead for the first time at 25-24 on a free throw by Chris Brust. Worthy gave the Heels their biggest lead of the first half at 29-26 on a patented turn-around.

But baskets by Pat Ewing and Eric "Sleepy" Floyd gave the Hoyas a 32-31 halftime lead.

The Tar Heels could not seem to get anything going for much of the first half except for Worthy's efforts and five goal-tending calls on Ewing.

Ewing did his share of scoring for his team too in the first half, canning 10, as did Floyd.

Worthy owned the half for the Heels, scoring 18 points.

But in the second half Jordan got the Heels started early with six points in the first four minutes to give them a 39-36 lead.

Georgetown's Ewing and Floyd, both all-tourney selections, combined for the next 11 points and the Hoyas were suddenly up 49-45 with 12 minutes left.

The game had many big plays, but perhaps the one that turned the tide and got the Tar Heel fans saying 'not this year Georgetown' was a Worthy dunk over fellow Gastonia native Floyd.

See CHAMPS on page 2

News Briefs

Columbia's landing site uncertain

WHITE SANDS MISSILE RANGE, N.M. (AP) — Space shuttle Columbia, diverted by wild desert winds from its scheduled landing Monday, will try again Tuesday in a suspenseful third-flight finale that could force the ship to bypass New Mexico and return non-stop to Florida.

It all depended on the morning weather and the condition of Northrup Strip on this barren Army missile base. NASA expected to make the decision by 7 a.m. EST — with a hoped-for landing four hours later.

Eugene Kranz, chief of flight operations, said in Houston that a Tuesday landing at 11:07 a.m. EST — 9:07 a.m. at White Sands — would be preferred. If the Northrup Strip was unsuitable, the shuttle would land at the Kennedy Space Center at Cape Canaveral, Fla. A Florida landing would come at 11:13 a.m. EST, or one orbit later at 12:47 p.m.

Kranz said the sandstorm that caused the postponement also brought some damage to the runway, but that it could be repaired overnight.

The runway at Cape Canaveral, 15,000 feet long, was ready and fully equipped. Columbia has never made a paved-runway landing, but the alternative is another try at wind-whipped Northrup, and NASA officials were pessimistic that conditions would improve.

No clear winner in El Salvador

SAN SALVADOR, El Salvador (AP) — Five right-wing parties that together won a majority in El Salvador's new constituent assembly agreed Monday to invite the Christian Democrats to join a "government of national unity," two opposition leaders said.

There was no immediate response from the Christian Democrats, who outpolled all other parties in Sunday's election of the 60-member assembly. The assembly will be empowered to install a provisional government to replace the civilian-military junta led by Jose Napoleon Duarte and dominated by his Christian Democrats.

With about one-fourth of the 4,600 voting stations reporting, the Central Election Commission gave the following output: the Christian Democrats, 136,829 votes, 40.5 percent; ARENA, 98,653 votes, 29.2 percent; National Conciliation Party, 54,187 votes, 16 percent; Democratic Action Party, 32,091 votes, 9.5 percent; Popular Sion Party, 4,134 votes, 1.2 percent.

Advising service being developed

By DEAN FOUST
Staff Writer

In an effort to reduce the academic advising burden currently delegated solely to the UNC faculty and administration, Student Government is developing a student advising service designed to complement the present system.

Faculty advisors will continue to handle all official paperwork, but the new student advising program will provide students with a more accessible medium than the faculty advisors, who often become overburdened by the heavy load of students each handles, said Darryl Thompson, chairperson of the Academic Advising Committee, which will direct the project.

"The academic advisors will be referral and resource individuals who will have the training to advise students of pertinent information concerning academics at this University," Thompson said.

"Their role in no way diminishes the faculty-student relationship," he said. "They are just there to allow that the faculty-student time be spent concerning more important issues. We will still refer students to their advisors."

Student advisors will serve as a source for information about general academic concerns. They will also be informed about more complex aspects such as the Carolina Course Review and the Undergraduate Bulletin, Thompson said.

Providing students with alternative forms of advising has been attempted several times before but none are currently operating. The Academic Resources Personnel program was created three years ago, in an attempt to locate student advisors in dormitories across campus. The program failed because of common problems inherent to advising programs — advisors being closed out of dormitories and the difficulty involved in updating all student advisors of every minute change in areas of academics — said Kari Schopler, former governor of Henderson Residence College and most recently the Special Projects coordinator for the Residence Hall Association.

HRC collaborated with General College for several years and provided some of the residents with a graduate student who acted as an official General College advisor. Although the advisor was given an office in the dormitory and even kept night and weekend office hours, a number of students still requested faculty advisors in South Building, Schopler said.

Last year, the N.C. Fellows Program designed a student advising program which was presented to Student Government, Thompson said. The program did not receive enough response from Student Government, and was shelved until the recent presidential campaign, when Student Body President Mike Vandenbergh promised such a service, Thompson said.

The academic advisors will be referral and resource individuals . . .

Darryl Thompson

With assistance from the Student Affairs and the Academic Affairs committee, along with the Department of University Housing, the Academic Advising Committee will coordinate the present student advising program.

The program will begin next semester in three residence halls — Morrison, Granville South and Henderson Residence College — with student advisors on each floor, Thompson said. These three areas were chosen as a cross-section of campus life, and because they traditionally house large numbers of freshmen, he said.

By beginning with only three dorms, Student Government hopes to avoid the problems encountered by the past student advising programs, in trying to grow too quickly, he said.

"That's why we will take only three dorms at first," he said. "We want to have a solid base of support that will help us establish credibility.

"The program itself has long term values but essentially we first want to establish this strong base of support," he said.

The committee eventually hopes to establish a central office in the Carolina Union to serve off-campus students. All future program expansions will be fully determined this summer, Thompson said.

To attract the most qualified students for the advising positions, the committee plans to recruit students from the Phi Eta Sigma and Phi Beta Kappa honor societies and the Dean's List, he said.

"We also want the advisors to be residents of dorm halls, so we will also go to the Resident Assistants (and Residence Directors) for student recommendations," he said. "We also want to work very closely with the Academic Lieutenant Governors in the dorms on this program," he said.

The first group of advisors will complete a brief training period in late April, and will return before classes next August for more extensive training through the General College, which also trains faculty advisors, he said. The student advisors will also assist Orientation Counselors with dormitory orientation, and may assist with course registration.

Each student advisor will be required to maintain regular office hours, although the number has not yet been determined. "We are exploring its possibilities as a work study job," Thompson said. "We're concerned about students who are interested in academics and who also might need the money."

The Academic Advising Committee has advocated a salary and guaranteed dormitory room for student advisors, he said. "We consider the job of the Academic Advisor just as essential as the duties of an RA."

Thompson said he had spoken with the Office of Stu-

See ADVISOR on page 2

Front page of the *Daily Tar Heel* published March 30, 1982, the day after the men's basketball team won the NCAA championship. North Carolina Collection, Wilson Library.

of mandatory student fees. The paper's critics charged that students should not have to pay for coverage that they disagreed with. By the 1980s the paper began a move toward financial independence by setting up a nonprofit. In 1993, 100 years after it was started, the *Daily Tar Heel* became an independent publication. By the 2000s the newspaper was facing challenges similar to newspapers everywhere: declining ad revenues and a readership that was increasingly looking to newer, online resources for news and information.

Many *Daily Tar Heel* alumni have gone on to prominent careers in journalism, several winning Pulitzer Prizes. Some of the university's best-known alumni were editors of the paper, including university presidents Edward Kidder Graham and Frank Porter Graham, novelist Thomas Wolfe, and journalist Charles Kuralt.

Dance Marathon. In February 1999 a group of around seventy-five UNC–Chapel Hill students danced for twenty-four hours to raise money for the North Carolina Children's Hospital. The Dance Marathon, inspired by a long-running student fund-raiser at Penn State, became an annual tradition. The number of student participants steadily increased, as did the amount of money raised. In 2014 the name of the program was officially changed to "Carolina for the Kids" and began to include other fund-raising activities.

Daniels Building. In 1963 the UNC Board of Trustees approved construction of a new building to house the campus bookstore, a relief to students who had complained about crowded conditions in the Book Exchange, located in the basement of Steele Building. The new bookstore was one of three new student services buildings built on the former site of Emerson Field. It was flanked on either side by the new House Undergraduate Library and Graham Student Union and faced the newly built sunken brick pit created during the construction of the new buildings. When it opened in time for the fall 1968 school year, the new Josephus Daniels Building housed the Book Exchange, which sold textbooks and school supplies, the Bull's Head Bookshop, and other offices and services. In addition to many other modern features, the Daniels Building was an early adopter of cameras and closed circuit television to guard against theft (and also, bookstore administrators argued, to analyze traffic patterns in the store). With the new building, the Book

Exchange name was retired and it was commonly referred to as Student Stores. In addition to selling books and supplies, Student Stores also offered a popular check-cashing service in the 1970s and 1980s. A 1973 *Daily Tar Heel* article reported that the store regularly cashed more than 1,000 checks a day for students.

In 2016, after more than a century of operating a textbook store on campus, the university outsourced the bookstore to Barnes and Noble, which renovated the interior of the building but retained the Student Stores and Bull's Head Bookshop names.

The building is named for Josephus Daniels, who had a long career in journalism and public service. Daniels attended law school at UNC in the 1880s and was an ardent supporter of the university throughout his life, serving on the board of trustees for more than forty years. In 1894, with support from Julian Carr, Daniels purchased the Raleigh *News and Observer* and turned it into a leading paper in the state, as well as one of the primary political tools of the North Carolina Democratic Party. The *News and Observer* was active during the 1898 statewide campaign and was an ardent supporter of the Democrats' white supremacy platform. Throughout the campaign, the paper repeatedly ran viciously racist political cartoons on the front page, many warning of the evils of "Negro domination" that would come if voters failed to elect Democrats. Following the successful campaign and the election two years later of his friend Charles B. Aycock as governor, Daniels was instrumental in developing the legislation that would effectively disenfranchise North Carolina's African American voters for the next half century. Daniels's political connections reached far beyond North Carolina and led to prominent posts in the federal government. He served as secretary of the navy during the administration of Woodrow Wilson, and then later as U.S. ambassador to Mexico under Franklin D. Roosevelt. Daniels returned to Raleigh in 1941 to resume his work on the *News and Observer* and work on his multivolume autobiography.

Danziger's was a legendary Franklin Street candy shop and restaurant. It was opened in 1939 by Edward G. Danziger, a confectioner from Vienna who a few years earlier had fled his native Austria ahead of the Nazi occupation. The candy shop and cafe at 153 East Franklin Street soon became a popular date spot with students. The success of the candy shop enabled Danziger and his family to open several other restaurants in town, including the Zoom Zoom Room and the Ram's Head Rathskeller.

Davie Hall was completed in 1908 to house the Departments of Botany and Zoology. Located at what was then the eastern edge of the campus, it was said to have all necessary modern conveniences, including elevators, a dark room, and rooms suitable for plants and animals. A new wing for botany was built in 1925, and underground lab space was added in 1940. The building did not age well and received a major renovation and addition in the 1960s: parts of the old building were torn away, and a new addition was built around the old one. The new addition added a distinctly modern style to the campus. It was designed by the architectural firm of Holloway-Reeves, which was also responsible for the State Legislative Building in Raleigh. When the new addition was completed in 1967, the Department of Psychology moved in.

Davie Hall is named for William Richardson Davie, the former Revolutionary War officer who is often called the father of the university. Davie graduated from the College of New Jersey (now Princeton) in 1776 and joined the military to serve in the Revolutionary War. After the war he was active in politics in North Carolina, serving as a delegate to the Constitutional Convention, in which he advocated for the interests of slaveholders and helped introduce and pass the Three-Fifths Compromise. At a ratification convention held in Fayetteville in 1789, in which Davie introduced the bill to ratify the federal constitution, he also successfully introduced a bill to establish the University of North Carolina. Davie was active in early university governance helping to establish a curriculum and hire its first faculty. As grand master of the North Carolina Masonic Order, Davie led the Masonic ceremony held at the laying of the cornerstone of Old East in 1793.

In the early 1800s, after an unexpected loss in a race for Congress and following a contentious argument about funding for the university, Davie retired from political life to his growing plantation in South Carolina. At the time of his death in 1820, Davie held 116 enslaved people.

Davie Poplar. The legendary tulip poplar at the heart of the UNC–Chapel Hill campus is older than the university. The earliest known reference to it is in the reminiscences of a member of the class of 1818. In his recollections of campus, he talks about the "old poplar," which shows

THE OLD DAVIE POPLAR U. N. C. CHAPEL HILL, N. C.

Postcard image of the "Old Davie Poplar," 1910. Durwood Barbour Postcard Collection, North Carolina Collection Photo Archives, Wilson Library.

that even in the university's first decades the tree was a landmark (and already considered old). The name Davie Poplar first began to be used in the 1890s, in honor of William Richardson Davie, whose early support has led many to call him the "father of the university." Cornelia Phillips Spencer is believed to be the one who named the tree for Davie.

The Davie Poplar used to be a popular gathering spot for students and a place to hold formal events, like the annual Class Day ceremony. The tree has seen some hard times. In 1902 a severe storm hit the campus and several large branches broke off. To the dismay of many alums, early newspaper reports said that the tree had fallen down in the storm. In 1918, fearing that the tree wouldn't last much longer, the Davie Poplar Jr., grafted from a branch of the original, was planted nearby. Throughout the years, there were continued concerns about the tree—both for its health and for the safety of the people passing underneath. In the 1950s a steel cable was put in place to attach the aging tree to stronger trees nearby, and concrete was used to reinforce the hollow interior of the Davie Poplar. In 1961 seven and a half tons of wood were trimmed from the tree.

The Davie Poplar was one of the focal points of UNC–Chapel Hill's 1993 bicentennial celebration. Public school students from each of North Carolina's 100 counties were invited to campus, each receiving a seedling from the Davie Poplar to plant in their home counties, symbolizing the statewide reach of the university and its ties to the public school system.

Davis Library. Following decades of rapid growth at the university, by the 1970s it became clear that the library collections and services were outgrowing the iconic Wilson Library building. In October 1975 the board of trustees approved the construction of a new central library on campus, using funds available from the sale of campus utilities. Built on the site of a former parking lot next to the Graham Student Union, construction began in 1979, and the new Walter Royal Davis Library opened in February 1984. It was designed by Italian architect Aldo Giurgola, also known for his work on the Wright Brothers National Memorial in Kitty Hawk, North Carolina, and the Australian Parliament House in Canberra.

The library is named for Walter Royal Davis, a donor and member of the UNC Board of Trustees. Davis is credited with persuading the state legislature to allow the university to use the proceeds of its recent sale of campus utilities for the construction of the new library. Davis was a Pasquotank County native who made a fortune in the oil industry in Texas. Despite never having attended college, he often made significant gifts to support higher education in North Carolina. He is possibly the only person to have served on the board of trustees for both UNC–Chapel Hill and Duke at the same time.

Dean Smith Center. As Carolina basketball continued its long run of success in the 1970s, many fans and alumni clamored for a new venue that would seat more people than Carmichael Arena. Fund-raising began as early as 1980 and would result in more than $34 million in private contributions. The building was to be named for coach Dean Smith, who initially resisted the idea until he was convinced that having his name on the arena would help with fund-raising.

The Dean E. Smith Student Activities Center opened on January 18, 1986. The first game was a 95–92 victory for UNC–Chapel Hill over Duke. The state-of-the-art building held more than 21,000 fans, more than double the capacity of Carmichael. Students and alumni quickly took to referring to the domed structure as the "Dean Dome."

It its early years the Dean Dome also hosted a wide variety of popular concerts. University administrators initially began booking concerts to defray operating losses from the expensive new venue. Many of the largest touring acts in the late 1980s and early 1990s performed in the Dean Smith Center, including Pink Floyd, Bruce Springsteen, Tina Turner, and the Grateful Dead.

With the fans spread out in the more spacious Dean Smith Center, the building received some criticism that the game environment was quieter than students and fans had been accustomed to in Carmichael. Some players and fans compared it unfavorably with the notoriously raucous atmosphere in Duke's Cameron Indoor Stadium. One of the more stinging criticisms came from Florida State University basketball player Sam Cassell, who said, after a 1991 game, "This is not a Duke kind of crowd. It's more like a cheese-and-wine crowd, kind of laid back."

In 2018 the Dean Smith Center court was named for men's basketball coach Roy Williams.

Dentistry, School of. *See* Adams School of Dentistry

Basketball coach Dean Smith in the nearly completed Dean E. Smith Student Activities Center at UNC, 1985. Photograph by Hugh Morton. Hugh Morton Photo Collection, North Carolina Collection Photo Archives, Wilson Library.

Dey Hall was completed in 1962 for the use of the university's foreign language departments. The building was praised for being fully air conditioned and for its language lab, which had 200 stations in which students could study languages using tape-recorded lessons and conversations. It is named for faculty member William Morton Dey, who led the department for more than forty years. He joined the faculty in 1909 and was named a Kenan Professor in 1934. He retired in 1950. Dey's specialty was French literature, and his knowledge and contributions were acknowledged by the French government, which made him Chevalier of the Legion of Honor in 1949.

Dialectic and Philanthropic Societies. Commonly known as the "Di" and "Phi," the Dialectic and Philanthropic Societies are the oldest student

organizations at Carolina and were at the heart of student life throughout the university's early history. Students founded a debating society
in 1795, less than a year after the university opened. A rival society was
founded shortly after, and the groups soon changed their names to the
Dialectic Society and Philanthropic Society. They competed for students
for several years before agreeing to divide incoming students geographi-
cally: those from west of Raleigh would join the Dialectic Society, while
those east of Raleigh would join the Philanthropic.

In an era before the university provided any support for student social and nonacademic life, the societies helped with entertainment (participating in and attending formal debates counted as entertainment)
and enforced student discipline with a series of fines for bad behavior.
They also purchased books, building libraries that, by 1850, would be
three times the size of the university's own library. Realizing the importance of the societies in promoting student self-governance, the UNC
Board of Trustees in 1885 passed a resolution requiring all students to
join one of the two groups. The requirement was in place for only ten
years, but the majority of students still joined one of the societies even
after they were no longer required to. The popularity of the societies
began to wane following World War I, as more student activities (including athletics) became available and the Campus Y emerged as the new
center of student life.

In their debates, the societies often took on controversial issues. An
1834 debate on the topic, "Ought slavery to be abolished?" was in favor
of abolition. However, when they debated in 1837 on whether "slavery
was an evil morally or politically," the answer was no. In 1945 the Di Society resolved that the system of racial segregation known as Jim Crow
should be abolished and that African Americans should be admitted
to UNC.

As the campus changed in the twentieth century, so did the societies. In 1930 they began to admit women. In 1959 they voted to merge
into a single organization, the Dialectic and Philanthropic Societies, or
DiPhi. Membership dwindled, but never to the point of dissolution;
there has always been a group of new UNC–Chapel Hill students interested in debate and in being part of the university's oldest tradition.

Dining. Campus dining halls have been a part of campus life—and students have complained about them—since the earliest days of the university. The second building built on campus, after Old East, was Stew-

ard's Hall, which opened in 1795. From the beginning students were unhappy with the food. In petitions to the faculty in 1809, students complained about the quality of food at Steward's Hall, citing "an insufficiency of butter," and beef that is "sometimes tainted, and impregnated with fly-blows." Steward's Hall was eventually leased to a local resident and run as a private business. Many UNC students in the nineteenth and early twentieth centuries got their meals from local boarding houses.

In 1898 the university converted an old gymnasium building into a new dining hall known as Commons Hall. Built on the current site of Phillips Hall, Commons served student meals until 1914, when the much more modern Swain Hall opened. Swain was the main campus dining hall for the next twenty-five years. The opinion of the students about the food offered there can be inferred by the nickname then in regular use, "Swine Hall."

Students never warmed to Swain Hall, and the campus soon outgrew the facility. In 1939 the university opened Lenoir Hall, a large, modern space that could seat up to 1,300 students at a time. Following World War II, students began to have multiple options for eating on campus, including the Pine Room, a snack bar in Lenoir, and the Monogram Club. When campus housing expanded to South Campus in the 1960s, student dining followed. The immediately unpopular Chase Hall cafeteria opened in 1965, and some dorms housed dining facilities.

Campus dining facilities were operated by the university until 1969. Almost immediately following a strike of cafeteria workers who were protesting low pay and poor working conditions, the university outsourced campus dining to Saga Corporation, a company that managed campus dining operations at schools around the country. Saga was soon replaced by Servomation, then by ARA, which later changed its name to Aramark and has managed dining at UNC for several decades.

One of the strangest periods in campus dining came in 1997, when privately operated food stands were placed around Polk Place to serve hungry students during a major renovation of Lenoir. The booths, which included one dedicated to corn on the cob, made the campus look like a county fair. When Lenoir reopened it was fully modernized and gave students a wide variety of dining options.

Dixie Classic was a popular basketball tournament held from 1949 to 1960 in Reynolds Coliseum in Raleigh. Started by N.C. State basketball coach Everett Case, the tournament featured North Carolina's "Big Four" teams (UNC, Duke, N.C. State, and Wake Forest) against top teams from around the country. It was popular with students and alumni and attracted a wide following statewide. The tournament ended in scandal when multiple players—including a couple from UNC—were caught fixing games in exchange for payment from gamblers. The charges cast a pall on basketball for several years. UNC System president William C. Friday limited the number of basketball scholarships and games. The scandal and subsequent reforms contributed to the resignation of UNC coach Frank McGuire and the hiring of his assistant coach, Dean Smith.

Dormitories. The university's first dorm was its first building. When Hinton James arrived on campus in 1795, Old East was the only building on campus. It was not long before the number of students outgrew the available space, even with six people in each room. Many of the earliest buildings have housed students at some point in their history, including South Building, Old West, New East, and New West. With the rapid growth of the university in the early twentieth century, there was a significant increase in the construction of dormitories. Vance, Battle, and Pettigrew Halls were completed in 1912 to house students. An additional ten residence halls were built in the 1920s, including Spencer Residence Hall, the first dorm built to house women students. The university continued to use land on the east side of campus for student housing through the 1940s. The post–World War II boom in enrollment saw the most serious housing crisis yet. With thousands of veterans returning to school, the dorms were filled to capacity and the university installed twenty-six Quonset huts as temporary housing. Even with the extra space, a few students were relegated to trailers and even tents on campus.

In the 1950s the university began to look toward South Campus as a growth area for student housing. In 1958 Avery, Parker, and Teague dorms were completed near Kenan Stadium. The most significant change in student housing came a few years later, in 1962, when the high-rise Ehringhaus and Craige dorms opened. The six-floor dorms were followed in 1965 and 1967 by Morrison and Hinton James dorms, both ten stories tall. Located far from north campus, the high-rises were an attempt to make the most economical and efficient use of the dwindling land available to the university. The push to build even bigger and higher dorms did not last long. There was discussion of building a twenty-one-story dorm on campus, but it was canceled. When the university built new dorms in early 2002, they were smaller and designed to bring more of a traditional campus feel to South Campus.

Dunce cap. When viewing Wilson Library from South Building, the top of the bell tower is visible, aligned with the center of the dome and looking like an old-fashioned dunce cap atop a student's head. One of the persistent rumors around campus is that this was done deliberately by John Motley Morehead, who was angry when Louis Round Wilson wouldn't let him put the bell tower on top of the library. In fact, Morehead's first suggestion was to put a bell tower on top of South Building. When the trustees rejected this plan, the library was suggested, but Wilson pointed out that loud bells reverberating over a quiet reading room would not make for the best study environment. Morehead was eventually persuaded that a freestanding bell tower would be best and the current site was chosen.

E

Eagle Hotel once stood on the present site of Graham Memorial Hall on the east side of McCorkle Place. The university's first steward, John "Buck" Taylor, opened a tavern on the site in 1796, which he and his son operated until the 1820s. It was known simply as the Tavern House and, like most such places at the time, was also an inn and gathering place. The property became a hotel in 1823. Sometime in the 1830s Ann Segur Hilliard, known as Miss Nancy, became the proprietor. The establishment was called first the Hilliard Hotel and then the Eagle Hotel. Hilliard added more space and boarded students there, reaching around ninety boarders by 1850. Hilliard ran the establishment with her sister and brother-in-law, Martha and Benton Utley, who enslaved forty-two people. The university paid for trustees to stay there, including their enslaved servants and their horses. As the only place to stay in Chapel Hill, the Eagle was popular with travelers, especially at commencement time. In 1847 Miss Hilliard built an addition to her hotel to welcome U.S. president and alumnus James K. Polk to that year's graduation.

After the Civil War the Eagle Hotel struggled financially. In the 1890s the owners tore down the original tavern building, replacing it with a large Queen Anne–style structure with a large porch. Known as the University Inn, the property did not thrive. The university bought the site in 1908 and used it as a dormitory until it was destroyed by fire in 1921.

In 1993–94 the faculty and students of the UNC Research Laboratories of Archaeology selected the site to conduct an archaeological field school to celebrate the university's bicentennial. The project demonstrated how the labs train undergraduate students in field and laboratory methods in historical archaeology and showcased the work for the public. Several thousand people visited the site during open houses,

The University Inn (formerly the Eagle Hotel), ca. 1890s. The building was located on the current site of Graham Memorial. North Carolina County Collection, North Carolina Collection Photo Archives, Wilson Library.

including hundreds of school children who participated in the excavations. This work provided new evidence and information about the early history of the town and campus.

Eddie Smith Field House. Completed in 2001, the Field House was built to serve as the indoor home for UNC–Chapel Hill's track and field teams. It was also used an indoor practice facility for the Tar Heel football team for many years before the team decided to build a dedicated indoor practice field. The Field House is named in honor of Eddie Smith Sr., whose son, Eddie Smith Jr., a 1965 graduate of Carolina, made a significant contribution to support its construction. The building houses the Dick Taylor Track, named in honor of one of the university's great track athletes. Taylor, class of 1950, was a star hurdler at Carolina. He was a native of Lumberton, North Carolina, and UNC–Pembroke, located in his hometown, also has a track named for Taylor.

Education, School of. The School of Education traces its origins back to 1877, when the university established a Summer Normal School to provide training for teachers in North Carolina. Teacher training was offered only during the summer until 1885, when the Department of

Normal Instruction was established. A graduate program was established in 1896. The name was changed to the Department of Education in 1903 and became the School of Education in 1913. That same year the school moved into Peabody Hall, a new building constructed with support from the Peabody Education Fund, which had long provided resources for teacher training at UNC and other schools.

Education was a popular major at the university in the post–World War II era, with school enrollment increasing around the state. In 1962 the university awarded more graduate degrees in education than in any other major. By the 1990s the school was consistently ranked among the top twenty-five education programs in the country.

The School of Education has often led the way at the university in hiring women faculty. Women began teaching at the Summer Normal School as early as 1878. In 1927 Sallie Marks became the first woman to join the faculty at UNC, and in 1970 Roberta Jackson joined the School of Education, becoming the first tenure-track African American woman at the university.

Ehringhaus Residence Hall was one of two high-rise dorms completed in 1962, as the university campus continued to move south in order to find a home for its expanding student body. The initial residents of the dorm were all first-year men students. Ehringhaus remained all men until 1972. In the 1970s the dorm developed the reputation as a "jock dorm." Explaining that the dorm was not as wild as some stories suggested, a resident told the *Daily Tar Heel* in 1976, "We don't throw Coke machines off the top floor anymore."

The dorm is named for former governor John Christoph Blucher Ehringhaus. A native of Pasquotank County, Ehringhaus graduated from UNC in 1901 and earned a law degree in 1903. He was North Carolina governor from 1932 to 1936, in the middle of the Great Depression. Ehringhaus managed to keep the state budget under control through cutting programs and introducing the state's first sales tax. After his term he returned to his law practice. In the late 1930s Ehringhaus served as head of the UNC General Alumni Association.

Emerson Field was completed in 1916 and used as the university's main athletic field for football, baseball, and track. It was named in honor of alumnus Isaac Emerson (class of 1879), who donated funds for the field.

Emerson, who studied chemistry at UNC, made a fortune when he invented and sold a new headache remedy called Bromo-Seltzer. Emerson Field was hailed as a state-of-the-art athletic facility when it was opened, boasting concrete bleachers holding up to 3,000 spectators, modern locker rooms, and a cinder running track. The football team quickly outgrew the field, moving to Kenan Stadium in 1927, and track events moved to Fetzer Field in 1935, but the baseball team remained at Emerson through 1965, leaving in time for the field to be cleared in 1967 for a major construction project. The field was located along Raleigh Street at the current site of the Graham Student Union and Davis Library.

Engineering, School of. The university began offering courses in applied sciences in the 1850s as part of an effort to prepare students for careers in engineering, mining, agriculture, and medicine. This was a new area for UNC and required some preparation: after Charles Phillips was selected to teach engineering, he left for a year to study the subject at Harvard before taking over classes in Chapel Hill. Engineering remained on the curriculum when UNC reopened in 1875, with specialties in mechanical engineering, civil engineering, mining, and military science. By the 1890s chemical and electrical engineering were being taught at UNC, and in 1922 the university created a School of Engineering. The school became of point of contention in the discussions over consolidation of the UNC System in the early 1930s. Both UNC and North Carolina State College of Agriculture and Engineering had strong engineering programs, but the consolidation plan sought to avoid this sort of duplication. In 1936, over the objection of the UNC faculty, the board of trustees accepted the recommendation of President Frank Porter Graham and voted to consolidate engineering instruction in Raleigh.

Escheats. To provide funding for the newly founded university in 1789, William R. Davie wrote and helped pass through the legislature an act that would give to the university all unclaimed land and property in the state. Known later as the Escheats Act, after a legal term for the reversion of property to the state, this would be the primary source of revenue for the university for decades. These funds were essential for the early growth of the school but also led to some unusual and troubling results. During the first few years of the university, a good bit of the land that was sold to fund the school was in far western North Carolina, in what is now Tennessee.

In the early to mid-nineteenth century, the unclaimed property allocated to the university sometimes included enslaved women, men, and children. Agents working on behalf of the university participated in the domestic slave trade, seeking to earn as much as possible for the university through these transactions. In some cases, including one described in Kemp Plummer Battle's *History of the University of North Carolina* (1907–12), this meant breaking apart families.

The state of North Carolina still has an escheats fund, but it is no longer earmarked solely for UNC–Chapel Hill. Money in the fund is used to support scholarships and other education initiatives statewide.

Eshelman School of Pharmacy is the only public school of pharmacy in North Carolina and one of the oldest in the nation. It began in 1897 with the hiring of Edward Vernon Howell as a professor of pharmacy. An earlier training program existed from 1880 as part of the first School of Medicine. The pharmacy school was in New West at first, moving to Person Hall in 1912 and to the old chemistry building, now named Howell Hall, in 1925. In 1960 the school opened Beard Hall, named for John Grover Beard, dean of the school from 1930 to 1946. The school added Kerr Hall in 2002, doubling its research and teaching space. A "building-inside-a-building" shared instrument facility was created to house and isolate nuclear magnetic resonance and advanced microscopy equipment. Along with the School of Medicine, the School of Pharmacy also occupies research space in the Genetic Medicine Building, which opened in 2008.

The school, which is one of the top ranked in the nation, has programs in pharmacy education, pharmacy practice, and pharmaceutical sciences. It maintains relationships with the other health affairs UNC–Chapel Hill schools, with international educational partners, and with pharmaceutical companies in Research Triangle Park.

The school became the Eshelman School of Pharmacy in 2008, in honor of alumnus Fred Eshelman, founder of the Wilmington-based contract research organization Pharmaceutical Product Development (PPD). A member of the class of 1972, Eshelman, who is also a dedicated philanthropist, has been a donor to the school's educational initiatives and cancer research. He made a $100 million commitment to the school in 2014, the largest gift to any pharmacy school in the United States.

Eve Carson Memorial Garden. Dedicated in 2010 in memory of students who have died while enrolled, the garden is named for Eve Carson, student body president when she was murdered in March 2008. The space is on Polk Place behind the Campus Y. It features a seating area and a curved marble slab inscribed with a quote from Carson: "Learn from every single being, experience, and moment. What joy it is to search for lessons and goodness and enthusiasm in others." Nearby is a blue butterfly bench donated anonymously in Carson's memory.

Everett Residence Hall was opened in 1928, one of several new dorms built around the same time. It has been popular with students over the years: the Men's Residence Council named it the best dorm for the 1963–64 school year. Everett remained an all-male dorm until 1984. It is named for William Nash Everett, class of 1886 and a longtime member of the UNC Board of Trustees. Everett, a businessman from Richmond County, served in the North Carolina state legislature, where he advocated for the university, and later became the state's secretary of state. The memorials for Everett after his death in 1928 were especially effusive, a testament to his popularity. University president Harry Woodburn Chase said, "Few men loved the University of North Carolina as he loved it, and wrought so consistently for its development."

F

FedEx Global Education Center. UNC–Chapel Hill emphasized its growing focus on international studies and programs with the opening of the FedEx Global Education Center in 2007. The modern building at the corner of McCauley Street and Pittsboro Street houses many of the university's centers with an international focus, offices, an auditorium, and classrooms. The building's construction was funded primarily from the North Carolina Higher Education Improvement Bonds Referendum, passed in 2000, but it received its name in recognition of a $5 million gift from FedEx. It was the first major building on the campus to be named for a corporation (although earlier research labs were named for their corporate sponsors). The decision to name the building after a corporation was somewhat controversial, attracting criticism from some faculty and alums who felt that the university either sold the name for too small an amount or missed an opportunity to honor an important figure from the university's past.

Fencing was a club sport at Carolina as early as the 1930s, when intramural matches were held in Memorial Hall. As interest in the sport grew in the 1960s, the university hired Ron Miller to come to Carolina to start a team. The reputation of the sport may not have been particularly high at the time, as shown by a 1967 *Daily Tar Heel* headline asking whether fencing was a "sissy sport." It was recognized as a varsity sport that year, and Miller would go on to become a legend in collegiate fencing, coaching for fifty-one years until announcing his retirement in 2018. The UNC–Chapel Hill men's fencing teams won eight Atlantic Coast Conference championships between 1971 and 1980, and the women's team, also coached by Miller, won their first ACC championship in 2018.

Fetzer Field was completed in 1935 as part of a Works Progress Administration project. The new athletic field was home to UNC's track and field team and featured a cinder track. The UNC soccer and lacrosse teams also played their home games at Fetzer Field. As the women's soccer team grew in national prominence, the attendance at home soccer games was one of the best in the NCAA. The field is named for Robert Fetzer, UNC athletic director from 1922 to 1947.

Fetzer Field was renovated in the late 1980s and reopened in 1990 with expanded seating and a signature Carolina Blue track. The new track was named in honor of Irwin Belk, a UNC alumnus and former president of Belk department stores, who provided support for the new facility.

In 2017, in order to provide updated and expanded facilities for popular soccer and lacrosse programs, the university demolished Fetzer Field to make way for the UNC Soccer and Lacrosse Stadium.

Fetzer Gymnasium. After four years of construction, Fetzer Gymnasium opened in 1981 on the site once occupied by the Tin Can. The new facility included three separate gyms, as well as offices and classrooms. It is named for Robert Fetzer, who came to UNC in 1921 to coach football and track. He later served as both director of the athletic department and chair of the Department of Physical Education. Fetzer remained as athletic director until 1952, overseeing a period of substantial growth for the program.

Field hockey. UNC students experimented with field hockey early in the twentieth century. A 1902 *Tar Heel* article describes a group of male students playing using an "ordinary cricket ball." The sport apparently did not catch on, as it was not mentioned again until the 1930s, when women students began playing it regularly as a club sport. Field hockey became a varsity sport in 1971, along with seven other women's sports as the university joined the Association of Intercollegiate Athletics for Women. The field hockey team has won multiple ACC and NCAA championships and is often recognized as one of the top programs in the country. In 2018 the university opened the new Karen Shelton Stadium for field hockey, named for coach Karen Shelton.

Finley Golf Course. Designed by George Cobb and opened in 1949, the Finley Golf Course was built to be used by Carolina students and fac-

The 1972 women's field hockey team was the first one to play a full schedule.
UNC Department of Athletics Records, University Archives, Wilson Library.

ulty. The university established an intramural golf program shortly after the course opened. In the 1990s golf course designer Tom Fazio oversaw a major renovation of the course. The redesigned course opened for use in 1999. The golf course was named for businessman and entrepreneur Albert Earle "A.E." Finley when it opened in 1949. Finley was the founder of North Carolina Equipment Company and owned the Pines Restaurant and University Motel in Chapel Hill. Finley was a frequent donor to Carolina and to North Carolina State University, where his name is on Carter-Finley Stadium.

First state university. UNC–Chapel Hill and the University of Georgia compete for the claim of first state university. Each has a fair case to make: Georgia was the first to be chartered, and UNC the first to open. The practice of public support for higher education predates both schools, and even the formation of the United States. Many of the earliest colleges in the country, including Harvard and William & Mary, received at least some direct support from their colonial governments. With the late eighteenth-century establishment of UNC and the University of Georgia, newly formed state governments took a more direct role by issuing charters and providing substantial funding for state universities. North Carolina's 1776 constitution declares, "All useful learning shall be duly encouraged, and promoted, in one or more universities."

The flower ladies were a mainstay on Franklin Street for decades.
This photo shows a group from the late 1960s. Durwood Barbour
Postcard Collection, North Carolina Collection, Wilson Library.

The legislature in Georgia issued a charter for the University of Georgia in 1785. The North Carolina legislature followed a few years later, chartering the University of North Carolina in 1789. But the North Carolinians were quicker to act. Construction of UNC began in 1793, the first students were admitted in 1795, and the first class graduated in 1798. The University of Georgia would not admit its first students until 1801.

Flower ladies. The flower ladies were a Franklin Street institution for most of the twentieth century. A group of local African American women began selling homegrown flowers on Franklin Street as early as the 1920s. They were popular with students and local residents. By the late 1960s more street vendors joined the flower ladies. The new "hippie vendors," selling albums, handmade goods, and drug paraphernalia, soon drew the anger of the Franklin Street store owners, who helped pass an ordinance prohibiting street vendors. Unfortunately, the ordinance also applied to the flower ladies. They moved to the alley adjacent to the Varsity Theatre and eventually to the NCNB Plaza (now called the Bank of America Center), where a few continued to sell flowers through the 1990s.

Action shot from an early game at Kenan Stadium. The old
field house is seen in the background. UNC Image Collection,
North Carolina Collection Photo Archives, Wilson Library.

Football as an organized sport at UNC began in 1888. The university's
first football game—and the first college football game played in North
Carolina—was a loss to Wake Forest in a game played at the state fair.
Many university traditions are tied to the growth of football and other
sports at UNC in the 1890s: to share news about the team, the Athletic
Association began publishing a weekly newspaper called the *Tar Heel*,
the predecessor to the *Daily Tar Heel*; the "tar heels" nickname began to
be more closely associated with the university during this period; when
the team needed official colors, it adopted light blue and white, the
colors of the two debating societies; and the words for the university's
alma mater, "Hark the Sound," were also written during this period.

In the early twentieth century, the football team's biggest rival was
the University of Virginia. The schools played several times in Richmond, Virginia, and the games were attended by large numbers of UNC
students who traveled by train. With the sport gaining fans in the 1920s,
UNC soon outgrew the limited seating at Emerson Field. Support from
alumnus William Rand Kenan Jr. enabled the university to build a
large, new stadium dedicated to football. Kenan Stadium, located in
the woods south of campus, hosted its first game in 1927.

In the years following World War II, Carolina had a series of successful football teams led by star halfback Charlie "Choo Choo" Justice. Jus-

tice was one of the best players in the country, twice finishing as a run-ner up in Heisman Trophy voting. The team went to several bowl games in the Justice era and rose to national prominence. One of the most memorable games of the period was a 1949 meeting between UNC and Notre Dame played in Yankee Stadium. Thousands of UNC students, many waving Confederate flags, traveled to New York for the game.

In the second half of the twentieth century, Carolina football entered the modern era. The university was one of the founding members of the Atlantic Coast Conference in 1953, and games began to be regu-larly broadcast on radio and television. In 1967 Ricky Lanier joined the team, becoming the first African American scholarship football player at the university.

Fordham Hall. Opened in 1988, Fordham Hall was built behind Mitchell Hall to house biology and biotechnology programs, with faculty offices and research laboratories. The building is named for Christopher C. Fordham III, chancellor of UNC–Chapel Hill from 1980 to 1988. Ford-ham was an alumnus (class of 1947) who returned to Chapel Hill in 1971 as dean of the School of Medicine. His tenure as chancellor was marked by a major revision of the undergraduate curriculum; by con-tinued expansion of the university, including the creation of new pro-grams such as the Area Health Education Centers; and by student anti-apartheid protests that culminated in the building of a mock shanty town on Polk Place.

Forest Theatre. Nestled in a natural bowl alongside Country Club Road in Battle Park, this outdoor theater space is defined by stone walls and light towers. It came into official use as a performing space in 1918, when the founder of the Carolina Playmakers, Frederick H. "Proff" Koch, came to Chapel Hill. The first theatrical performance there, Wil-liam Shakespeare's *The Taming of the Shrew*, was presented by summer school students in July 1919. Those first audiences sat on a sloping lawn; the tiered seating and stonework were added in 1940 as a WPA (Works Progress Administration) project. During that work, designers added a stone brought from Roanoke Island that is believed to be a bal-last stone from the ships that carried Sir Walter Raleigh's first colonists in the 1500s. The theater was dedicated to Koch in 1953, and the name was formally changed to Koch Memorial Theatre. The North Carolina

Early performance at Forest Theatre before the addition
of seating in 1940. UNC Photo Lab Collection, North
Carolina Collection Photo Archives, Wilson Library.

Botanical Garden now maintains the space, which is still used as a performance space and venue for receptions, weddings, and picnics.

Franklin Street. The main street of Chapel Hill is named in honor of Benjamin Franklin for his promotion of education. Students and townspeople famously take over the street to celebrate basketball championships and Halloween. It has been the site for parades and protests, as well as for annual street fairs, including Festifall and Apple Chill. Franklin Street has been there from the beginning of the town in 1793. It grew from a modest path to a tree-lined and often muddy thruway lined by wooden sidewalks, until it was paved in the 1920s. Business establishments have come and gone through the years. Some of the oldest still in business on the street are the Carolina Coffee Shop, Julian's, Sutton's Drug Store, the Varsity Theatre, and the Chapel Hill Tire Company. Two curious markers stood on the south side of Franklin Street near Battle Hall. The one still standing marks the Boone Trail Highway, first erected in 1923 as part of an ambitious plan to raise awareness for the need for better roads in North Carolina. The second marker was for the

Celebration on Franklin Street following the men's basketball team's 2017 NCAA championship. Photo by Justin Smith, UNC–Chapel Hill.

Jefferson Davis Highway, a transcontinental highway project started by the United Daughters of the Confederacy in 1913, which was never completed. In 2019 the Davis Highway marker was removed by the Town of Chapel Hill.

Frank Porter Graham Child Development Institute. Established in 1966, the Frank Porter Graham Child Development Institute was founded to encourage and facilitate research that would improve the lives of children. The institute supports the work of more than 200 researchers from a variety of disciplines. Major projects have included work on developmental disabilities, early childcare and education, and public policy. The institute operated an on-site daycare facility for more than forty years. It is named for former UNC president Frank Porter Graham.

Fraternities and sororities. The first fraternity on campus was the Beta chapter of Delta Kappa Epsilon, organized in April 1851. It was soon followed by Phi Gamma Delta, Delta Psi, Chi Psi, and Sigma Alpha Epsilon. They disbanded during the Civil War and university closing, returning to campus soon afterward. Alpha Tau Omega, active since 1879, is the longest consecutively active fraternity at UNC–Chapel Hill. In 1890 the Greek letter fraternities published the first yearbook, *The Hellenian*,

Members of Alpha Pi Omega, UNC's (and the nation's) first Native American sorority. *Yackety Yack*, 2000, North Carolina Collection, Wilson Library.

which was replaced in 1901 by the university-wide *Yackety Yack*. Professional fraternities established chapters at UNC in the 1910s, starting with Alpha Chi Sigma, a chemistry fraternity, in 1912.

Although women began attending the university in the 1890s, the first sororities did not open until 1923, with Pi Beta Phi and Chi Omega. Their number increased from the 1930s through the 1970s, as women students gained a greater foothold. The first Jewish fraternity at UNC came in 1924, with the Omega chapter of Tau Epsilon Phi. In 1973 the Psi Delta Chapter of Omega Psi Phi became the first historically black Greek fraternity at Carolina; and the Kappa Omicron chapter of Delta Sigma Theta the first African American sorority on campus. In 1994 UNC–Chapel Hill undergraduates organized the nation's first sorority for Native American women, Alpha Pi Omega, which has grown to nineteen chapters across the country.

A number of cultural fraternities and sororities have joined these since the late 1990s, representing students interested in Asian, South Asian, Latinx, and multicultural experiences. All of the Greek fraternities and sororities are official student organizations at Carolina, and in 2018 about 17 percent of the students were affiliated with one.

Fraternity Row originally stretched from the site of Porthole Alley south to Cameron Avenue. A fire in January 1919 destroyed three of the ten houses and nearly burned down the new Carnegie Library (Hill Hall). The trustees decided to deal with the hazards of frame fraternity houses by moving them off-campus. They purchased lots on the west side of Columbia Street and exchanged the fraternities on campus property for new spaces there. The newly dubbed Fraternity Court was completed in 1926. Until recently, only two of the original fraternity houses remained: Hill Hall Annex, located just to the north of Hill Hall, was built in the 1890s as the Delta Kappa Epsilon Fraternity. It served many subsequent functions until it was demolished in 2017. The sole remaining structure is Evergreen House, which was built around 1890 as the Kappa Sigma Fraternity and now houses the Department of Psychology community clinic.

Friday Center. The William and Ida Friday Center for Continuing Education opened in 1991 to serve as a conference facility for the university. Located a few miles from campus and convenient to Interstate 40, the site offers an expansive space and plenty of parking, features increasingly hard to find on the crowded main campus. The Friday Center also serves as the home of UNC–Chapel Hill's continuing education efforts, offering programs and classes to anyone interested in learning, regardless of their affiliation with the university.

The center is named for one of UNC's most influential leaders, William C. Friday, and his wife, Ida Friday. William Friday earned his undergraduate degree at North Carolina State College of Agriculture and Engineering and a law degree from UNC. He spent his entire career in higher education, serving first as dean of students at UNC and then as assistant to the president of the UNC System. Friday was appointed president of the consolidated university (later the UNC System) in 1956 and remained in the job until 1986, making him the longest-serving president in the system's history. Ida Howell Friday was a graduate of Meredith College and the UNC School of Public Health. A painter and sculptor, she also supported local historic preservation, civil rights, women's rights, and the arts.

Friday's tenure as president was marked by incredible growth and change. The system grew from three schools to sixteen as the state substantially increased its commitment to public higher education. Friday's time as president also saw multiple controversies. Early in his tenure he had to deal with the Dixie Classic gambling scandal and the state's Speaker Ban Law. For much of the 1970s Friday struggled to refute and then respond to accusations from the federal Department of Housing, Education, and Welfare that the UNC System was not providing equal funding and support for African American students.

Friday remained wary of the influence of college athletics throughout his career. In his retirement he was one of the cofounders of the

Knight Commission on Intercollegiate Athletics, which sought to provide analysis and support for universities trying to manage the rapid growth and influence of athletics. For many years Friday hosted the *North Carolina People* interview program on UNC-TV and was one of the best-known figures in the state.

G

Gardner Hall. Opened in 1953, Gardner was one of three new buildings built for the School of Business Administration (Carroll and Hanes were the others). The new buildings were designed to match the older buildings directly across Polk Place (Saunders, Manning, and Murphey). It has served as the home for several academic departments. Since the 1970s the Department of Economics has been based in Gardner Hall. The building is named for former North Carolina governor O. Max Gardner. A native of Shelby, he received his undergraduate degree from North Carolina State College of Agriculture and Engineering (now North Carolina State University) and attended law school at Carolina. He played football for both schools. Serving as governor from 1928 to 1932, during the Great Depression, he sought several cost-saving measures, including consolidation of the state's three public universities: UNC, North Carolina State College, and the North Carolina College for Women (now UNC-Greensboro). After leaving office, Gardner established a law firm in Washington, D.C., where he was a successful lobbyist and an adviser to President Franklin D. Roosevelt.

Genetic Medicine Building. This multidisciplinary research facility opened in 2008 to house scientists and laboratories from the School of Medicine's Departments of Biochemistry and Biophysics, Genetics, and Pharmacology, and from the Eshelman School of Pharmacy's Institute of Pharmacogenomics and Individualized Therapy, the Center for Integrative Chemical Biology and Drug Discovery, and the Center for Nanotechnology in Drug Delivery. At seven stories and some 330,000 square feet, it is one of the largest buildings on campus.

Genome Sciences Building. This building was a major component of a campus-wide effort initiated in 2004 to expand research facilities at UNC–Chapel Hill. Completed in 2012, the building houses the Carolina Center for Genome Sciences, which brings together faculty from across campus working on genomics research. It contains auditoriums, classrooms, and laboratories. Built to be more environmentally friendly than older campus buildings, it includes several innovative features, including rooftop greenhouses used by researchers working on plant genomics.

George Watts Hill Alumni Center. In 1993, after several years of construction, the General Alumni Association dedicated the George Watts Hill Alumni Center, located on Stadium Drive. The center was designed to be used both as a gathering place for alumni and as an event center. It houses the offices for the Alumni Association, including the *Alumni Review*, and alumni records. The building includes a library, meeting rooms, and the Carolina Club, a private membership club with dining and event spaces established in 1993 for alumni association members and UNC faculty and staff. The center is named for alumnus George Watts Hill (class of 1922), a successful business leader from Durham who donated $3.5 million toward the construction of the center. Hill's father, John Sprunt Hill, had also been a prominent donor to the university, funding the construction of the Carolina Inn and providing support to the university libraries.

German Club. This student organization oversaw campus dances for many years. The name comes from a style of formal social dancing in the nineteenth century called a "German cotillion" or simply "German." At Carolina throughout the first half of the twentieth century, the formal dances organized by the club were known as the "Germans."

UNC students were organizing formal dances as early as the 1830s, when they hosted a Commencement Ball. Dances were primarily organized by campus clubs. In 1923, following a dance that was, according to the *Tar Heel*, "characterized by excessive drinking and other loose conduct," students sought to provide more oversight of campus dances and charged the German Club with their management. At one point open to all students, the club was later composed of representatives from UNC's social fraternities.

The spring and fall Germans were major events in Carolina student life. They often featured prominent national acts, such as Woody Herman, Fats Domino, and Louis Armstrong (who performed on campus at least twice). The entertainment was not limited to musical acts — comedian Woody Allen performed at a German Club dance in 1965. By the late 1960s, as the student body grew larger and more diverse, fewer students attended the formal dances and they eventually ended. There was a brief revival of the German Club dances in the 1980s, but these lasted only for a few years.

Gerrard Hall (New Chapel). This modest building is now little noticed on Cameron Avenue between South Building, the Campus Y, and Memorial Hall. Construction took place between 1822 and 1837, halted by the lack of funds. It was the university's second chapel, replacing Person Hall for that purpose, in an era when students began each day with mandatory religious services. Gerrard was also used for commencement and other official functions. President James K. Polk (UNC class of 1818) spoke there for commencement in 1841, as did President James Buchanan in 1859 and President Andrew Johnson in 1867.

Gerrard, along with Old West and the extant design of the quad around the Old Well, are the work of noted architect William Nichols. Along with the other antebellum buildings, Gerrard was built using an enslaved labor force, including people enslaved by Nichols and by university trustee William Polk.

Gerrard has entrances on two sides, a feature that shows how university plans change over time. Not long after it was completed a portico was added on the south side, as university officials thought to face the entrance toward a planned east-west avenue in that direction. In 1900 the portico came down, as the anticipated avenue had not been built, and two entrances were built into the building's east side. Between the two is a marble dedicatory plaque with the biblical phrase from Micah: "To do justly and to love mercy, and to walk humbly with thy God." In the early 2000s university architects rebuilt the south portico.

The building is named for Charles Gerrard, a Revolutionary War veteran who bequeathed the university nearly 14,000 acres in Tennessee, part of which he received for his service to the state in the Revolutionary War. Funds from the sale of these lands paid to complete the chapel construction in 1837.

Gillings Center for Dramatic Art. This facility, located on Country Club Road adjacent to the Old Chapel Hill Cemetery, is the home of the Department of Dramatic Art and PlayMakers Repertory Company. The building has offices, classrooms, rehearsal spaces, production shops, and two theaters. The Paul Green Theatre, which seats 500, is named in memory of Paul Green, the Pulitzer Prize–winning playwright and human rights activist who was a UNC alumnus and professor. The theater features an innovative thrust stage designed by renowned scenic artist Desmond Heeley. The Elizabeth Price Kenan Theatre, a performance space with flexible seating, hosts student productions, the PRC2 series, as well as guest shows. The space's name recognizes the support of local philanthropist Betty Kenan for the performing arts at UNC. The opening of the center in 1998 meant that for the first time all of the UNC Department of Dramatic Art operations were together in one location. The building was named the Joan H. Gillings Center for Dramatic Art in 2017 in recognition of Gillings's support for performing arts programming at UNC–Chapel Hill. A resident of Chapel Hill and Wilmington, North Carolina, Gillings has been a committed supporter of programs both at Carolina and at the University of North Carolina–Wilmington.

Gillings School of Global Public Health. Public health programs at UNC began in the 1920s as part of the university's efforts to address the needs of the state. It set up training programs for county health officers and public health nurses in collaboration with the State Board of Health. These programs were part of the School of Medicine, eventually becoming a separate school and awarding its first degrees in 1940. Graduate and research programs helped the school grow exponentially in the decades after World War II. It developed international research endeavors such as the Carolina Population Center, and multi-institutional efforts to address cancer, HIV/AIDS, aging, and environmental pollutants.

In 2008 the school became the Gillings School of Global Public Health in recognition of a transformational gift from local business owners and philanthropists Dennis Gillings and Joan Gillings. Adding the word "global" to the school's name illustrated its reach. Its faculty and students work in all 100 counties of the state and in more than 60 countries worldwide. Consistently ranked as one of the top public

Hippol Castle, home of the Order of the Gimghoul, ca. 1930s.
Photo by Bayard Wootten. Bayard Wootten Photo Collection,
North Carolina Collection, Wilson Library.

health programs in the country, the Gillings School has departments in biostatistics, environmental sciences and engineering, epidemiology, health behavior, health policy and management, maternal and child health, and nutrition, and a program in public health leadership.

Gimghoul. In 1889 a small group of UNC students founded a club called the Order of Dromgoole. They were likely inspired by the example of secret societies at other colleges, such as the well-known Skull and Bones at Yale. The name came from a former student named Peter Dromgoole, who disappeared from campus mysteriously in the 1830s and was never heard from again. The name was soon changed to the Order of the Gimghoul, "in accord with midnight and graves and weirdness," according to one of the founders. The club was open only to male students, junior class or higher, and to faculty. In its early years the names of the club members were published in the yearbooks; the names of members are now kept secret. There are other long-running private societies on campus, including the Gorgon's Head, another secret society, and the Golden Fleece, an honorary organization. But the Order of the Gimghoul is the only one with a castle.

In 1915 the Order of the Gimghoul purchased a large tract of land east of campus. They sold part of it, gave part of it to the university to be used as Battle Park, and kept the remainder to build a home for the order. Completed in 1926 using designs by architect and UNC alumnus Nathaniel Cortlandt Curtis, the large stone building, known as Hippol Castle, is located at the end of a residential street on the east side of campus called Gimghoul Road. The Order of the Gimghoul still exists, with new members added regularly, but its activities and traditions remain a mystery to the majority of UNC–Chapel Hill students.

Glee Club. One of the university's oldest student clubs, the UNC Glee Club was founded in 1848 at the suggestion of math instructor Charles Phillips. The club soon became a fixture at celebrations and official events and helped introduce at least a couple of notable songs. In 1878 the Glee Club was the first group to perform "The Old North State," which would later become the state song of North Carolina. At the club's 1897 commencement performance they introduced a new piece, "Hark the Sound," which was soon adopted as the university's alma mater. In 1934 women students at the university organized a Women's Glee Club. The men's club often performed outside of Chapel Hill, traveling around the state and country for concerts and going on extended tours of Europe in 1927 and 1966. In June 1966, the Men's Glee Club performed before a national audience in an appearance on the Ed Sullivan Show. The Men's and Women's Glee Clubs remain active on campus and are now overseen by the Department of Music.

Golden Fleece. The Order of the Golden Fleece was founded in 1904 at the suggestion of philosophy professor Horace Williams, who was worried that the university was becoming too factional. Williams, along with faculty members Edward Kidder Graham and Eben Alexander, wanted to promote service to the university. The order was open to all students, faculty, and alumni, though new members were primarily rising seniors. Women began to be admitted starting in 1972. The name comes from the story of Jason and the Golden Fleece. The president of the club is known as the Jason, while the members are called Argonauts.

The induction or "tapping" ceremonies are now private but used to be held in a dramatic public ceremony. In the 1930s students would gather in Memorial Hall to hear a lecture on the subject of character, followed by a ritual in which current members of the Golden Fleece, wearing black hooded robes, would walk among the audience and select the students to be inducted into the order. The Order of the Golden Fleece continues to add new members every year. The Golden Fleece typically works in a quiet way through individuals and other organizations to promote unity and address timely issues. On rare occasions, the order has worked publicly on campus issues such as hazing and the student honor code. The organization remains private, but the names of members are not kept secret and have included many well-known UNC–Chapel Hill administrators and alumni.

Gore Cogeneration Facility. Located near the intersection of West Cameron Avenue and Merritt Mill Road, the so-called Cogen Facility is the fourth power plant at UNC–Chapel Hill, completed in 1992. The plant, which is coal powered, provides about 20 percent of campus electricity needs, including the hospitals. It also generates steam as a byproduct, which is used for heating and other uses, thus the term "cogeneration." While the facility is recognized as efficient and clean for this type of energy production, it is responsible for 50 percent of the greenhouse gases that the university emits every year. The university is in the process of modifying it to also use natural gas, which will reduce coal burning, and instituting further measures to reduce emission and improve air quality.

The facility is named in memory of professor Joshua W. Gore, who came to UNC in 1882 to teach physics and engineering and lead the School of Mines, which became the Department of Applied Science. Gore installed the first electrical systems on campus in 1890 and helped design and build the first telephone system. He also helped design the first power plant in 1895, which he oversaw until his death in 1908.

Government, School of. Now located in the Knapp-Sanders Building on the eastern edge of campus, the School of Government is the oldest program of its kind in the nation. It was created to train and support local officials at all levels of government in North Carolina. Since its inception it has been the destination for generations of new mayors, legislators, city managers, county attorneys, judges, budget directors, tax supervisors, planning and zoning personnel, and more. More than

12,000 public officials participate annually in a training program. The school also has a residential and online master of public administration degree program.

Law professor Albert Coates began to offer classes for elected officials who needed to learn the laws they were expected to enforce. He soon realized there was a constant flow of new officials who needed this training. In 1931, with the help of his wife, Gladys Hall Coates, he created the Institute of Government as a private enterprise. It became part of the university in 1942 and was the foundation for the School of Government, established in 2001.

Governors. When Roy Cooper was sworn in on January 1, 2017, he became the 32nd governor of North Carolina to have attended Carolina. The first was William Miller, who attended UNC during the 1802 school year, left without graduating, and was elected governor in 1814. Miller's story is not unusual—many early governors left the university before graduating, a sign that possession of a college degree was not seen as a prerequisite for many professions in the nineteenth century. Twenty-one governors (including Cooper) earned degrees from the university.

Graham Memorial Hall. Not long after the death of beloved university president Edward Kidder Graham in 1918, alumni announced a plan to raise money to build a student union, which would be named in honor of Graham. The Campus Y had served as the center of student activities since 1907 and was running out of space. Construction on the union began in 1922 but took nearly a decade, delayed in part by lack of funds. Students eventually decided to pay for the finishing touches themselves, voting in 1931 to pay a union fee of one dollar each academic quarter for furnishings and maintenance.

The Graham Memorial Student Union opened in the fall of 1931. It featured a large, wood-paneled lounge, game rooms with billiards and table tennis, a bowling alley, and a barber shop. It also housed student organizations and publications, including the *Daily Tar Heel* and the *Yackety Yack*. It would remain the center of student life until the new Frank Porter Graham Student Union was built in the late 1960s.

Graham Memorial is named for Edward Kidder Graham. A native of Charlotte, he graduated from UNC in 1898 and was hired the following year as a librarian. He soon joined the English department as an instructor and was frequently promoted, serving as department chair and later dean of the College of Liberal Arts. He was appointed acting president of UNC in 1913 and was elected to succeed Francis Venable in 1914. He served until his death from influenza in 1918. Despite his short tenure as president, Graham has had a lasting influence on the university. He continued the work begun by Venable to develop UNC into a research university. Graham was also especially interested in expanding the university's role in North Carolina. He helped establish the Bureau of Extension, which brought lectures and lent books to communities across the state.

When the student union moved to its new home in 1968, the Department of Dramatic Art took over Graham Memorial. In 2000, following renovations, the building became the home of the honors program and other campus offices.

Graham Residence Hall opened in 1924, alongside two other new dorms (Aycock and Lewis). It was named in 1928 for John Washington Graham, the son of former governor and U.S. senator William A. Graham. After graduating from UNC in 1857 and serving in the Confederate army, where he was wounded twice, he had a successful career as a lawyer. Graham was an active member of the conservative party that sought to overturn Reconstruction-era reforms in the state. As a member of the state senate in the early 1870s, he was active in the ultimately successful effort to impeach Governor William Holden. During the trial Graham suggested that the crimes committed by robed Ku Klux Klan members in the late 1860s were actually done by disguised African Americans. Graham was a member of the UNC Board of Trustees for more than fifty years.

Graham Student Union. Carolina students began advocating for a new student union as early as the 1950s. The Graham Memorial Building, dedicated in 1931, was ill-suited for the needs of the post–World War II generation of students. The new union was part of an effort to expand and modernize student services at the university, built at the same time as the new Student Stores building and House Undergraduate Library. The modern architectural style of the new buildings was not popular with everyone, as seen in debates in the *Daily Tar Heel* at the time, but the increase in space was definitely welcomed. The Graham Student Union opened for students in 1969. The new building featured expanded office space, meeting rooms, lounges, snack bar, and a bowling alley. It was expanded in 1981 and again in the early 2000s.

The building is named for Frank Porter Graham, one of the most beloved figures in UNC–Chapel Hill history. A 1909 graduate of Carolina, Graham was a popular history professor at UNC before being elected as president of the university in 1930. In 1931 he was appointed president of the consolidated University of North Carolina. Graham oversaw the university system through the difficult years of the Great Depression and the subsequent boom in enrollment and building during and after World War II. He is usually remembered best for his concern for students and for his progressive politics.

Graham was widely popular with students, especially in Chapel Hill. Future university and state leaders, such as UNC System president William C. Friday and state governor Terry Sanford, cited Graham as a formative influence on their careers. Graham was often less popular around the state and was criticized for his support of organized labor and civil rights. His willingness to speak out on social and political issues was tempered by his reluctance to do anything that he felt would harm the university. When Pauli Murray applied to attend graduate school at UNC in 1939, Graham responded that it was too soon for him to publicly advocate for admitting African Americans to the university, fearful that doing so would "cause a throwback to a darker time."

In 1949 Graham was appointed to serve out the remainder of a vacant term in the U.S. Senate. Widely expected to win reelection in 1950, he was defeated in the primary by Willis Smith, whose campaign focused heavily on Graham's support of civil rights and integration. The loss was a blow not just to Graham but to his many devoted supporters among students and alumni. Graham would spend the remainder of his career working at the United Nations but was a frequent presence in Chapel Hill until his death in 1972.

Granville Towers opened in 1966 as an experiment in a new type of campus housing. The two high-rise buildings on Franklin Street, built on the site of the old Chapel Hill High School, would house more than 1,000 students in the country's first example of a private dorm. Granville Towers was built by a private company in cooperation with the university. While students enjoyed more amenities than those in traditional dorms, they still had to follow university rules about drinking and hours, and there were graduate counselors on every floor. More expensive than campus housing options, Granville Towers offered a more luxurious and more independent living experience, with furnished rooms, private bathrooms, a cafeteria, parking, and, perhaps most coveted by students, air conditioning in every room.

The towers were originally divided by gender: men in the west building, women in the east. In 2009 UNC–Chapel Hill purchased Granville Towers and the adjacent shopping center, but the towers continued to be run by a private company in cooperation with the university.

Greenlaw Hall. In the mid-1960s construction began on a new building for the English department, which was the largest on campus and had long outgrown its home in Bingham Hall. Opened in 1970, Greenlaw Hall contained over 100 faculty offices, classrooms, and an auditorium. The original plans also called for a second-floor bridge connecting Greenlaw to Bingham, but it was abandoned due to lack of funds.

The building is named for former faculty member and administrator Edwin A. Greenlaw. Although he spent only twelve years at Carolina (1913–25), he had a lasting influence. Hired as an English professor and later promoted to department chair and then dean of the graduate school, Greenlaw helped grow the department, starting a program in comparative literature. He led the university's efforts to join the prestigious Association of American Universities and helped establish the University of North Carolina Press. He was also one of the original group of Kenan Professors. In *The Web and the Rock*, a novel by his former student Thomas Wolfe, the character of Randolph Ware is based on Greenlaw.

Green Theatre. *See* Gillings Center for Dramatic Art

Grimes Residence Hall opened in 1922, along with Mangum, Ruffin, and Manly dorms. During World War II the four dorms housed U.S. Navy cadets. There is some question as to whom this naming honored. The UNC Board of Trustees minutes record that the honoree was Bryan Grimes (1828–1880), while later accounts note that the honoree was his, son J. Bryan Grimes (1868–1923). The elder Grimes was a university alumnus and trustee and UNC's second-highest-ranking Confederate officer (Leonidas Polk was the highest-ranking alumnus). Grimes came from a prominent eastern North Carolina family that grew wealthy through the use of enslaved labor. After the war he was a conservative and an advocate for white supremacy. In 1880 he was assassinated under mysterious circumstances. His alleged killer was acquitted but subsequently lynched. An early twentieth-century account of Ku Klux Klan activity in the state claimed that the elder Grimes was an organizer in eastern North Carolina. His son, J. Bryan Grimes, was also an alumnus and trustee and was North Carolina secretary of state. The younger Grimes chaired the trustee committee that oversaw development of Polk Place. He was also an agricultural and cultural leader, helping organize the Tobacco Growers Association and form the State Literary and Historical Association.

H

Halloween. Carolina students began celebrating Halloween with an informal gathering on Franklin Street in the 1980s. Town police closed off the main blocks of Franklin Street for an informal parade of costumed students. Within a decade it was the biggest party of the year. By the early 1990s attendance was growing as students from other universities flocked to Chapel Hill. Word spread, and it quickly grew into a very big event. By the late 1990s Chapel Hill police were estimating crowds of between 40,000 and 60,000 people. The peak was probably in 2007, when an estimated 80,000 people crowded into downtown. Concerned about increasing costs for crowd control and crime (thirteen people were arrested in 2007), the university and town began promoting a "Homegrown Halloween," taking steps to limit the size of the crowds. By the 2010s the Halloween crowds had been reduced to a still large but more manageable average of 20,000–30,000 students.

Hamilton Hall was built in 1972 to house the departments of history, political science, and sociology. The Research Laboratories of Archaeology occupies the basement. When it opened the university celebrated the fact that they had managed to preserve an old oak, located on the building's southeast side, throughout the construction process. That tree still shades Hamilton's entrance.

The building is named in honor of Joseph Grégoire de Roulhac Hamilton. Hamilton chaired the history department from 1908 to 1930 and then turned his attention to the collection and preservation of personal papers and historical records from throughout the Southeast. Equipped with the selling point of the new university library building (now Wilson Library), Hamilton and his wife and colleague, Mary

Cornelia Hamilton, traveled widely and convinced many families to donate their family and business papers to UNC. Dubbed "Ransack" by those who claimed he was robbing their states of their history, he gathered materials that would be the foundation of the newly established Southern Historical Collection. Hamilton was an avowed white supremacist whose own historical works helped construct the "Lost Cause" version of American history and justified Ku Klux Klan violence and Jim Crow segregation. Yet he was a meticulous scholar who preserved the primary sources that a younger generation of historians would use to challenge and eventually discredit the work of Hamilton and other Confederate apologists.

Hanes Art Center. The Frank Borden and Barbara Lasater Hanes Art Center is the home of the Department of Art and Art History. Completed in 1982, the building allowed the department to centralize all of its activities. The center includes classrooms, offices, studio spaces, and the Joseph Curtis Sloane Art Library, named in honor of a former department chair.

Frank Borden Hanes and Barbara Lasater Hanes were active arts and civic supporters at Carolina and in their hometown of Winston-Salem. Frank was the first chairman of the university's Arts and Sciences Foundation, which generates private support for the College of Arts and Sciences.

Hanes Hall was dedicated in 1953 as one of three new buildings for the School of Business Administration (Gardner and Carroll were the others). For several decades Hanes Hall was also the home of the university registrar and career services offices.

The building is named for Robert March Hanes, UNC class of 1912 and veteran of World War I. The Winston-Salem native had a very successful career in business, most notably as president of Wachovia Bank. He served in the state legislature, where he advocated for the establishment of a statewide sales tax, and on the UNC Board of Trustees. He was also active in the establishment of Research Triangle Park—the main administrative building at the park is named in his honor.

Hardin Residence Hall opened in 2002, one of four new dorms completed around the same time (along with Craige North, Koury, and Horton). The new dorms were smaller than their high-rise counterparts, an intentional decision to help foster more of a sense of community in UNC–Chapel Hill residence halls. The new dorms were situated in a way that would create open, outdoor quad areas in an attempt to duplicate the popular spaces on the old campus.

Originally named Morrison South for its proximity to nearby Morrison dorm, the building was renamed in 2007 for former chancellor Paul Hardin. A native of Charlotte and a Duke alumnus, Hardin had an itinerant career in higher education. Before coming to Chapel Hill, he served as president of Wofford College, Drew University, and Southern Methodist University. Hardin was chancellor from 1988 to 1995, a period highlighted by the student-led activism in support of a freestanding black cultural center and by the university's 1993 bicentennial celebration.

Health Sciences Library. In 1971 UNC–Chapel Hill dedicated a new Health Sciences Library, bringing together the separate departmental libraries from the five health affairs schools: medicine, dentistry, nursing, public health, and pharmacy. At first many services were available only to graduate students; in 1976 the Health Sciences Library began circulating its collection to undergraduate students. The original three-story building was expanded in the early 1980s.

He's Not Here opened in 1972 in a courtyard between Franklin and Rosemary Streets. By the late 1970s it was described by the *Daily Tar Heel* as one of the two most popular bars in town (Troll's was the other). He's Not Here is known for its balcony, outdoor seating, and legendary plastic blue cups holding thirty-two ounces of beer that have been offered at the bar since at least the mid-1980s. There is no consensus on where the bar got its memorable name; most likely it is a reference to a common refrain of bartenders fielding calls from concerned spouses or friends.

Hickerson House. The two-story historic house on Battle Lane is the home of the Center for Urban and Regional Studies. The house was built between 1915 and 1925 by Thomas Felix Hickerson, a Carolina alumnus and longtime faculty member. He deeded the house to the university in 1952, but it was not used by the university until he died in 1968. The Center for Urban and Regional Studies, created in 1957, is one of the oldest university-based research centers of its kind. Its focus is on basic and applied research on urban, regional, and rural planning and policy issues.

Hickerson taught engineering and mathematics at UNC from 1909 to 1952. He was an authority on highway engineering, producing authoritative works on road and bridge building and advising on numerous projects, including the Blue Ridge Parkway. At UNC he was one of the longest-serving trustees of the Order of the Gimghoul. He helped plan the Gimghoul Road development and oversaw the construction of the order's Gimghoul Castle.

High Noon. In the early 1970s small groups of Carolina students began gathering at the bell tower at noon to smoke marijuana—they called it High Noon. The location was likely selected because of its central location and also due to the tall hedges that used to surround the bell tower. Their meetings were an open secret on campus and a source of concern for university officials. After the *Daily Tar Heel* and other statewide newspapers began writing about the gatherings, parents and others contacted the university to express their displeasure. The publicity led to more students participating, with as many as 300 joining in by early 1975. While there were no arrests, repeated threats by university administrators—including the use of photographers on top of Wilson Library taking pictures of the smokers—helped discourage most students from joining in, though smaller groups would continue to meet and smoke for many years.

Hillel. The first Jewish student organization at UNC was the Menorah Society, active in the 1910s and 1920s. The group was the center of a minor controversy when university president Frank Porter Graham offered the group space in the campus YMCA, despite objections from the YMCA national organization. The Menorah Society and its successor, the Carolina Jewish Society, were short-lived, most likely due to lack of interest from students. In 1935 students began advocating to open a chapter of the Hillel Foundation, the national Jewish student organization. One of the leading advocates was student Maurice Julian, who would later open Julian's clothing store on Franklin Street. The UNC chapter of the Hillel Foundation formally opened on October 9, 1936, with a ceremony attended by Frank Porter Graham. The rabbi who served as director had an office in the Campus Y and began offering religious services in Graham Memorial Hall. The group had a house on Rosemary Street in the 1940s before moving to its current location on Cameron Avenue in 1952. In 1966 the Hillel House hosted a speech by Frank Wilkinson, after he had been prohibited from speaking on campus under the state's Speaker Ban Law.

Hill Hall was completed in 1907 as a new library, replacing separate spaces for the libraries of the Dialectic and Philanthropic Societies, and a small university collection. Its construction marked a step in the university's evolution into a research institution, based on the model of German universities that trained specialists as faculty and emphasized the discovery of new knowledge. Industrialist and philanthropist Andrew Carnegie provided the funds, with the requirement that the university match his gift to provide for upkeep and expansion. When it opened, the Carnegie Library Building, as it was originally called, had 45,822 volumes, with room to accommodate 200,000. The UNC Bureau of Extension and the University of North Carolina Press had its beginning in this building until they outgrew their space there. In 1930, following the completion of the new University Library (now Wilson Library), the Department of Music moved into the Carnegie Building. The department added an auditorium and an organ. Durham philanthropist John Sprunt Hill and his family funded the new construction and renovations, and the university renamed the building in their honor.

John Sprunt Hill was an 1889 university graduate who built a fortune in banking, insurance, and real estate. He served as a university trustee for many years. In addition to his support for the music department, Hill donated $5,000 to the library to be used for collecting historical and literary material about North Carolina, an enterprise now known as the North Carolina Collection. During the 1920s Hill built the Carolina Inn and later donated it to the university, stipulating that its profits support the North Carolina Collection.

After a major renovation, the auditorium reopened in 2017 as the James and Susan Moeser Auditorium. It was named in recognition of former chancellor James C. Moeser and his wife, Susan. Moeser, who was chancellor from 2000 to 2008, served in administrative positions at various universities and as chancellor at the University of Nebraska–Lincoln. During his tenure at Carolina, Moeser oversaw campus-transforming construction funded through a bond referendum and the successful Carolina First fund-raising campaign; he also oversaw the creation of the Carolina Covenant. Susan Moeser is a member of the music department faculty. Both Moesers are concert organists.

Hinton James Residence Hall. Completed in time for the fall 1967 semester, Hinton James was (and remains) UNC–Chapel Hill's largest residence hall. Housing close to 1,000 students, "HoJo" continued the 1960s trend of building high-rise dorms on South Campus. The dorm was the first to house both women and men when, in the fall of 1969, UNC began "Project Hinton," an experiment in coed living, with women occupying the top two floors of the dorm. By the 1970s Hinton James housed more African American students than any other campus dorm, leading to accusations that the university was enabling student "self-segregation."

The building is named for UNC's first student, Hinton James. A native of what is now Pender County, James arrived at the newly established University of North Carolina on February 12, 1795. For two weeks he was the only student. He lived in Old East (the only building on campus at the time) and studied alongside the few other students who found their way to Chapel Hill. He graduated in 1798, one of seven members of the university's first graduating class. James had a successful career as an engineer and later as a politician, serving in the state legislature and as the mayor of Wilmington. The legend of Hinton James looms large not just because he was the first student but because of the way he got to campus. James is said to have walked all the way from his home, a journey of around 140 miles. There is no documentary evidence to support the idea that James walked, and one early account suggested that he came on horseback. Whether true or not, the story of Hinton James's long walk began to emerge in the early twentieth century and is now a common campus legend.

Holi Moli. In 2008 members of the Hindu YUVA (Youth for Unity, Virtues and Action) student group held the first on-campus celebration of the Hindu holiday Holi, the "festival of colors." The event expanded in 2009, bringing in more students for the traditional ceremony, during which participants showered each other with packets of colored powder. Sponsored by several South Asian student groups, the event quickly grew, with more than 2,000 students participating in 2016. During the chaotic celebration, clouds of colorful powder rise into the air and students emerge coated with different colors. The ceremony has moved around campus as it grew. It was held for several years on Polk Place before moving to Hooker Fields.

Homecoming. Through much of the nineteenth century, commencement served as a sort of unofficial homecoming for alumni. Former students often returned to participate in the ceremonies and connect with former classmates. The modern homecoming tradition began in the early twentieth century, coinciding with the rising popularity of intercollegiate sports. The University of Missouri is credited with starting the trend when it held a homecoming celebration in 1911 complete with pep rallies and a parade leading up to a football game. At UNC, the General Alumni Association worked to build a homecoming tradition. The first official homecoming weekend at Carolina came in 1923. Students began electing a homecoming king and queen in the 1930s and held a homecoming parade beginning in the 1950s (however, the homecoming parade was never as popular or as rowdy as the annual Beat Dook Parade).

The tradition of electing a homecoming queen evolved from a process that resembled a beauty pageant in the mid-twentieth century to a more democratic system in the 1970s. The changes resulted in both a more diverse group of winners and a number of challenges to a tradition that was increasingly seen as sexist and outdated. In 1975 students elected a male student, Delmar Williams. The athletic department threatened to cancel the ceremonies before reaching a compromise in which a female student was picked as honorary homecoming queen and Williams was honored as homecoming king. In 1976 student Sheri Parks was elected the first African American homecoming queen. By the 1980s the annual election was frequently used as a vehicle for pranks. Students ran a dog for homecoming queen in 1980 (she was eventually disqualified because the rules stated that the candidate had to be a currently enrolled student), and in 1983 students elected Steve Latham, who ran under the pseudonym "Yure Nmomma."

Despite changing student attitudes, homecoming continued to be a major event for alumni. The General Alumni Association expanded its programming, hosting large reunions for classes and for affinity groups such as Black Alumni Reunion, band members, and student government. Activities take place throughout what is now called Alumni Weekend.

Honors Carolina is a program of the College of Arts and Sciences for qualified undergraduate students that features courses, special events, and learning opportunities to enhance a student's degree work. Some students enter the program when they enter the university, and others apply at the end of their first year. Honors students must maintain a cumulative grade point average of 3.000 or higher and complete a minimum number of honors credit hours by graduation in order to receive the "Honors Carolina Laureate" distinction on their transcript. Honors courses are open to all academically qualified students, although members of Honors Carolina receive priority registration. To graduate from the university with honors or highest honors, students must complete a senior thesis in their academic major.

The honors program began in 1954 for academically gifted freshmen. Over the years it expanded its scope to cover all undergraduates and a larger cohort, more programs, and more outside-the-classroom learning opportunities. The program renovated and moved into its current location in 2000 and changed its name to Honors Carolina in 2011.

The campus home for Honors Carolina is the James M. Johnston Center for Undergraduate Excellence, located in Graham Memorial Hall. The center is named in recognition of the James M. Johnston Charitable Trust, which supported the 1999–2000 renovation of the building. Johnston was an alumnus who created the trust in his will. The trust has also made over $25 million in scholarships gifts to Carolina since 1967.

Hooker Fields. The university's intramural fields have been located along South Road across from the Old Chapel Hill Cemetery since the 1930s. The fields are used by students participating in intramural and club sports. To accommodate increasing demand for use of the fields, lights were added in the 1960s and artificial turf was installed in 2000.

The fields are named in honor of former chancellor Michael Hooker, who graduated from UNC–Chapel Hill in 1969 (a semester later than many of his classmates, after Hooker put off the then-required swim test until the last minute and failed on his first try). Hooker earned his Ph.D. from the University of Massachusetts and soon moved into higher education administration. He served as president of Bennington College and chancellor of the University of Maryland–Baltimore County and the University of Massachusetts system before returning to Carolina as chancellor in 1995. Hooker's tenure was marked by an emphasis on advancing technology on campus and a commitment to statewide service. While chancellor he visited all of North Carolina's 100 counties. Only forty-nine when he was named chancellor, Hooker was successful in connecting with students. He was a fixture at UNC sporting events and on several occasions crowd-surfed in the student section at men's basketball games. He was only a few years into his tenure as chancellor when he was diagnosed with leukemia. Hooker died in 1999.

Horace Williams Airport. The university-owned Horace Williams Airport closed in 2018 after eighty years of operation. It opened in 1928 when local contractor Charlie Lee Martindale purchased fifty acres from UNC professor Horace Williams and built a small airfield that came to be called the Chapel Hill Airport. Throughout the 1930s and early 1940s Carolina and Duke student pilots could be seen flying over Chapel Hill in Piper Cubs and other trainers, under a program sponsored by the federal Civil Aeronautics Agency. UNC bought the airport in 1940 when it received 870 adjacent acres through Williams's will. They renamed it for Horace Williams, who had been a popular professor of philosophy at Carolina from 1890 to 1940.

In 1942 Horace Williams Airport and UNC–Chapel Hill became one of five U.S. Navy pre-flight schools. By 1945 more than 18,000 cadets had trained there, including baseball great Ted Williams, Paul "Bear" Bryant, and future presidents Gerald Ford and George H. W. Bush. The airport always saw a lot of activity around big sporting events. After the war the airport was a popular destination for private plane owners and visiting alumni. On the day of the 1948 UNC-Texas football game, ninety-seven planes used the airport.

Since the late 1960s, with the rapidly expanding Raleigh-Durham airport (RDU) nearby, university administrators and town leaders have frequently debated the necessity of having an airport in Chapel Hill. One of the most compelling arguments to leave the airport in place was its use by UNC–Chapel Hill doctors traveling around the state with the Area Health Education Centers (AHEC) program. The call to remove the airport was especially strong in the early 2000s as the university began planning for Carolina North, a major expansion of the campus to be built primarily on the land used by and surrounding the airport. In preparation to carry out that plan, the Chapel Hill Flying Club relocated to the airport in Sanford, North Carolina, and the AHEC air operations moved to RDU in 2007. Although those plans still remain on hold, the university finally closed the airport to air traffic in 2018, citing the cost to keep it open.

Horney, Giles F., Building. Located on Airport Road, the Horney Building and its annex house physical plant and facilities support shops, offices, and work areas. Completed in 1962, it was named in honor of Giles Foushee Horney (1908–1986) in 1981. Horney, who worked for the university for forty-four years, served for twenty-nine years as superintendent of buildings and grounds. Horney was a champion for campus beautification and oversaw the installation of brick sidewalks in the 1950s.

Horton Residence Hall opened in 2002, one of four new dorms completed around the same time (Craige North, Koury, and Hardin were the others). The smaller dorms were an effort to bring more of a traditional campus feel to South Campus, which had been dominated by the high-rise dorms built in the 1960s and 1970s. The dorms, which included seminar rooms to bring residence and academic life closer together, were in high demand among students when they first opened.

Originally named Hinton James North, the building was renamed in 2007 for George Moses Horton. An enslaved African American writer living in Chatham County, just south of Chapel Hill, Horton was a presence on campus for many years in the early to mid-nineteenth century. He initially came to Chapel Hill to sell produce, but students and local residents soon discovered his talent for writing and memorizing poetry. He sold love poems to students, who were said to have passed them off as their own. Assisted by Caroline Hentz, the wife of a faculty member, in 1829 Horton published *A Hope for Liberty*, a collection of poems, making him the first African American man to publish a book in the South. Horton published another book in 1845 and drew the attention of local residents and UNC administrators. Yet he remained enslaved, finally escaping at the end of the Civil War with a Michigan regiment on its way north. Horton lived the remainder of his life in Philadelphia.

Hospitals. The North Carolina legislature appropriated funds for a teaching hospital at the university as part of the plan to create a four-year school of medicine at UNC. The hospital opened in 1952 and was named North Carolina Memorial Hospital in honor of North Carolinians who had given their lives in military service. The hospital was

North Carolina Memorial Hospital shown shortly after its opening in 1952.
UNC Photo Lab Collection, North Carolina Collection
Photo Archives, Wilson Library.

heavily used, welcoming its 100,000th patient in 1960. It expanded rapidly, adding new programs and expanding the facilities. In 1965 the hospital was the subject of an investigation under the Civil Rights Act. In response, the university announced that it would no longer segregate hospital patients by race.

In 1989 the hospital and its constituent services were organized under the new name UNC Hospitals. In 1998 the North Carolina General Assembly authorized the creation of the UNC Health Care system, which recognized the statewide impact and importance of the UNC hospitals and health care services. The major hospital services in Chapel Hill grew to include the Neurosciences Hospital (opened in 1995), the Women's Hospital (2001), the Children's Hospital (2001), and the Cancer Hospital (2009), home of the Lineberger Comprehensive Cancer Center.

House Undergraduate Library. As early as 1960, library and university administrators began discussing the need for a library space devoted to the needs of undergraduate students. The Robert B. House Under-graduate Library opened in 1968, around the same time as the new Student Stores and Graham Student Union buildings. The three build-ings, designed by the Charlotte architectural firm Cameron Associates, marked a major expansion of the campus and a new commitment to student services. The House Undergraduate Library has focused on the needs of undergraduate students, staying open later than the other cam-pus libraries and offering or hosting support services, including a term paper clinic in the 1970s, one of the university's first computer labs in the 1980s, and, more recently, reserve readings, and spaces and equip-ment for design and media production.

The library is named for Robert B. House, who served as chancellor from 1945 to 1957. A Halifax County native who graduated from UNC in 1916, House spent the majority of his career at Carolina. He joined the administration in 1926 and was appointed dean of administration for the Chapel Hill campus in 1934, after the creation of the consolidated UNC System. In 1945 the name of his job changed and he became the first person at the university to hold the title of chancellor. House led Carolina through a period of dramatic change, first helping the univer-sity endure the Great Depression and then World War II, and then over-seeing the subsequent rapid expansion of the campus and student body and the admission of the first African American students in the 1950s.

Howell Hall. Completed in 1906 to house the Department of Chemistry (which had been in Person Hall), this building was the first on campus to be funded by a direct appropriation from the state. When the chem-istry department moved to Venable Hall in 1925, the building, which had been known as the Chemistry Building, became home to the School of Pharmacy and was renamed for the pharmacy dean. When the phar-macy school moved to a new home in Beard Hall in 1960, Howell Hall was renovated for the School of Journalism, which was there until 1999. The Department of Psychology and Neuroscience moved to the build-ing after the journalism department left. A renovation in 2016 added new laboratories for research in human neurostimulation, physiologi-cal monitoring, brain imaging, and behavioral observation.

The building is named in honor of Edward Vernon Howell, Caro-lina's first pharmacy dean. Born in Raleigh, Howell came to campus in 1897. He headed the pharmacy school for thirty-three years. During his tenure Howell worked to enhance professional standards for the state's pharmacists. At a time when faculty could join the varsity football team, Howell was an outstanding player. He is also believed to have been the first person in Chapel Hill to own an automobile.

Hyde Hall is home to the Institute for Arts and Humanities, which provides support and training for faculty through a variety of programs. The decision to place a new building for the institute in McCorkle Place, the oldest part of campus, symbolized the institute's centrality to nurturing the historical commitment to the arts and humanities at Carolina. Completed in 2002, Hyde Hall was funded entirely through private donations. *Conversation,* a sculpture by North Carolina artist and Carolina alumnus Thomas Sayre, sits in the garden at Hyde Hall. The stone work symbolizes the interdisciplinary dialogues that take place at the institute.

The building is named in honor of Barbara Rosser Hyde (UNC–Chapel Hill class of 1983) and her husband, J. R. "Pitt" Hyde (class of 1965). Both are committed philanthropists for civic and educational programs in their hometown of Memphis and at Carolina.

Infirmary. The university did not have a campus infirmary until 1895. The *Tar Heel* described it as a place where "the indisposed, the drooping, the lame and the halting may retreat." In an era when transportation was slow and unreliable and the nearest hospital was in Durham, the college infirmary often handled serious illnesses, including a case of smallpox in 1900 that had the whole campus on high alert. As student health needs increased, a new infirmary was built in 1900, only to be replaced again in 1907. In 1919 the campus hired its first physician, Dr. Eric Abernethy, who brought modern ideas about sanitation and medical practices to the campus. The infirmary building was later named Abernethy Hall in his honor. In an era with very different ideas about privacy, the names of sick students who were admitted were published in the "Infirmary List," a regular feature of the student newspaper through the early 1960s.

Influenza. The influenza pandemic that swept the world in 1918 and 1919 had a very visible effect in Chapel Hill, claiming two consecutive university presidents. Edward Kidder Graham, the popular young president who was leading the university's growth and transformation into a modern research university, died from complications from the flu in October 1918. His successor, Marvin Hendrix Stacy, died from influenza just a few months later. Other than the tragic loss of Graham and Stacy, UNC did not suffer great losses during the pandemic, with only a few students dying. Concerned about future outbreaks, in 1919 UNC hired its first physician, Dr. Eric Abernethy, and began the work of modernizing the university infirmary and sanitation practices on campus.

Information and Library Science, School of. The university began offering courses in library science as early as 1904, as part of the summer school, and added them to the regular curriculum a few years later. Librarian Louis Round Wilson was an early proponent of professional library training and spoke often about the need for a library school on campus. Wilson's advocacy increased in the 1920s, and the university agreed to add the new program. In 1931, supported by a grant from the Carnegie Foundation, UNC began offering classes in the School of Library Science, with Wilson as the director. The school was located in the new University Library (now Wilson Library). Wilson was succeeded after a few years by Susan Grey Akers, one of the original faculty members. When her title was changed to dean in 1941, Akers became the first woman to hold an academic deanship at the university.

The school moved to Manning Hall in 1970 after the building was vacated by the law school. In 1988 the name was changed to the School of Information and Library Science, and in 1999 it was ranked by *U.S. News & World Report* as the top library and information science graduate program in the country.

Institute of Marine Sciences. Founded in 1947 as the University Institute of Fisheries Research, the institute was established to give Carolina students and faculty an opportunity to learn and conduct hands-on research on coastal issues, and to advise local and state government. Located along the coast near Morehead City, the institute includes research labs and teaching facilities.

Integration. Under Jim Crow laws from 1900 to 1951, North Carolina's public schools at all levels were segregated institutions with separate schools for whites, African Americans, and Native Americans. In the 1930s university administrators successfully fought the entry of African Americans to graduate programs by helping open a law school and other graduate programs at the North Carolina College for Negroes in Durham (now North Carolina Central University). In 1951, however, in *McKissick v. Carmichael*, the courts ruled that the two law schools were not equal and ordered UNC to admit the African American plaintiffs to its law school. Following their legal victory, Harvey Beech, James Lassiter, J. Kenneth Lee, and Floyd McKissick enrolled in the summer of 1951. The same year Carolina admitted Edward Oscar Diggs, an African American student, to the medical school because there were no comparable schools in the state, and Gwendolyn Harrison, a teacher, to summer school graduate courses.

Native Americans who sought entrance to UNC had a more arbitrary experience, as admittance sometimes depended on individual administrators. While there had been one or two American Indians in UNC programs in the 1920s, the 1950s court rulings also opened the doors to them. Cecil B. Lowry (Lumbee) entered as a junior in 1951, and the following year Genevieve Lowry (Lumbee) transferred to UNC as a junior and Otis M. Lowry (Lumbee) entered the medical school.

UNC continued to have a reluctant approach to integration. The first African American students were restricted to their own floor in Steele Dormitory (now Steele Building) and denied seating in the student section of the football stadium. Once the Supreme Court outlawed all forms of segregation in *Brown v. Board of Education* in 1954, the university had no further legal recourse. In the fall of 1955 the first African American undergraduates entered Carolina: brothers LeRoy and Ralph Frasier and John Lewis Brandon. Enrollment grew slowly; by 1963 only eighteen African American students were at Carolina.

Despite this step toward integration, local businesses continued to maintain racial segregation. In February 1960 nine African American high school students in Chapel Hill staged a sit-in at Colonial Drug Store, setting off years of boycotts, sit-ins, and marches. They were soon joined by university students from Carolina, North Carolina A&T in Greensboro, and other nearby colleges. Many clergy members, faculty, and town residents joined the protests. In March 1964 two African American activists and two white university students staged a weeklong Easter fast in front of the Franklin Street post office. The Ku Klux Klan responded by staging a rally in Chapel Hill. Student government generally supported the protests, and the honor court acquitted all of the student protesters who appeared before it. In contrast, the university administration, by far the largest employer in town, tried to maintain a publicly neutral stance despite its tacit support for segregation. The university's North Carolina Memorial Hospital still maintained segregated facilities, the university television station had refused to air a national program about desegregation, and the athletics program refused to move its weekly press luncheons from a segregated Chapel Hill restaurant. Passage of the Civil Rights Act in the summer of 1964 ended this phase of resistance to integration.

Harvey Beech (*left*) and J. Kenneth Lee entering Manning Hall
on June 11, 1951, their first day as law students at UNC.
J. Kenneth Lee Papers, Southern Historical Collection, Wilson Library.

The university's first black athlete, Edwin Okoroma of Nigeria, joined the soccer team in 1963. Charles Scott became the first African American scholarship athlete in 1966 when Coach Dean Smith recruited him to join the basketball team. That same year, the School of Social Work hired Hortense McClinton, the first African American faculty member at Carolina.

Internet. The university entered the age of networked computing as early as 1966 as a partner in the Triangle University Computation Center in Research Triangle Park, which linked computers at UNC–Chapel Hill, N.C. State, and Duke. In 1984 the university joined a computer network sponsored by the Association of American University Students to facilitate communication between member universities. By 1991 the university was offering e-mail as a service to campus users. To get access, students and faculty had to go to Phillips Hall and sign up. They received a thirty-eight-page manual explaining how to use e-mail. For faculty and staff who wanted to stay in touch but were dubious about the new service, the university provided "Papermail," which would print e-mails and send them through the campus mail. By 1993 over 1,000 students signed up for e-mail in a single month. UNC–Chapel Hill launched its first website in the mid-1990s and began the processing of moving more and more information and services online.

Intimate Bookshop. Although it no longer exists, the Intimate Bookshop lives on in Chapel Hill's reputation for creative writing and independent thinking, both of which were nurtured throughout the twentieth century at the Intimate by Carolina faculty and students. The bookshop began in 1931 when Carolina student Milton "Ab" Abernethy set up shop in his boarding house room and invited people to explore the world of books and literature. Abernethy had also just started a literary magazine called *Contempo* with his fellow student and friend Anthony Buttitta. That endeavor survived only three years but introduced the work of a number of influential writers and thinkers to the small college town.

The bookshop, however, continued. In 1933 it moved into its first Franklin Street location. The store quickly became the center for radical activity and gatherings, in part because of the printing press in the back, where Abernethy printed *Contempo* and materials for radical campus organizations.

Team from the coed intramural bowling league, 1973. The campus bowling alley was on the ground floor of the Frank Porter Graham Student Union. UNC Photo Lab Collection, North Carolina Collection Photo Archives, Wilson Library.

In 1964 Wallace Kuralt and his wife, Brenda, bought the store. During their tenure the Franklin Street store thrived, competing with the campus textbook store and expanding its selections to better serve a general audience. The Kuralts eventually opened nine more stores around the state and in Atlanta. A fire decimated the Chapel Hill store in 1992. The Kuralts rebuilt, adding space and special touches such as squeaky floorboards so that it seemed like the old familiar store. The growth of chain bookstores in the 1990s eventually forced Kuralt to close all of the Intimate stores, including the Franklin Street location in 1998.

Intramural sports. UNC students began participating in organized intramural sports in the 1920s. These casual but competitive activities have been popular with students ever since, though the games have changed over the years. Some sports, like tennis, basketball, and softball, have been popular for decades, but other sports have come and gone depending on the interests of the students. In the 1920s and 1930s indoor track, water polo, boxing, and horseshoes were among the sports offered. Whiffle ball and ultimate Frisbee were popular in the 1970s. More recent intramural sports have included inner tube water basketball, kickball, and street hockey. Dorms and fraternities have traditionally been the most active in fielding teams, though the programs at UNC–Chapel Hill have drawn interest from a wide variety of campus organizations. In 2018 UNC Campus Recreation reported that on average two out of three students participate in intramural sports during their time at Carolina.

Invisible University of North Carolina. In the fall of 1970 graduate student Nyle Frank started the Invisible University of North Carolina. The (very) informal "invisible university" offered alternative classes in the style of 1960s teach-ins. Anyone interested could sign up to take a class, or to teach one. The first course, taught by campus police chief Arthur Beaumont, was called Cooperation between the Fuzz and the Fuzzies. Other courses included graffiti interpretation and pumpkin carving. Frank, a native of Los Angeles, was a well-known figure on campus in the early 1970s. He was easily recognizable by his elaborate, colorful clothing and his distinctive "goastache" (half mustache, half goatee). Not satisfied with just an invisible university, in December 1970 Frank was crowned King of the Invisible Universe in a three-and-a-half hour ceremony in the Pit, attended by more than 2,000 students.

J

Jackson Hall. The building now known as Blyden and Roberta H. Jackson Hall was originally built in 1942 to house the campus's U.S. Navy pre-flight school. After World War II a kitchen and dining room were added and it housed the Monogram Club, an organization of current and former varsity athletes. The building became known as the Monogram Club and contained the popular Circus Room soda fountain and snack bar. After a brief stint as a faculty club, the Monogram Club building was renovated again and became the home of the Office of Undergraduate Admissions. In 1992 it was renamed in honor of Blyden and Roberta Jackson. Blyden Jackson, hired in 1969 in the English department, was the first African American full professor at Carolina. When his wife, Roberta Jackson, was hired in 1970 by the School of Education, she was the first tenure-track African American woman in the Division of Academic Affairs.

Joyner Residence Hall. Completed in 1948, Joyner was one of several new dorms built in response to the post–World War II increase in enrollment. Originally housing only men, the building was converted to a women's dorm in the early 1960s. It is named for James Y. Joyner, UNC class of 1881. Joyner had a long career in education, first as a school teacher and then as a faculty member and administrator at the North Carolina College for Women (now UNC-Greensboro). He was a classmate and friend of future governor Charles B. Aycock, who appointed Joyner to be superintendent of public education in North Carolina, a position he held until 1919. Joyner was a prominent supporter of public education throughout his life.

JubiLee

A SALUTE TO SPRING

Brochure from the
first Jubilee festival,
held in 1963.
Carolina Union Records,
University Archives,
Wilson Library.

Jubilee was an annual music festival held at the end of the spring semester from 1963 to 1971. It was popular from the beginning. The headliners of the first Jubilee, the Four Preps, drew around 5,000 people to their performance on the lawn in front of Graham Memorial Hall. The concerts grew in popularity as they continued to bring in national acts, including Flatt and Scruggs, Neil Diamond, Johnny Cash and June Carter, and B.B. King. The 1970 festival, held in Kenan Stadium, was a three-day affair that included not just concerts but carnival rides, poetry readings, fireworks, and a 3:00 A.M. showing of Rocky and Bullwinkle cartoons. By 1971 the event got a little too big. An estimated 23,000 people attended the concert on Navy Field featuring Chuck Berry, Muddy Waters, and the Allman Brothers. The crowd included many people without tickets who rushed past the security barriers. Citing increasing costs and concerns over safety, the university discontinued Jubilee.

Julian's. In 1942 alumnus Maurice Julian opened a men's clothing store on Franklin Street to cater to the cadets in the U.S. Navy pre-flight school on campus. After the war Julian's College Shop catered to students and faculty in an era when most of the people on the still predominantly male campus wore a suit and tie every day. At the time, the 100 block of Franklin Street had nine men's stores, including Varley's, Town and Campus, and Milton's Clothing Cupboard, owned by Maurice Julian's brother, Milton. As times and fashion changed, the other stores gradually closed, leaving Julian's as the last of the old-school menswear stores on Franklin Street. After Maurice Julian's death in 1993, the business was inherited by his children. Originally located at 140 East Franklin Street, near the Carolina Coffee Shop, the business moved across the street to 135 East Franklin in 2007.

The influence of Julian's has extended well beyond the store largely through the work of Maurice Julian's son, Alexander, who went on to become a successful fashion designer and was known as a master colorist. The university has called on Alexander Julian, also an alumnus, at least twice to help revitalize the UNC style: in 1993, by redesigning the men's basketball team uniforms (he added the signature argyle to the uniforms), and in 2010, when he redesigned the university's graduation gowns. After many years of lamenting that the gowns were more turquoise than true Carolina blue, Julian was given the task of redesigning them. The new, "true blue" gowns were first worn at the 2011 commencement. One of the most prominent of Julian's regular customers is probably UNC–Chapel Hill basketball coach Roy Williams. After the Tar Heels won the national championship in 2005, Coach Williams joked, "I owe it all to my lucky Alexander Julian suit and tie."

K

Kenan-Flagler Business School. UNC first established a School of Commerce in 1919 to train students to "meet the more complex and changing conditions of modern commercial and industrial life," according to the *Tar Heel*. Housed originally in Alumni Hall, the school held classes in Saunders Hall and then in Bingham Hall. The early 1950s was a period of growth and change for the school: the name was changed to the School of Business Administration, the program moved into larger facilities in the newly built Carroll Hall, and the school launched a master's of business administration program. In 1991, following gifts from the W. R. Kenan Jr. Charitable Trust and the Kenan family, the school name became the Kenan-Flagler Business School. The name recognizes Mary Lily Kenan Flagler Bingham, sister of William R. Kenan Jr., who established the Kenan Professorships with a bequest, and her husband, oil and railroad magnate Henry Morrison Flagler. With the completion of the McColl Building on a hill near the Dean Smith Center, the school moved to South Campus in 1997.

Kenan Laboratory was completed in 1971 as laboratory and office space for the Department of Chemistry. It was funded by legislative appropriation and named in honor of William Rand Kenan Jr., UNC class of 1894. As a student Kenan assisted in experiments that helped identify calcium carbide and acetylene, work that helped lead to the development of the Union Carbide Company. Kenan worked on the development of acetylene production and later became business partners with oil executive Henry Morrison Flagler. Kenan supported many projects at UNC, most notably the football stadium, which he asked to be named in memory of his parents.

When it opened, Kenan Laboratory was the largest example yet of "modern architecture" on a campus that had largely built in the colonial revival style. Its gray concrete utilitarian appearance struck many people as ugly, although it and the later-built Morehead Laboratory are now considered valuable examples of midcentury modern architecture.

Kenan Music Building. Opened in 2008, the Kenan Music Building was a part of the Arts Commons envisioned under Chancellor James Moeser, who led efforts to expand and upgrade facilities for the arts at UNC–Chapel Hill. The effort received substantial support from the Kenan Charitable Trust, which earned naming rights to the new building. The trust also provided funding for sixteen full scholarships for students studying music. According to Moeser, the facility provided students and faculty with first-class teaching and rehearsal spaces for the first time since 1930.

Kenan Professorships. Kenan family members have supported the University of North Carolina since its beginning. The family and its related philanthropies are among the largest donors to the university. Arguably this support has had its greatest influence in the endowed professorships that bear the surname. The first of these, the Kenan Professorships, was established in 1917 through the bequest of Mary Lily Kenan Flagler Bingham. One of the first endowments to UNC and the largest gift to a state university at the time, her gift enabled the university to pay higher faculty salaries to attract and keep outstanding professors. The William R. Kenan Jr. Professorships, created by the namesake's bequest in 1965, added another twenty-five faculty positions. The Graham Kenan Professorship was established in the School of Law in 1965, and the Sarah Graham Kenan Professorships, created in 1968, benefit the law, medical, and business schools. The most recent addition to this aspect of Kenan family philanthropy are the Kenan Eminent Professorships, set up in 2003 to create five faculty appointments and to match gifts from other donors who also contribute to such an endowment.

Kenan Residence Hall was completed in 1939, at the same time as McIver Residence Hall, both of which would serve as women's dormitories for the rapidly expanding population of female students at Carolina. The building is named in honor of Mary Lily Kenan Flagler Bingham, whose bequest to the university in 1917 helped establish the Kenan Professorships.

Kenan Stadium. As college football grew rapidly in popularity in the early twentieth century, the Tar Heels soon began attracting more fans than could fit in Emerson Field, which could hold only around 3,000 people. A group of alumni led an effort to build a new stadium and began raising money. The fund-raising effort reached William Rand Kenan Jr., a graduate of the class of 1894 and a member of one of Carolina's earliest football teams. Kenan initially gave $1,000 and eventually agreed to donate the entire amount required for the stadium, around $275,000. It was to be named Kenan Stadium in memory of his parents, William R. Kenan Sr. and Mary Hargrave Kenan.

In 2018 a faculty committee and some journalists—including from the *Daily Tar Heel*, which ran a front-page story on the stadium—criticized the university for honoring Kenan Sr., one of the leaders of the 1898 Wilmington coup that overturned a multiracial government and murdered numerous African American citizens. Following public discussion and criticism, the university announced that the plaque honoring William Kenan Sr. would be changed to focus instead on William Kenan Jr. in recognition of his substantial financial support of the university.

The stadium was built south of campus in a natural valley over Meeting of the Waters Creek. It was designed by Atwood and Nash, a prominent North Carolina firm that had worked on many significant buildings around the state and on campus. The new stadium was so well received that it attracted the attention of other universities. Atwood and Nash were later hired to provide designs for new stadiums at the University of Georgia and the University of Alabama. Kenan Stadium hosted its first football game, a UNC victory over Davidson, on November 12, 1927. It was formally dedicated a few weeks later, on Thanksgiving Day, during the UNC-Virginia game.

The stadium has undergone several additions and renovations. In 1963 upper decks were added, increasing the seating capacity to 43,000. More seats were added in each of the following three decades, with a major renovation and expansion taking place in 2010–11. This renovation resulted in the demolition of the original field house to make way for the Loudermilk Center for Excellence, an academic support program for UNC student athletes.

Kenan Stadium, University of North Carolina, Chapel Hill, North Carolina

Kenan Stadium, ca. 1930s. Durwood Barbour Postcard Collection,
North Carolina Collection Photo Archives, Wilson Library.

The university's annual spring commencement has been held in Kenan Stadium since the 1930s. It has hosted speeches by U.S. presidents (John F. Kennedy in 1963 and Bill Clinton in 1993) and major concerts, including U2 in 1983 and Bruce Springsteen in 2003.

Kenan Theatre. *See* Gillings Center for Dramatic Art

Kerr Hall was dedicated in 2002 as a teaching and research building at the School of Pharmacy. The building is named for School of Pharmacy alumnus Banks Kerr, who donated $2 million toward its construction. After graduating from UNC, Kerr opened a drugstore in Raleigh, the beginning of a successful statewide chain of stores. At its peak, there were ninety-seven Kerr Drug stores.

Kessing Pool is the university's outdoor swimming pool. It was originally built for use by navy cadets attending the pre-flight school at UNC, one of five U.S. Navy pre-flight schools established across the country during World War II. The pool is named for Oliver Owen Kessing, who was the first commanding officer of the campus pre-flight school. The swimming pools on campus were among many spaces on campus that remained segregated when the first African American students enrolled in the early 1950s. In an oral history interview, Floyd McKissick, one of the first African American students to attend UNC when he entered the law school in 1951, remembered the swimming pools: "There were some incidents of some of the kids [going] to the swimming pool to swim and they wouldn't let them in, and I told them this pool was going to get integrated today, and I just went on and jumped into the pool. After I jumped into the pool, I walked on out and nobody said anything to me and I said nothing to anybody else. I said, 'It's integrated now.'"

Knapp-Sanders Building. Located on the eastern edge of campus at Country Club and Raleigh Roads, Knapp-Sanders the home of the School of Government. The building was completed in 1956, funded through a gift from the Knapp Foundation and from a legislative appropriation.

The building is home to a series of large historic murals by artist Frances Vandeveer Kughle. Painted in the style of earlier WPA (Works Progress Administration) murals, the fourteen works, installed in 1960, depict scenes from North Carolina history. After many years of hearing criticisms that the murals overlooked or misinterpreted significant aspects of state history, the School of Government removed many of the murals and arranged to have a new mural painted that would recognize major figures and events from North Carolina African American history. This new mural was installed in 2010.

Joseph Palmer Knapp was a publisher, financier, philanthropist, and conservationist who came to know the state through a vacation home in Currituck County along the North Carolina coast. He became involved in helping local government leaders on improvement projects, which led him to extend his philanthropy to the government and schools of the county. His recognition that public officials needed training just as other professionals did led him to correspond with Albert Coates, founder and first director of the Institute of Government, which later evolved into the School of Government. Knapp died before he could do more, but his wife, Margaret Rutledge Knapp, saw to it that the family foundation funded the institute's new building. The Knapp Foundation has continued its support of the School of Government, also contributing to the 1998 addition, which added the name Sanders.

John Lassiter Sanders was the institute's second director, taking over from Coates in 1962. Over the years Sanders served as an adviser to state government on reapportionment, the creation of the community college system, and the rewriting of the state's constitution. He worked for the UNC System from 1973 to 1978, where he helped complete its first long-range plan. In 1979 Sanders became institute director again and retired in 1992.

Koury Natatorium. The Maurice J. Koury Natatorium is the home of the Tar Heel swimming and diving teams. Located on South Campus, adjacent to the Dean Smith Center, the natatorium hosted its first competition on October 31, 1986. The modern facility was a significant improvement for the Tar Heel swim teams over Bowman Gray Memorial Pool, which was built in the 1930s. The state-of-the-art natatorium featured a 1,700-seat grandstand and held over a million gallons of water. The new pool received national attention when it hosted swimming and water polo during the 1987 Olympic Festival. It is named for Maurice J. Koury, an alumnus, major donor, and successful fund-raiser for the university. Koury's ongoing support for the university is marked by the many places his name appears on campus: a residence hall, an auditorium at the Kenan-Flagler Business School, a library in the alumni center, and a building at the UNC School of Dentistry.

Koury Oral Health Sciences Building opened in 2012 as a teaching and research facility for the School of Dentistry. The building is one of several spaces on campus named for alumnus Maurice J. Koury. A successful business leader in the textile industry, Koury first became involved with the School of Dentistry as a patient. Built with a number of environmentally friendly features, the Koury building has earned Leadership in Energy and Environmental Design (LEED) gold certification.

Koury Residence Hall was completed in 2002, one of four new dorms finished around the same time (Craige North, Hardin, and Horton are the others). The new dorms, in high demand with students, featured modern technology, single-sex suites, and coed floors. Originally named Ehringhaus South for its proximity to the nearby larger dorm, the building was renamed in 2008 for alumnus Maurice J. Koury. A 1949 graduate of UNC, Koury was president of Carolina Hosiery Mills. He was active in alumni groups and a successful fund-raiser, helping lead the campaign to raise money for the Dean Smith Center in the 1980s and the adjacent natatorium, which is also named for Koury.

Lacrosse. Carolina students began playing lacrosse as a club sport in 1937, gathering enough support to elevate it to a varsity sport in 1949. By the 1970s the UNC–Chapel Hill team was competitive at the national level. The team won national championships in 1981, 1982, 1986, and 1991. While the team was successful, lacrosse still lagged in popularity at Carolina. In 1989 the *Daily Tar Heel* published "A Southerner's Guide to a Northern Sport" for students who were unfamiliar with the sport and its rules. Carolina began offering women's lacrosse as a varsity sport in 1994. The team quickly found success, making it to their first NCAA Final Four in 1997, and it won its first NCAA championship in 2013. The year 2016 was a high point for lacrosse at UNC–Chapel Hill when both the men's and women's teams won national championships.

Late Night with Roy is a celebration of the opening of the college basketball season. First held in 2003 by head coach Roy Williams, it follows in the tradition of "midnight madness" events held by other universities on the first day of basketball practice. The celebration usually features prepared skits, dances, and an introduction to that year's basketball team.

Latinx Center. The UNC Latinx Center, which opened in new quarters in Abernethy Hall in late 2019, coordinates a number of educational and outreach programs for the Carolina community, including a Latinx Mentoring Program, Latinx Heritage Month, Exitos graduation ceremony, and a Latinx Alumni Reunion. The center was the culmination of an initiative launched by the Carolina Latino/a Collaborative in 2013, although the efforts began in 2007 with a small group of students who began the conversation to provide a space for this growing segment of the student body. The Latinx Center sponsors engagement and outreach programs and provides a space to support Latinx students.

Law, School of. Carolina's oldest professional school, and the oldest law school in the state, began in 1845 with the hiring of William Horn Battle. A North Carolina Superior Court judge, Battle led the program during its formative years. The program became a school in 1899. It was a charter member of the American Association of Law Schools in 1920 and has been approved by the American Bar Association since 1928.

The program at first had rooms in various buildings, including Old West and South. The school's first building was Smith Hall (now historic Playmakers Theatre) from 1907 to 1923, when Manning Hall was built. The school moved to Van Hecke–Wettach Hall in 1968.

The School of Law has had numerous distinguished alumni, including North Carolina governors, state supreme court justices, and elected representatives. Some 40 percent of active attorneys in the state are UNC–Chapel Hill law school alumni. Among its notable alumni are governors Terry Sanford and James Hunt; civil rights lawyer and activist Julius LeVonne Chambers; Susie Marshall Sharp, the first female chief justice of the state supreme court; and Katherine Robinson Everett, the first woman to argue a case before the North Carolina Supreme Court, which she won.

The law school has on occasion been a target of conservative politicians. Recent examples include the 2015 mandate from the UNC System Board of Governors to close the school's Center on Poverty, Work and Opportunity; and in 2017, a vote to bar litigation by the school's Center for Civil Rights. The school established the North Carolina Poverty Research Fund to replace the former, and the latter continues to produce research and analysis to advance civil rights and social justice. The law school, in partnership with the Hussman School of Journalism and Media, also hosts the UNC Center for Media Law and Policy.

Lenoir Hall. As the university enrollment grew in the 1920 and 1930s, the main campus cafeteria in Swain Hall could not keep up with demand. Lenoir Hall was built using Public Works Administration funds during a boom in campus construction in the late 1930s. When the new dining hall opened in January 1940, it was able to seat more than 1,000 students at a time and serve as many as 10,000 meals a day. According to the *Daily Tar Heel* it was the largest cafeteria of its kind in the country. Lenoir has always been a dining hall but has undergone frequent changes over the years, with significant renovations in 1984, 1997, and 2011.

The most dramatic period in Lenoir Hall's history came in 1969, following a strike by cafeteria workers who were advocating for better wages, back pay, and improved working conditions. After demonstrations led by students in the Black Student Movement drew the attention of Governor Bob Scott, the governor ordered highway patrol troops to campus to assure that Lenoir could open and operate peacefully. There were no documented clashes between students and the highway patrol, but the sight of uniformed guards lining the walkway to Lenoir was one that the university community would not soon forget.

The building is named for William Lenoir, the first chairman of the UNC Board of Trustees. A native of Virginia, Lenoir spend most of his life in North Carolina, working as an educator in eastern North Carolina and later as a surveyor in the western part of the state, near the town that now bears his name. He served in the Revolutionary War, rising to the rank of general. He was a slave owner and a member of the state legislature, where he joined the committee that would become the first board of trustees of the university.

Lewis Residence Hall opened in 1924, around the same time as nearby Aycock and Graham dorms. The dorm houses around 100 students. It remained an all-male dorm (one of the last remaining on campus) until 1985. In 1987 it underwent an extensive renovation, which included the installation of central air conditioning. It is named for Richard Henry Lewis, a Pitt County native who attended UNC from 1866 until the school closed in 1868. He finished his education in Virginia and Maryland and went on to a successful career in medicine. He worked as a practicing doctor, served as secretary of the North Carolina State Board of Health, and taught at both UNC and the Leonard Medical School at Shaw University in Raleigh. He was a member of the UNC Board of Trustees for thirty-five years.

LGBTQ Center. In the early 2000s, citing concerns over a campus climate that was not supportive of and often hostile to LGBTQ students, the provost's office convened a Committee on LGBTQ Life. Among the recommendations was the creation of a center to provide services and support and to foster a sense of community for LGBTQ students and staff at Carolina. The center was established in 2003 with a full-time director. The LGBTQ Center holds events and programs, leads Safe Zone training for the campus community, and advocates for LGBTQ students at Carolina.

Libraries. The university began building a library before the first brick was laid for the campus. The first book, a copy of sermons distributed by the U.S. Congress to each of the states, was given to the newly established university in 1792 and placed in a school in New Bern until suitable facilities could be built in Chapel Hill.

Through most of the first century of the university, there were three libraries on campus: the University Library, much of which had been purchased by UNC president Joseph Caldwell on a trip to Europe in the 1820s, and the separate libraries of the Dialectic and Philanthropic Societies. While the University Library languished, the society libraries were where many students turned to find books to support their studies and for general reading. The three libraries were merged in 1885, and the University Library was formally established as a separate unit of the university in 1905.

The first building built to house the University Library was Smith Hall (now historic Playmakers Theatre), which opened in 1851. In an arrangement that was indicative of the size and importance of the library at the time, the building was also used as a ballroom, with movable shelves that could be pushed against the wall to make room for dancers. UNC's first dedicated research library opened in 1907 with support from Andrew Carnegie. The Carnegie Library (later renamed Hill Hall) represented the university's commitment to building a research library to support its growing needs.

The rapid expansion of the university through the twentieth century is mirrored by the continued construction and expansion of library buildings. The landmark Wilson Library (originally known as the University Library) opened in 1929, with additions added to hold more books and archival collections in 1952 and 1977. The university opened a dedicated House Undergraduate Library in 1968 and a new, modern library building, Davis Library, in 1984. After Davis Library opened, Wilson Library was renovated to house special collections on campus.

The libraries have grown and changed to adapt to the digital age, often leading the way on campus. They began using a computer catalog in 1969 and opened one of the first public computer labs on campus in the 1980s. Documenting the American South, a digital library program started in the mid-1990s, received national recognition for making rare and hard-to-find primary sources about southern history easily accessible online. By the 2010s UNC Libraries was consistently ranked, in number of volumes, as one of the top twenty academic libraries in the country.

Love House and Hutchins Forum. Located at 410 East Franklin Street next to the President's House, Love House has been the home of the Center for the Study of the American South since 2007. The house was built in 1887 by university mathematics professor James Lee Love, who lived there with his wife, Julia Spencer Love, and her mother, Cornelia Phillips Spencer. Mrs. Spencer was a well-known writer and university booster. The university bought the house in 1890 and used it to house faculty. In 2003 the house was renovated and expanded with the Hutchins Forum to be the home for the center. The added name honors James A. Hutchins Jr., UNC class of 1937, who worked at the Department of Agriculture on programs to feed children and eliminate hunger.

Lux Libertas. The university's motto is Lux Libertas, Latin for "light and liberty." It was adopted in 1897 at the same time as the new school seal, which included a crest with the words on it. In their minutes approving the new seal, the UNC Board of Trustees noted that the seal (and presumably the motto) was presented by university president Edwin Anderson Alderman.

M

MacNider Hall opened in 1939, built in part with funds from the Public Works Administration. The new building had long been desired by the Schools of Medicine and Public Health, which had outgrown their space in Caldwell Hall. The location helped establish a new home for the university's health affairs programs on South Campus. In 1951 the building was named for former dean William de Berniere MacNider, who was a native of Chapel Hill and graduated with the first class of the medical school, in 1903. He spent more than fifty years working at UNC, first appointed as a teaching assistant in 1899 and retiring in 1950. He was dean of the School of Medicine from 1937 to 1940. MacNider organized the university's Department of Pharmacology in the medical school, which focuses on the study of chemical interactions on biological systems, including but not limited to the effects of pharmaceutical drugs. UNC's department is one of the ten original pharmacology departments in the United States.

Mangum Residence Hall opened in 1922, around the same time as nearby Grimes, Ruffin, and Manly dorms. It is named in honor of three members of the Mangum family. Willie Person Mangum, UNC class of 1815, was a prominent politician, representing the state in the U.S. House and Senate and also serving for decades as a member of the UNC Board of Trustees. Adolphus Williamson Mangum, a Methodist minister, served as a chaplain in the Confederate army and later joined the UNC faculty. William Preston Mangum was an 1860 graduate of Carolina who died in the Civil War fighting for the Confederacy.

In the 1980s and 1990s dorm residents turned Mangum into a haunted house for Halloween. The tradition began in 1981 as a way to raise money for an ice machine for the dorm. One of the organizers told the *Daily Tar Heel* it would contain "madmen, a hell scene, a ceme-tery scene, and a lot of other scary scenes." In subsequent years the haunted house was held as a fund-raiser for the North Carolina Jaycee Burn Center.

Manly Residence Hall. Opened in 1922, Manly was one of several new dorms built in the early 1920s (nearby Grimes, Ruffin, and Mangum opened around the same time). It is named for brothers Charles and Mathias Manly, from Chatham County. Charles Manly, an 1814 gradu-ate of UNC, was a lawyer and politician, serving as governor of North Carolina from 1849 to 1851. Matthias Manly, class of 1824, was also a lawyer and served for many years as a judge. Both brothers were long-serving members of the UNC Board of Trustees. In 1938 the dorm made news in the school paper by holding a formal banquet for its residents in Swain Hall, featuring formal table settings, a steak dinner, and enter-tainment. Future governor Terry Sanford, then a resident of Manly, pre-sided over the ceremonies. In 1985 Manly changed from being an all-male dorm to a women-only residence hall.

Manning Hall opened in 1923 as the home of the UNC School of Law. The modern building, built as part of the expansion of the campus around what is now known as Polk Place, included classrooms and a library. It was expanded beginning in the late 1940s, adding a new wing containing more classrooms, a library reading room, and a courtroom. However, within a few decades the law school had outgrown the build-ing again and in 1968 moved into Van Hecke–Wettach Hall. While the building was vacant it played a role in the 1969 strike of campus cafe-teria staff. While the cafeteria workers were on strike, student support-ers set up a Soul Food cafeteria in Manning as a way to raise money for the workers and encourage other students to avoid using campus din-ing services in Lenoir Hall. As the demonstrations within Lenoir grew more disruptive, Governor Bob Scott ordered the state highway patrol to campus with orders to vacate the students from Manning Hall and close the building. Manning was renovated soon after and reopened in 1970 as the new home of the UNC School of Library Science.

Manning Hall is named for John Manning, professor of law at UNC from 1881 to 1899. Under his leadership the law school enrollment grew from just seven students when he began to eighty-seven students by the end of the 1890s. Manning graduated from UNC in 1850 and began a long career in law, interrupted by service in the Confederate army. He also served in the state legislature, where he lobbied successfully to give an annual state appropriation to the university.

Marching band. The tradition of music at Tar Heel sporting events goes back to 1903, when the University Brass Band played at a baseball game on campus. The band played occasionally at games in subsequent years but did not become a fixture at sporting events until the 1920s, especially after the opening of Kenan Stadium. By the 1940s marching band performances were common at halftime of home football games and featured creative formations by the band members. The Marching Tar Heels prospered under the leadership of John Yesulaitis, who took over in 1964 and led the band for more than twenty years. Yesulaitis grew the marching band to include more than 200 students, and it became known as the "Pride of the ACC."

Marsico Hall was dedicated in 2014, serving primarily to house imaging facilities for the School of Medicine and other health affairs programs. Built using state appropriations, it was the only new building to receive state support in 2009. The building is named for Thomas F. Marsico, an investment manager, father of two UNC–Chapel Hill alumni, and donor to the School of Medicine.

McColl Building. Located on a hill above the Smith Center, the McColl Building is the home of the Kenan-Flagler Business School. It was completed in 1997 and named for alumnus and Charlotte businessman Hugh McColl, retired chairman and CEO of Bank of America. McColl has offices, classrooms, and a 400-seat auditorium.

McCorkle Place, the forested quad stretching from Franklin Street to Cameron Avenue, is the center of the university's original campus. This space holds some of the university's iconic emblems and monuments, including Old East, the Old Well, the Davie Poplar, Caldwell Monument, Unsung Founders Memorial, and Confederate Monument (removed in 2018–19). The quad is on the National Register of Historic Places.

It is named in honor of Samuel Eusebius McCorkle, farmer, slave owner, Presbyterian minister, and educator. McCorkle, along with William R. Davie, successfully campaigned for a state-supported university.

He was a founding member of the UNC Board of Trustees and is credited with influencing the quadrangle-based design of the campus, modeled after universities in England.

McGavran-Greenberg Hall, completed in 1990, is part of the complex that houses the Gillings School of Global Public Health. The building houses administrative offices, teaching areas, and laboratories. It was named in honor of two early deans of the School of Public Health. Edward G. McGavran, who led the school from 1947 to 1963, oversaw a major expansion that added three departments. Bernard George Greenberg was the founder and first chair of the school's biostatistics department and dean from 1972 to 1982.

McIver Residence Hall was part of a late-1930s rush to provide more on-campus housing for women students. It was completed in 1939, at the same time as neighboring Kenan Residence Hall, also built as a dormitory for women. The building is named for alumnus Charles Duncan McIver (class of 1881), who was the founder and the first president of the State Normal and Industrial School for Girls, the institution that is now UNC-Greensboro.

Media and Journalism, School of. The English department began courses in journalism in 1909, and UNC set up a separate Department of Journalism in 1924. Gerald W. Johnson, who went on to a distinguished journalism and writing career, served as the first department chair. The department became the School of Journalism in 1950, expanded to the School of Journalism and Mass Communication in 1990, and adopted the name Media and Journalism in 2015. In 2019 it became the Hussman School of Journalism and Media, in honor of Walter E. Hussman Jr. (class of 1968) and the Hussman family. The school's first dean was Oscar J. Coffin, a *Daily Tar Heel* editor and Carolina alumnus, who led the department and the school for twenty-seven years.

In 1924, there were seventeen students, including five women. It had space in New West, along with the *Daily Tar Heel* offices. Over the years the department and school have been in Bynum Hall, Howell Hall, and Carroll Hall. Today it has more than 900 students in bachelor's, master's, and doctoral programs, with areas of study in advertising and public relations, journalism, and business journalism. It also offers special programs in environment and science communication, health communication, Latino journalism and media, sports communication, and a joint M.A./J.D. degree with the School of Law.

The school has a number of distinguished alumni who have advanced the profession, including twenty-four alumni or faculty who have won or been part of twenty-eight Pulitzer Prizes. Graduates are Emily Steel of the *New York Times*, Brooke Baldwin of CNN, editorial cartoonist Jeff MacNelly, and Stuart Scott of ESPN, among many more.

Medicine, School of. The university first established a School of Medicine in 1879. It was a two-year program, designed to provide students with the fundamentals of medical education, with the understanding that they would continue their education elsewhere. This first effort was short-lived, with the school closing in 1885 after the first dean resigned. It reopened in 1890 as a "special school of medicine and pharmacy."

The School of Medicine moved around campus, housed at different times in New East and Person Hall before moving into the university's first building constructed for medical education, Caldwell Hall, in 1912. The school also used a small wooden building south of campus as a "dissecting hall." Students were required to take a course in dissection as part of their study of anatomy. This introduced the problem common at nineteenth-century medical schools: finding bodies to operate on. The university, not unlike other medical schools at the time, was believed to have employed grave robbers to secure cadavers. The majority of bodies used by the students during that era were African Americans.

In 1902 UNC began a "University of North Carolina Medical Department at Raleigh," offering classes in the state capital. But this closed in 1909, as the university had difficulty funding both programs. As the university advocated to expand to a full four-year medical program, the university system and legislature explored other options, including a rumored proposal from Bowman Gray to fund the school, provided it move to Winston-Salem. In the late 1940s the legislature finally agreed to support a four-year medical program and the establishment of a teaching hospital in Chapel Hill. The North Carolina Memorial Hospital opened in 1952 and the first class of the four-year program graduated in 1954.

Since the establishment of the four-year program, the School of Medicine and related programs in health sciences have seen rapid growth. In 1971 the school significantly expanded its statewide reach with the establishment of Area Health Education Centers. These re-

In this photo, taken between 1896 and 1905, the original Memorial Hall is visible on the right, with Old West, South Building, and Gerrard Hall (*left to right*) in the background. Collier Cobb Photo Collection, North Carolina Collection Photo Archives, Wilson Library.

gional centers provide continuing education opportunities for health professionals across North Carolina.

The school grew throughout the late twentieth and early twenty-first centuries, expanding throughout South Campus and establishing new programs and centers focused on genome sciences, maternal and infant health, infectious disease, cardiovascular biology, cancer research, and many others. By the 2010s the School of Medicine was consistently recognized as one of the nation's leading medical schools.

Meeting of the Waters Creek passes through and, in some cases, under the university campus. The creek has been channeled into tunnels passing underneath several campus buildings, including Kenan Stadium. It emerges in the Coker Pinetum, south of Ehringhaus dorm, and flows into the North Carolina Botanical Garden, where it joins Morgan Creek. Coker Pinetum is a twenty-five-acre area that connects the campus with the Botanical Garden. Botany professor William C. Coker gave the property to the university to be used for teaching and as a living laboratory.

Memorial Hall is Carolina's main performing arts venue and the second building to bear the name and the marble tablets inside. The first

Memorial Hall was built in 1885 as a new assembly space for a growing university. It was a combination memorial to the late UNC president David Lowry Swain, alumni who died fighting for the Confederacy, and notable men (and, later, women) of the state. University leaders raised money to build the hall through the sale of marble tablets to commemorate this last group, which they then displayed on its walls. That first building was eventually declared structurally unsound, and in 1930 the university demolished it and erected the present Colonial Revival building. They preserved the marble tablets and placed them into the new building, although not in their original organization. Currently, more than one hundred and sixty marble tablets grace the walls.

Memorial Hall has been the site of commencements, baccalaureates, University Days, speeches, protests, and performances of all kinds. A renovation in 2005 finally gave the hall a fly system, off-stage areas, dressing rooms, and, most important, air conditioning. Memorial Hall is the main performance space for Carolina Performing Arts, which brings to campus an array of productions by prominent and popular performing artists from around the world.

Miller Hall. Opened as 1942, Miller was one of several new buildings constructed for the U.S. Navy pre-flight school on campus during World War II. Miller housed navy cadets and later UNC students before being converted to office space in 1950. In 2010 the building was demolished to facilitate repairs to underground steam tunnels. The site was then used to expand the parking lot of the Carolina Inn. Miller Hall was named for William Miller (1783–1825), who was the first North Carolina governor to have attended UNC.

Mi Pueblo was established as the Carolina Hispanic Association (often shortened to CHispA) and was the earliest student organization for Latinx students at UNC–Chapel Hill. Founded in 1990, the group brought together students for social events and support. Early programs included Latin American dance classes and performances and invited lectures. With the rapid growth of the number of Latinx students at Carolina in the 1990s and 2000s, CHispA expanded to include several subgroups. By then it was one of many student organizations created by and for Latinx students. In 2018 members of the group voted to change the organization's name to Mi Pueblo.

Members of the Carolina Hispanic Association. *Yackety Yack*, 1995, North Carolina Collection, Wilson Library.

Mitchell Hall opened in 1964 to serve as the home for the Department of Geology and has done so for more than fifty years. The building is named for Elisha Mitchell, a native of Connecticut and graduate of Yale who was hired in 1818 as chair of mathematics at UNC. Mitchell, also a Presbyterian minister, would remain at Carolina for nearly forty years, serving at various times as bursar, superintendent of property, and acting president. He was also a slaveholder and, in 1848, published a sermon he gave in defense of slavery, in which he referred to African Americans as a race "of inferior moral and mental endowment." Nevertheless, Mitchell was influential in broadly expanding the curriculum in natural sciences at the university. He also made a lasting contribution to the landscape by ordering and supervising the construction of the low stone walls around campus. He is recognized statewide for his efforts to measure the elevation of the mountains in western North Carolina. On one of these visits in 1857, during an attempt to determine the highest peak in the state, Mitchell fell and died. The mountain he was measuring was named Mount Mitchell in his honor.

Monogram Club. In 1908 a group of current and former Carolina varsity athletes organized the "North Carolina Club" as a social organization and to promote sports at the university. The name was changed in the early 1920s to the Monogram Club, a popular name for student-athlete groups used by several other universities. Club members advocated for athletic teams and facilities and for a while oversaw the cheerleading squads. The club also hosted social events that were open to everyone. In the mid-1940s the club moved its offices into the building recently vacated by the campus's navy pre-flight school following

World War II. The building housed the popular Circus Room soda fountain and snack bar and became known informally as the Monogram Club until its name was changed to Blyden and Roberta H. Jackson Hall in 1992.

Morehead-Cain Scholarship. In 1951 the Morehead Foundation, which was created by alumnus and donor John Motley Morehead, announced a $2 million endowment to support student scholarships. The Morehead Scholarships were modeled after the Rhodes Scholarships at Oxford University. The initial criteria for the scholarships, as established by John Motley Morehead, included "qualities of manhood," "evidence of moral force of character," and "physical vigor," along with exceptional scholastic ability. In the early years of the program, around forty to fifty scholarships were awarded annually. As the endowment grew with additional gifts, the number of scholarships increased, topping 100 in some years. Initially limited to men only, the scholarship was first awarded to a woman student in 1971. In 2007 the Morehead Foundation announced a $100 million gift from the Gordon and Mary Cain Foundation and changed the name of both the foundation and scholarships to Morehead-Cain. The Cain Foundation gift was unusual in that neither Gordon nor Mary Cain had a direct connection to the university. Like Morehead, Cain was a chemist who went on to a successful business career. He and his wife learned about and came to admire the Morehead Scholarships through Carolina alumni they knew in Texas and when spending their summers in Linville, North Carolina.

Morehead Chemistry Laboratory. Completed in 1985 as undergraduate lab and classroom space for the Department of Chemistry, the lab was built with a legislative appropriation and named in honor of John Motley Morehead III (UNC class of 1891). He became a chemical engineer, working with a company cofounded by his father. There he helped develop the large-scale manufacture of calcium carbide and acetylene gas. The company eventually became part of Union Carbide. In addition to supporting chemistry and the University of North Carolina Press, Morehead built the Morehead Planetarium and established the Morehead (now Morehead-Cain) Foundation.

Morehead Planetarium and Science Center. John Motley Morehead III was interested in providing a "silk hat" for the university—a landmark building that was unlikely to be built using taxpayer funds. When a Harvard professor told Morehead, "Your state needs cosmic awakening," Morehead made the decision to build a planetarium. When it opened in 1949, the Morehead Planetarium was the first in the South and one of only six in the United States. From 1959 to 1975 the planetarium hosted training programs for U.S. astronauts, including the members of the *Apollo 11* mission to the moon.

The planetarium expanded in 1973 with the addition of an observatory, a banquet hall, and an art gallery. The expansion also included guest quarters, with a large parlor and eight bedrooms. It has been used to host distinguished guests to campus, including Gerald Ford, Andrew Young, Martha Graham, and Princess Anne of Great Britain.

The Morehead Planetarium has always served a dual purpose: as a research laboratory for faculty and students and as a center for education for school children across North Carolina. The planetarium expanded its education and outreach work in the 2000s. In 2002 the name was changed to the Morehead Planetarium and Science Center, and in 2010 the planetarium led the first annual North Carolina Science Festival.

Morrison Residence Hall. Completed in 1965, Morrison continued the expansion of the campus to the south. It was built in the style of nearby Craige and Ehringhaus dorms, which opened a few years earlier. Morehead is a little larger than these other two dorms, housing around 900 students. In 1970 Morrison became the first permanent coed dorm on campus, and the first in which men and women lived on the same floor.

The dorm is named after former governor and U.S. senator Cameron Morrison. A native of Richmond County and longtime resident of Charlotte, Morrison never attended college but was awarded an honorary degree from UNC in 1922. Morrison was governor of North Carolina from 1921 to 1925, a period of rapid growth for both the state and the university. Known as the Good Roads Governor, he supported heavy investment in infrastructure and education, and he supported UNC's ambitious expansion plans. Morrison's political career touched on many of the most controversial issues of his time. He was active in the bitter 1898 and 1900 elections, known as the white supremacy campaigns. Morrison was one of the leaders of the Red Shirts, a terrorist organization devoted to the intimidation of African American voters and their political allies. When he was governor Morrison weighed in on the controversy that erupted when the state textbook commission was considering adopting a textbook that taught evolution. Morrison said, "I don't want my daughter or anybody's daughter to have to study a book that prints pictures of a monkey and a man on the same page."

Murphey Hall was completed in 1923 for use as classrooms and offices. The building originally housed the Departments of English, German, Greek, Latin, and Romance Languages. As the academic departments grew, most eventually moved to new homes: languages to Dey Hall and English to Greenlaw Hall. The Department of Classics, which has been in the building since the 1930s, has been the primary resident of Murphey since the 1970s.

The building is named for Archibald DeBow Murphey, an early graduate of UNC (class of 1799) and a member of the UNC Board of Trustees for several decades. Murphey has been called the father of public education in North Carolina for his strong advocacy for public schools when he was in the state legislature. In this aspect he was ahead of his time: the state would not pass its first public school act until seven years after Murphey's death.

Muslim Students Association. The UNC–Chapel Hill Muslim Students Association was founded in 1975 with the goals of fostering community, providing opportunities for fellowship and prayer, and promoting understanding of Islam on campus and in the community. In 1989 the association announced plans to build a mosque and Islamic center near downtown Chapel Hill. The plans were approved by the town planning board, but the mosque supporters were ultimately unable to raise enough money to purchase the property. Throughout the history of the organization its members have worked to counteract hate speech and violence directed at Muslims through education and outreach. The organization has also worked with and cosponsored educational and cultural events with numerous campus organizations, including Hillel, the Black Student Movement, the Stone Center, and others.

N

Nash Hall opened in 1942, one of several new buildings used for the U.S. Navy's pre-flight school on campus during World War II. Located near the corner of McCauley and Pittsboro Streets across from the Carolina Inn, it housed cadets and later students before being converted to office and lab space in the early 1950s. The building was demolished in 2006 to facilitate work on underground steam pipes, and the space was converted to a parking lot. Nash Hall was named for the Nash family of Hillsborough, including Frederick Nash, a lawyer, judge, university trustee, and, in the 1850s, chief justice of the North Carolina Supreme Court.

The **National Pan-Hellenic Council** is composed of the nine historically African American Greek lettered fraternities and sororities. The organizations are popularly known as the Divine Nine. Established when the United States was racially segregated, the organizations no longer restrict membership but continue to commemorate and celebrate their origins in African American history and culture. Planning is currently under way for an NPHC Garden, in the courtyard of the Student and Academic Service Building. The Garden, intended to evoke traditional fraternity and sorority "plots" at historically black universities, will be a gathering space for members as well as the entire campus community. The NPHC organizations with chapters at Carolina are listed here with charter date:

> Alpha Kappa Alpha Sorority, Inc. (1974)
> Alpha Phi Alpha Fraternity, Inc. (1976)
> Delta Sigma Theta Sorority, Inc. (1973)
> Kappa Alpha Psi Fraternity, Inc. (1976)
> Omega Psi Phi Fraternity, Inc. (1973)

Phi Beta Sigma Fraternity, Inc. (1982)
Sigma Gamma Rho Sorority, Inc. (1990)
Zeta Phi Beta Sorority, Inc. (1978)

Native Americans. North Carolina has the largest native population east of the Mississippi River, including eight sovereign American Indian tribes. The site of the University of North Carolina and the Town of Chapel Hill in the central Piedmont was home to Indigenous peoples for thousands of years before Europeans and Africans arrived here. The campus is located on land that Europeans took from local tribes—the Enos, Occaneechis, Shakoris, and Sissipahaws—through war and treaty. As the forces of colonization disrupted lives through disease, enslavement, and displacement, some of the Piedmont indigenous peoples moved to join the Catawba Nation south and west of here, while the Occaneechis moved north to join the Saponi Confederation. Others remained, sought ways to accommodate European settlement, and built new communities. In its early years, the university also benefited from the sale of vast tracts of land in western North Carolina and Tennessee that had once belonged to the Cherokees and Chickasaws.

Legal segregation barred American Indians from attending the university. There is mention of a Chickasaw man who attended in the 1880s, but little is known about his time here. Henry Owl, a member of the Eastern Band of Cherokee Indians, was the first American Indian man to earn a UNC degree. Owl received a master of arts in history in 1929. The following year Owl presented his master's thesis as proof of his literacy when he registered to vote. Continuing attempts to disenfranchise him eventually led to his testifying in Congress and to a state law that reaffirmed the right to vote for Cherokees. Owl's determination is honored on campus with the Henry Owl Fund, established in 2011 to support graduate students studying the Cherokee language.

Genevieve Lowry Cole (Lumbee) was the first American Indian woman to earn a degree from Carolina. She graduated from UNC's medical technology program in 1954. Cole went on to work in health care in North Carolina in various capacities, including as the UNC hospital supervisor of clinical hematology, the senior technologist in Duke Hospital's Microbiology Laboratory, and the branch head of three laboratories at the North Carolina State Laboratory of Public Health in Raleigh. She currently is a member of the UNC–Chapel Hill Board of Visitors and an advocate for Carolina's Native American students.

Naval Armory. As the campus ramped up military training facilities during World War II, the U.S. Navy funded the construction of an armory. Initially used by the navy for the campus pre-flight school, the building has housed the campus Navy ROTC since 1943. It was built to support the training needs of navy cadets and included classrooms, a drill floor, and an indoor rifle range. The armory currently houses UNC–Chapel Hill Navy, Air Force, and Army ROTC programs. Beginning in the early 2000s, the university has discussed razing the armory to make way for new construction (other nearby buildings built during the World War II expansion have suffered a similar fate). In 2002 navy cadets successfully lobbied to keep the building, but its future on campus continues to be discussed.

Navy Field was located along Ridge Road behind Fetzer Field and across from Boshamer Stadium. It was originally used for military exercises when the U.S. Navy pre-flight school was on campus during World War II. The field was later adapted for use by UNC athletics, serving as a practice field for the football team and hosting home games for the field hockey and lacrosse teams for many years. Use of the field was discontinued in the 2010s to make way for the new indoor football practice facility.

Navy pre-flight school. During World War II, the university served as a major training center for the U.S. Navy. President Frank Porter Graham successfully lobbied the Roosevelt administration to select Chapel Hill to host one of the navy's pilot training centers. First announced in 1942, the UNC pre-flight school led to the construction of several new buildings to host the cadets and the renovation of many older ones. By the end of the war more than 20,000 people had received military training in Chapel Hill. Many notable people spent time on campus at the navy pre-flight school, including future presidents Gerald Ford and George H. W. Bush. When pressed for staff to support the cadets, the navy brought in German and Italian prisoners of war from Camp Butner to serve as dining hall attendants.

In addition to the many ways that the navy transformed the campus during the war years, the pre-flight school was especially notable for its baseball team and its band. Nicknamed the "Cloudbusters," the school's baseball team had several professionals who were preparing to serve in the navy, including Ted Williams. The navy program also in-

The B-1 Band at the U.S. Navy pre-flight school on campus, ca. 1944.
U.S. Navy Pre-Flight School Photo Collection, North
Carolina Collection Photo Archives, Wilson Library.

cluded the B-1 Band, an African American band containing musicians from North Carolina, many of whom were students at North Carolina A&T. The band members were the first African Americans to serve in the U.S. Navy above the rank of dining hall workers and porters. When university officials refused to house them on campus, the band was welcomed into the community center in the Northside neighborhood west of campus. Each morning they would march to campus to play at the raising of the colors.

NC logo. The interlocking "NC" logo has been associated with the university since at least the 1890s. It was used on uniforms worn by the early baseball and football teams and appears on sweaters worn by students in the late nineteenth and early twentieth centuries. When UNC–Chapel Hill entered its first trademark and licensing agreement in 1982, the "NC" logo was one of the symbols registered by the university.

New East. With enrollment increasing in the 1850s, the university built two new dorms to house the additional students. They were placed on either side of the east and west buildings and were called New East and

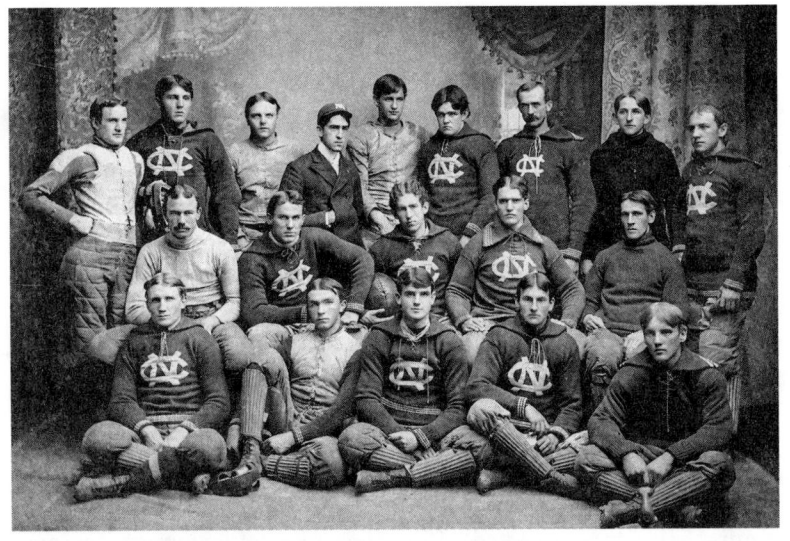

The interlocking "NC" design has been on UNC athletic uniforms since the early days of organized sports on campus. This photo shows the 1898 football team. UNC Image Collection, North Carolina Collection Photo Archives, Wilson Library.

New West. As New East was on a downhill slope, architect William Percival designed it with an additional story to balance the height of the buildings on the landscape. New East was not without its critics. The supposedly modern heating system failed to work as designed. When a committee surveyed the campus in the 1870s in preparation to reopen the university, New East was called "the most ill[-l]y constructed of all the buildings." In addition to dorm rooms, New East also housed the debating hall and library of the Philanthropic Society. Students lived in the building until the 1890s, when it was converted to serve as office space and classrooms for academic departments. Several departments have used the building at different times, including biology, geology, and most recently, city and regional planning. The Philanthropic Society continued to meet in the building for many years, and at one point New East hosted meetings of the student legislature.

New West was built in the late 1850s as a dorm to house the expanding population of students. It was designed by architect William Percival to match New East, except that it is one story shorter. In what was an innovation at the time, the building did not include fireplaces in each room.

Instead, they would be heated by a basement furnace and a system of pipes. It didn't work—the rooms on the bottom floor were much too hot while the top floors stayed cold. When the Dialectic and Philanthropic Societies combined in 1959, they agreed to hold their meetings in New West. The building has had many different uses over the years. In the 1890s New West was home to university printing and a pharmaceutical lab. Departmental occupants have included music, psychology, computer science, and, most recently, Asian studies.

Nike has provided shoes, uniforms, and other items for Tar Heel athletic teams since 1993. The switch to Nike was a big change for UNC's basketball teams, which had worn Converse shoes since 1962. The university's relationship with Nike has not been without controversy. When UNC–Chapel Hill was negotiating a renewal of the contract in 1996, a group of students protested, citing allegations of low wages and poor working conditions for Nike's factory workers in Asia. Student objections continued through the next couple of years and were investigated in detail in a spring 1998 class called Economics, Ethics, and Impacts of the Global Economy: The Nike Example. The course drew national attention, including coverage on ESPN, and had a surprise visitor at the end of the semester when Nike CEO Phil Knight came to campus and sat in on the students' final presentations, which contained multiple recommendations for the company. Nike promised to take a closer look at its labor practices, and the athletic department continued to renew its Nike contracts, with the most recent extension announced in 2018.

Nobel Prize. Two UNC–Chapel Hill faculty members have been awarded a Nobel Prize: Oliver Smithies, who won the Nobel Prize in Physiology or Medicine in 2007 for his work on gene modifications using embryonic stem cells, and Aziz Sancar, who won the 2015 Nobel in Chemistry for his work on DNA repair. Smithies used part of his award to establish the Oliver Smithies Nobel Symposium to bring a Nobel laureate to campus each year for a visit and lecture. Carolina alumnus Robert Furchgott, class of 1937, earned a Nobel Prize in Physiology or Medicine in 1998, for discoveries concerning nitric oxide as a signaling molecule in the cardiovascular system.

North Carolina Botanical Garden. The UNC Board of Trustees first approved the use of university-owned land for a botanical garden in 1952.

The original land was supplemented by private gifts, and the North Carolina Botanical Garden now manages more than 1,000 acres. The garden, overseen by the university's botany department, first opened to the public in 1966. It was designed as a conservation garden, cultivating and maintaining thousands of different native plant species. The garden supports both education and research, attracting a large number of visitors each year and serving as a resource for faculty and students in the botany department. One of the many specialized collections in the garden is devoted to carnivorous plants, including pitcher plants and Venus flytraps. In addition to the main gardens located southeast of campus, the North Carolina Botanical Garden also oversees the Coker Arboretum, Battle Park, the Mason Farm Biological Reserve (a natural area preserved for research and education), and the UNC Herbarium, a collection of natural history specimens founded in 1908 that has grown into one of the largest collections of its kind in the country.

North Carolina Collection. The North Carolina Collection, part of the Wilson Special Collections Library, traces its origins back to 1844, when university president David Lowry Swain created the North Carolina Historical Society and began collecting books and other materials about North Carolina history. Mary Lindsay Thornton was hired as the first curator of the collection in 1917 and remained in the job for more than forty years, helping grow the collection into one of the largest state historical libraries in the country. In 1935 alumnus John Sprunt Hill, who was already a dedicated supporter of the collection, donated the Carolina Inn to the university with the direction that profits from the inn would be used to support the North Carolina Collection. In addition to its printed materials about North Carolina, the collection also supports a gallery in Wilson Library and a large photographic archive and hosts the North Carolina Digital Heritage Center, which provides digital library services for cultural heritage organizations across the state.

Nursing, School of. The School of Nursing was founded in 1950 as the first four-year school of nursing in the state to offer a bachelor's degree. (Duke University already had a three-year degree program.) UNC had offered summer extension classes for nurses beginning in the mid-1930s and a bachelor's degree in public health nursing in the School of Public Health starting in 1941. A nursing program was part of a major effort by the state legislature in the late 1940s to improve health care statewide. The effort included expanding UNC's medical program to four years from two years, building a state hospital, and adding dental and nursing schools to the existing pharmacy and public health programs.

The first class of twenty-seven white women that started the program in fall 1951 were the first full class of freshmen women to enroll at the university, as female enrollment was still limited elsewhere in the university. Their first dormitory was Smith Building. Residence halls, offices, and classrooms of the School of Nursing occupied space in a number of buildings over the years, including the hospital, until Carrington Hall opened in 1969.

The School of Nursing now offers bachelor of science and master of science degrees in nursing, a doctor of philosophy, and a doctor of nursing practice. Its focus remains on practice, research, teaching, and administration.

O

Odum Institute for Research in Social Science. The Institute for Social Sciences was established in 1924 with funding from the Rockefeller Foundation and encouragement from university president Harry Woodburn Chase. It was the first program of its kind in the country. Led by sociologist Howard Odum, the institute focused most of its research on social and economic problems facing the American South, including poverty and race relations. The early work of the institute helped raise the academic reputation of the university, especially among other regional schools, but it also drew criticism and accusations of a liberal or even Communist influence at the university. The institute evolved throughout the twentieth century, adding equipment and staff to adapt to the increasingly complex data-processing needs of social scientists. In 1999 the name was changed to the Howard W. Odum Institute for Research in Social Science in honor of the institute's founding director.

Odum Village. In 1960 the university opened new housing for married students in order to replace the ramshackle Victory Village units. The new community, eventually named Odum Village after UNC faculty member Howard W. Odum, included brick buildings (a big improvement from the prefabricated metal Victory Village units) and modern amenities, including a large television antenna. The two complexes continued side by side on South Campus for several years before demolition began on the Victory Village buildings. Odum Village served as the primary housing for married students until Baity Hill Graduate and Family Housing opened in 2005. In 2016 the UNC–Chapel Hill Board of Trustees approved demolition of the Odum Village buildings to make way for future projects.

Old Chapel Hill Cemetery, located at the corner of South and Country Club Roads, is as old as UNC itself. The first recorded burial was a white student, George Clarke of Bertie County, who died unexpectedly in 1798. He was buried in the woods at the top of a knoll that was then well east of campus and town. The earliest known African American person buried there was Ellington Burnett in 1853. A low rock wall near the center of the cemetery historically separated the graves of black and white persons. For many years it was known as the College Graveyard or Village Cemetery, and both university and town cared for it. Now officially owned by the town, the cemetery is on the National Register of Historic Places as a burial site of formerly enslaved people and of noteworthy faculty and university leaders. In 2004 the Black Student Movement erected a plaque on South Road to honor those buried in the African American section. In 2005 Carolina officials dedicated Memorial Grove, a space for the scattering and interment of ashes. Perhaps the best-known epitaph in the cemetery belongs to Jane Tenney Gilbert: "I was a Tar Heel born and a Tar Heel bred / and here I lie a Tar Heel dead. / BORN JAN. 1896 AND STILL HERE 1980."

Old East is the first building at the university and is listed on the National Register of Historic Places as the first building on a public university campus in the United States. The original structure, located just to the east of the Old Well, was designed to be the north wing of a larger building. It was built by James Patterson and remodeled in 1822 by William Nichols, adding a third floor, and in 1848 by Alexander Jackson Davis, all of whom used enslaved laborers. Known as simply as the College, later East, and then Old East as the campus grew, the structure has been in continuous occupation since beginning as a dormitory.

Old East and Old West have undergone multiple repairs and renovations over the years. A major restoration project in the mid-1990s removed virtually all of the interiors and restored the exteriors to resemble their 1848 appearance. This effort included recreating the Philanthropic Society library space on the third floor of Old East.

Old Students Club. Founded in 1936, the Old Students Club is a section of the General Alumni Association for people who were students more than fifty years ago. In the 1950s the group considered changing the name. "That word Old is the point of criticism," the club president

This 1797 drawing of Old East by student John Pettigrew is one of the earliest known images of the UNC campus and a rare glimpse of Old East before its third story was added.
Pettigrew Family Papers, Southern Historical Collection, Wilson Library.

wrote. "We just don't like to be called Old." But after discussing it, the group decided to keep the name.

Old Well. Early UNC students and faculty relied on wells and nearby springs and creeks for water. The Old Well is probably one of the original wells dug in the 1790s. Located near Old East, the well was at the center of the small campus following the construction of South Building and Old West. Photos from the 1890s show the well surrounded by a rough wooden structure that would have been built to cover the open well and provide shelter for students. Students and others retrieved water from the well using a wooden bucket and a chain. In 1897 university president Edwin Anderson Alderman, whose office in South Building looked out on the well, wanted to "add a little beauty to the grim, austere dignity of the old Campus at Chapel Hill." He was inspired by the small temples he had seen in English gardens and at Versailles. Using some of these as models, campus builders constructed a domed

"The Well," ca. 1892. This photo shows the well a few years before it was renovated to its now iconic design in 1897. Kemp Battle Photograph Album, North Carolina Collection Photo Archives, Wilson Library.

structure with white columns, which is the design of the Old Well we know today. A pump was installed in 1900, replaced by a water fountain in 1925, at which point it ceased to operate as a well: the fountain was connected to the university's water system.

By the 1950s the Old Well was showing signs of decay, and university officials decided that it needed to be completely rebuilt. The original structure was demolished in the summer of 1954, and a replica was built in its place, containing sturdier pillars, marble bases, and a copper dome. The Old Well has become one of the most recognizable symbols of the university. It is a registered trademark of UNC–Chapel Hill and is used on everything from clothing to institutional letterhead.

Old West. Completed in 1823 as a companion to Old East, located to the west of the Old Well. Construction was under the direction of architect William Nichols, who also designed a third floor for Old East at the same time to make the buildings match. Nichols and architect Alexander Jackson Davis, who oversaw an addition and renovation in 1848, used enslaved laborers on this construction. In the 1880s Old West was home to the North Carolina Historical Society for a brief period. It also housed faculty offices and lecture rooms for the early medical school faculty, making it the first building used exclusively for medical instruction in Chapel Hill.

Old East and Old West have undergone multiple repairs and renovations over the years. A major restoration project in the mid-1990s removed virtually all of the interiors and restored the exteriors to resemble their 1848 appearance.

Olympics. The university has several interesting connections to the Olympic games. Faculty member Eben Alexander was serving as ambassador to Greece in 1896 during the revival of the modern Olympics and was instrumental in recruiting American athletes to participate. UNC's first Olympian was Harry Williamson, who competed in track in the 1936 games in Berlin. The first medalist from Carolina was Floyd "Chunk" Simmons, who won the bronze medal in the decathlon in 1948. UNC gold medalists include several in men's basketball and women's soccer. In 1987 UNC hosted several events during the Olympic Festival, an Olympic-style competition held in non-Olympic years. In 1996 the Olympic torch passed through campus on its way to the Atlanta games.

P

Parker Residence Hall opened 1958, at the same time as nearby Avery and Teague dorms. Originally all male, Parker became a women's dorm starting in 1968. It is named for John J. Parker, a lawyer and judge. Parker graduated from UNC in 1907 and went on to a long and successful legal career. In 1930 Parker was nominated by President Herbert Hoover to fill an empty Supreme Court seat. His nomination was narrowly defeated, due in large part to opposition from organized labor and the NAACP. Labor unions opposed Parker due to some of his decisions on the U.S. Court of Appeals, and the NAACP campaigned against his nomination due to remarks he had made during an unsuccessful gubernatorial campaign in 1920 when he referred to the participation of African Americans in politics as a "source of evil and danger to both parties." Parker was a member of the UNC Board of Trustees for several decades and a strong supporter of university president Frank Porter Graham.

Patch Adams. In the summer of 1998 the UNC–Chapel Hill campus was transformed into the fictional Virginia Medical University for the filming of the movie *Patch Adams*. Based on the true story of an unorthodox doctor who used humor to help his patients, the movie starred Robin Williams, who was in Chapel Hill for several weeks for filming. Many Carolina students, staff, and local residents had roles as extras in the movie. Alumni will recognize many campus locations in the movie, including Polk Place, Gerrard Hall, Wilson Library, and Carroll Hall. While it was exciting to see the campus on the big screen, it received many poor reviews, and film critic Gene Siskel picked it as the worst movie of the year.

Peabody Hall has always served as the home for the School of Education. It opened in 1913 and received a major renovation and expansion in 1960. It is named for philanthropist George Peabody, who established the Peabody Education Fund after the Civil War to support teacher training, primarily in the South. The fund provided support for the university's first Summer Normal School for teachers in 1877 and in 1911 contributed $40,000 toward the construction of a new building for the School of Education.

Person Hall was the third building completed after Old East and Steward's Hall. Completed in 1797, Person served as the College Chapel and village church for almost forty years. In 1877 the building was renovated to house the Departments of Physics and Chemistry. Shortly after they moved in, the building caught fire and the interior was destroyed. Trustee Julian Carr paid for its rebuilding, and in 1886 and 1892 the building was enlarged to better accommodate chemistry labs and instruction. The School of Medicine later occupied Person Hall, followed by the School of Pharmacy, and then the Department of Music.

In 1936, using New Deal funds, the university turned Person Hall into an art gallery and home to the art department. The distinctive gargoyles and statue of Archbishop of Canterbury Stephen Langton were added to the exterior at this time. The music department returned to the building in the mid-1970s and has occupied it since then.

Person Hall is named in honor of Brigadier General Thomas Person, a Revolutionary War officer and wealthy planter who used and profited from enslaved labor. He was also a founding UNC trustee. It is the first university building named for a donor. When the university needed funds to complete its construction, Person gave 1,050 silver dollars for the project.

Pettigrew Hall, part of the three-part Battle-Vance-Pettigrew building, opened in 1912 as a dormitory. Built on northwest corner of McCorkle Place on Franklin Street, the modern dorm featured steam heat, water, and shower baths on every floor. The building served as a dorm until the late 1960s, when it was converted to office space, used most recently by the Office of Scholarships and Student Aid. The building is named for alumnus and Civil War general James Johnston Pettigrew. Valedictorian of the class of 1847, Pettigrew was one of the most acclaimed students of his generation. After graduation he traveled, wrote, and practiced law in South Carolina. Initially a reluctant secessionist, he eventually joined the South Carolina militia and was appointed to lead a North Carolina regiment in the Civil War. He rose to the rank of brigadier general, was wounded in battle multiple times, and eventually died from wounds suffered while leading his regiment in the ill-fated Pickett's Charge at the Battle of Gettysburg.

Pharmacy, School of. *See* Eshelman School of Pharmacy

Phillips Hall opened in 1919 to house many of the university's science departments, which had been scattered around the campus. The Departments of Math, Physics, and Engineering were the first occupants. As Phillips was being built, the *Tar Heel* boasted that the new building would be the "best equipped of its kind in the South" and that it would "equal those at Harvard and Yale." In addition to modern scientific facilities (including a "dynamo room"), it contained reinforced steel and concrete that were supposed to make it fireproof. It has been expanded several times since 1919, including the addition of the Phillips Annex, built in 1960 to house the university's Computation Center.

The distinctive style of Phillips Hall, called English Collegiate at the time it was built, has led to one of the most unlikely, although persistent, myths about the campus. Students have suggested that it was not designed for UNC–Chapel Hill at all, that the campus architect received plans meant for another campus. The design of Phillips Hall, however, was intentional, with the building style specified in the construction contract. It was built during a period of architectural experimentation on campus, with buildings such as the Smith Building, Campus Y, and Battle-Vance-Pettigrew departing from the style of the older buildings. It has not been one of the more popular buildings on campus. Historian Archibald Henderson wrote that "the general effect was that of an industrial plant, suggesting automobiles or sewing machines."

The building is named for three members of the Phillips family, all of whom taught at UNC in the nineteenth century: James Phillips, an early math instructor; Charles Phillips, who taught math and engineering and briefly served as acting president of the university; and William Battle Phillips, who earned the university's first doctorate when he received a Ph.D. in chemistry in 1883.

Physical education. While early Carolina students often participated in outdoor games, the university did not require physical education until 1891. To encourage physical fitness among the student body, students were required to take part in exercises at the gymnasium (then located in Commons Hall) three times a week. These early classes were organized by the campus YMCA. The requirements have changed many times over the years. In 1896 all students had to exercise at the gym for thirty minutes a day. By the early twentieth century this was reduced to a varying number of hours a week, with different requirements by class. World War I brought about an increased focus on physical training, and a Department of Physical Education was established soon after, with a separate physical education department for women created in 1933. In 1938 the two were combined into the Department of Physical Education and Athletics.

In the 1930s and 1940s the physical education department was closely aligned with the athletic department and recreational sports. By the 1950s the different functions separated and the Department of Physical Education focused exclusively on teaching. The curriculum received a full revision in the 1980s, reflected in the change of the name to the Department of Physical Education, Exercise, and Sport Science. In 1999 it was shortened to the Department of Exercise and Sport Science.

Piney Prospect is a promontory on the east edge of campus and the site of Gimghoul Castle. In his first description of the site, William Richardson Davie called it Prospect Point, a place from which one could view the land to the east, including the high points near the Eno, Little, and Flat Rivers. According to Kemp Plummer Battle, the name became "Piney" through the common practice of pronouncing "point" as "pi'nt," which eventually just became "piney." Battle grew up exploring the woods in this area, eventually making trails and naming many of its features. When the Order of the Gimghoul purchased the land in the 1920s, a seat was placed at the point using rocks Battle had gathered there, in his memory. The Piney Prospect overlook is on the Lover's Loop Trail, part of Battle Park.

The Pit. The beloved gathering space at the heart of the campus, the Pit was created, possibly unintentionally, during construction projects in 1967 and 1968. Formerly the site of Emerson Field, the area was cleared to make way for three new student services buildings: Graham

Student Union, Student Stores building, and House Undergraduate Library. During the construction, crews left a large dirt depression in front of the new bookstore. The hole remained while work continued during the fall and winter of 1968–69, creating a major navigational headache for students, especially during the rainy spring. The *Daily Tar Heel* referred to it at various times as a "man-made mud crater" and "big, ugly mud hole." By late in the spring of 1969 the campus grounds crew announced plans to cover up the dirt with a "sunken brick patio surrounded by brick steps" and "two shade trees planted in the center." In the fall of 1969 students returned to find the newly improved area. The student handbook and *Daily Tar Heel* began to refer to the space as the Pit, and the name stuck.

Pit preachers. The promise of a ready audience and a tolerance for free speech on campus has long made the Pit a popular location for preaching. The "pit preachers" are usually evangelical Christians seeking to educate, chastise, or convert passing students. Many are noted for their fiery rhetoric, not to mention their powerful voices. Arguing with the preacher is a favorite pastime of students, and a crowd often gathers to mock, dispute, or simply listen. While there have been many different preachers on campus, the best known and most persistent is Gary Birdsong, an itinerant preacher who travels to schools around North Carolina (at North Carolina State he is known as the Brickyard Preacher). A fixture in the Pit since the early 1980s, Birdsong's deep voice resonates across campus, and his inflammatory descriptions of the sinful lives of college students ("Homo Hill" is his nickname for Chapel Hill) are a fixture of his confrontational style. He was banned from the Pit by campus police for two years in 2007 after refusing to leave when the space was reserved by a student group. He spoke elsewhere on campus and promptly returned to the Pit as soon as the ban expired.

PlayMakers Repertory Company is a professional regional theater company in residence at UNC–Chapel Hill. Resident and visiting professional artists work in conjunction with graduate students in acting, costume production, and technical production from the Department of Dramatic Art. It is a member of the League of Resident Theatres in the United States and one of the oldest professional theater companies in North Carolina. The company produces a full season of classical and re-

Playmakers Theatre, originally Smith Hall, was the home of the UNC School of Law at the time of this ca. 1920 photo. Durwood Barbour Postcard Collection, North Carolina Collection Photo Archives, Wilson Library.

gional plays, staged in the Paul Green Theatre and the Kenan Theatre in the Joan H. Gillings Center for Dramatic Art. PlayMakers' first official production was *The Crucible* in January 1977, held in the Playmakers Theatre.

Playmakers Theatre (Smith Hall). Designed by architect Alexander Jackson Davis, Playmakers Theatre is a National Historic Landmark and one of the most significant architectural works on campus. Built in 1850 as a combination library and ballroom, the building was named for its benefactor, Benjamin Smith. A significant architectural feature is the use of wheat and corn decorations on the column capitals instead of the traditional acanthus leaves. Over the years the building housed a chemistry laboratory, and in 1893 it became the university bath house, with six tubs installed for 500 students. The law school occupied the building until 1925, when the university turned it into a theater for the Carolina Playmakers, with the help of a grant from the Carnegie Corporation. It was the main indoor performing space for the Carolina Playmakers until the Paul Green Theatre opened in 1978. Playmakers Theatre continues to be used as a performance space, despite its lack of accessible restrooms and air conditioning.

View of Polk Place, ca. 1960s, probably taken from one of the
upstairs windows in South Building. UNC Image Collection,
North Carolina Collection Photo Archives, Wilson Library.

Polk Place. The quad that stretches from South Building to Wilson
Library is named for James K. Polk, the only university alumnus to date
to become president of the United States. If McCorkle Place, to the
north of South Building, represents the nineteenth-century campus,
then Polk Place represents the early twentieth century and the beginning of the modern research university. The quad was planned to accommodate dramatic growth in the student body. Most of its classroom
buildings, along with Wilson Library, were built over about ten years.
The architect firm of McKim, Mead and White designed the quad, and
architect Arthur C. Nash oversaw its development and construction. To
accommodate the construction pace, a railroad spur was extended tem-
porarily into the center of the quad so that materials could be delivered
to the site.

Presidents of UNC. Carolina's early history is marked by long presidential tenures. The campus leader was at first designated as presiding pro-

fessor. Four men served under that title, from 1794 to 1804, when the trustees opted to promote Joseph Caldwell to president. He served until 1812 and stepped in again four years later to serve another twenty-three years. Caldwell was followed by David Lowry Swain, whose thirty-three-year tenure remains a record. In the political turmoil of Reconstruction, mathematics professor Solomon Pool attempted to keep the university open for three years in the face of virulent Democratic opposition. After reopening in 1875 the university gained new prominence and stability under the twenty-year tenure of Kemp Plummer Battle. Presidents Francis Preston Venable and Harry Woodburn Chase began to build a research enterprise, while the brief tenure of Edward Kidder Graham saw the creation of an extension program to serve the state. Although Frank Porter Graham's nineteen years as president spanned the change from a single university to a consolidated system, his influence on Carolina as a progressive dedicated to academic freedom shaped the university's reputation for the remainder of the twentieth century.

Presiding Professors
>David Ker: 1794–96
>Charles W. Harris: 1796 (July–December)
>Joseph Caldwell: 1796–97
>James S. Gillespie: 1797–99
>Joseph Caldwell: 1799–1804

University Presidents
>Joseph Caldwell: 1804–12
>Robert Hett Chapman: 1812–16
>Joseph Caldwell: 1816–35
>Elisha Mitchell (acting): 1835 (February–December)
>David Lowry Swain: 1835–68
>Solomon Pool: 1869–72
>Charles Phillips: 1875–76
>Kemp Plummer Battle: 1876–91
>George Tayloe Winston: 1891–96
>Edwin Anderson Alderman: 1896–1900
>Francis Preston Venable: 1900–1913
>Edward Kidder Graham (acting): 1913–14, (president): 1914–18
>Marvin Hendrix Stacy (acting): 1918–19
>Harry Woodburn Chase: 1919–30
>Frank Porter Graham: 1930–34

Prisoners of war. A small group of prisoners of war worked briefly at the university during World War II. Camp Butner, located in Granville County about thirty miles northeast of Chapel Hill, began receiving German prisoners of war in the spring of 1944. By the summer some of the prisoners were working as dining hall attendants on campus. They worked in Lenoir Hall, which was used exclusively by the U.S. Navy cadets for the navy pre-flight school located on campus. It is not clear how long the prisoners were on campus or how many there were, but occasional mentions of them in the *Daily Tar Heel* from August 1944 show that students were aware of the prisoners and were in occasional contact with them.

Public Health, School of. *See* Gillings School of Global Public Health

Pulpit Hill is the name of a fictionalized version of Chapel Hill that appeared in Thomas Wolfe's 1929 novel, *Look Homeward, Angel*. Wolfe's heavily autobiographical first novel has his protagonist, Eugene Gant, attending the state university there. He describes the campus as a "charming" place where "a young man was able to loaf comfortably and delightfully through four luxurious and indolent years." The novel also includes fictional versions of several of Wolfe's professors, most notably philosophy professor Horace Williams. The university appeared in Wolfe's fiction again in his posthumous novel *The Web and the Rock* as Pine Rock College. Although he called it an "old, impoverished backwoods college," the references to the university were clear when he wrote about "its unfinished spareness, its old brick and its campus well." Despite these sometimes harsh descriptions, Wolfe (class of 1920) retained fond memories of his alma mater. In a letter to a classmate in 1929 he wrote, "So far from forgetting the blessed place, I think my picture of it grows clearer every year: it was as close to magic as I've ever been."

Q

Quail Hill. *See* Chancellor's residence

R

Radio, Television, and Motion Pictures, Department of. This department, popularly known by its acronym, RTVMP, existed from 1954 to 1993. It was the brainchild of Earl Wynn, a faculty member in drama and speech, who developed the first courses in broadcasting at Carolina. Wynn also led the closely allied Communication Center based in Swain Hall to centralize all of the equipment needed for radio, television, motion picture, photographic, and record production.

Wynn produced the university's first radio program, which occurred on May 26, 1940, through the Extension Division, and taught the first course in radio in 1942. After he returned from service in World War II, Wynn set up a department of radio, which became RTVMP in 1954. The department offered undergraduate and master's degrees, in addition to developing the radio station that became WUNC-FM and the television station that became UNC-TV.

The College of Arts and Sciences abolished the RTVMP department in 1993. Parts of its curriculum moved into the School of Journalism and Mass Communication (now the Hussman School of Journalism and Media), and other parts merged with the Department of Speech Communication (now the Department of Communication). The latter continues to operate studio facilities in Swain Hall.

Rameses. The tradition of having a live ram at home football games began in 1924. Cheerleader Vic Huggins, looking for inspiration during a lackluster season, wanted to find a live animal mascot for the team. Inspired by star fullback Jack Merritt, known as the Battering Ram, Huggins decided to use a ram. He paid $25 for a live ram from a farm in Texas. Dubbed Rameses, the ram made its debut at a game on November 8, 1924. A live ram, often with its horns painted Carolina blue, has

RTVMP students in a campus recording studio, ca. 1959. UNC Photo Lab Collection, North Carolina Collection Photo Archives, Wilson Library.

been a fixture at Tar Heel home football games ever since. When not at football games, Rameses lives at a farm near campus in the care of the Hogan family, who have cared for at least twenty generations of the Rameses line.

The university included Rameses as one of its trademarks when it began its licensing program in the early 1980s. The first Rameses costume was introduced during the 1987–88 basketball season. The ram costume, worn by a student, was more popular than the short-lived "Tar Heel Tim" in the 1970s, a student dressed as a large foot. The Rameses costume design went through a couple of changes over the years but quickly became a regular part of the Carolina athletics experience and

In this photo from the early 1940s, Rameses is posing with the Duke Blue Devil mascot before a football game. Photograph by Hugh Morton. Hugh Morton Photo Collection, North Carolina Collection Photo Archives, Wilson Library.

a visible symbol of the university at events around campus. In 2015, to handle increasing demands for Rameses at events and to try to connect more with kids, the university introduced Rameses Jr., another costumed ram, this one with Carolina blue horns and a more friendly expression on its face.

Rathskeller. The Ram's Head Rathskeller, opened in Amber Alley off of Franklin Street in 1948, was beloved by generations of Carolina students. It was run by the Danziger family, owner of several successful restaurants in Chapel Hill. It was a combination of a formal restaurant and beer hall but turned into a college town classic, with dishes that remained on the menu for decades and carved initials from students over many years in the walls. "The Rat" was the first restaurant to serve imported beer in Chapel Hill. Some of the best-known menu items were the lasagna, known informally as the "bowl of cheese," and a sizzling steak called The Gambler. The "Rat" was also notable for its beloved and long-serving staff, with some waiters staying at the restaurants for decades, providing a sense of continuity for generations of Carolina students. The Rathskeller closed in 2007, though a few of the classic menu items have been revived at S&T's Soda Shoppe, a Pittsboro restaurant owned by longtime fans of the Rathskeller.

Reconstruction and closing. The defeat of the Confederacy and the emancipation of one-third of the people of North Carolina in 1865 brought change at every level to the university and Chapel Hill. Fewer than 100 students remained enrolled, and the university's finances were ruined by investments that were now worthless. Potential new students would have come from families likewise impacted by the economic collapse. Political divisions played out over control of the campus. A provisional state government led by Republicans was hostile to a university that they identified with the elite wealthy people who had led the state into secession and defeat. UNC president David Lowry Swain eventually persuaded the legislature to appropriate funds to pay faculty salaries. He also gained access to the state's share of the Morrill Act, passed in 1862 by the U.S. Congress to create land-grant colleges.

When Congress took over Reconstruction in 1867, it imposed new requirements on the former Confederate states. Under a new state government and a new state constitution ratified in 1868 by a multiracial assembly, control of the state university shifted to the State Board of Education. The Republican state government replaced Swain and the faculty with new appointments, making professor Solomon Pool president. Democrats, comprised largely of the former slaveholding elite who had lost the war, imposed a virtual boycott on the university. In Chapel Hill the opposition included Cornelia Phillips Spencer, who excoriated Republicans and Pool's administration in weekly newspaper columns. Students stayed away, while the Republican legislature, mired in its own financial troubles, offered no support.

At the 1869 commencement, Republican governor William Woods Holden called for a more egalitarian approach to higher education and for UNC to truly be a "people's university." He proposed opening a school elsewhere for African Americans that would be part of UNC, a plan that led conservative opponents to make untrue claims about the integration of the university. Terrorist activity by the Ku Klux Klan in Orange County targeted university faculty and Republicans, adding to social turmoil and uncertainty. Holden's attempt to fight the Klan with state militia helped mobilize Democratic voters, who in 1870 elected a majority in the state house and senate. The legislature impeached and convicted Holden, removing him from office.

President Pool still tried to keep the university open, but the threat of Klan violence and the lack of financial resources ensured that no new students enrolled. By the beginning of 1871 the university was closed, and faculty and students were gone. Four years would pass before the university's allies could muster the political support under Democrats to reopen the campus.

Religion. Despite its status as a public university, the university had a close relationship with Christianity for much of its first 100 years. Students had to attend daily chapel or Sunday church service, and the distribution of Bibles to graduating seniors was a commencement tradition until the mid-1970s. In 1859 the Young Men's Christian Association (YMCA) opened a chapter on campus and students held their own religious services and Bible study groups. The YMCA Building opened in 1907, funded by private donations. The Young Women's Christian Association arrived in 1935 and then merged with the YMCA in 1963 to form what is now known as the Campus Y. Today more than forty student organizations have a faith or religious affiliation, which reflects the variety of religious traditions among the student body.

Religion has also been the focus of controversy in university history. In the early decades President Joseph Caldwell and later President David Lowry Swain had to refute religious leaders who argued that the state university was a threat to the growth of church-affiliated schools. Other critics claimed at various times that the campus was dominated by Presbyterians or Episcopalians, although the facts never supported this charge.

UNC had a small number of Jewish students and even faculty members before the twentieth century. That number began to grow in the 1920s. UNC never imposed a quota for Jewish students at the undergraduate level, as many American colleges and universities did around this time. In 1933, however, Isaac Manning, dean of the medical school, denied admission to an applicant because he was Jewish. Manning maintained a quota because, he claimed, it was difficult to place Jewish students in further study at other schools. Morris Krasny, the applicant, appealed to UNC president Frank Porter Graham, and Graham ordered the medical school to accept him. Manning resigned rather than change his decision.

In 2002 the book selection committee for the annual Summer Reading Program for new students chose *Approaching the Qur'an: The Early Revelations*, by Michael Sells. Committee members saw a need for Americans to better understand Islam after the attacks of September 11, 2001. After criticism from conservative journalists about the selection, the Family Policy Network (FPN) filed suit against the university (*Yacovelli v. Moeser*) on behalf of several students. FPN claimed that the university had violated the Establishment Clause of the First Amendment, but the network lost in court and on appeal. Meanwhile, for students who did not wish to take part in discussions, the university offered the option of writing a paper.

The university has had a Department of Religious Studies since 1946, which has bachelor's, master's, and doctoral degree programs. Faculty teach and conduct research in historical and contemporary topics across an array of religious traditions, including Christianity, Judaism, Islam, Buddhism, and Hinduism.

Research Laboratories of Archaeology. The university began offering courses in archaeology as early as the 1920s. These were primarily lecture classes focused on historical archaeology, with an emphasis on ancient Greece and Rome. In the mid-1930s, following an increased interest in the archaeology of North Carolina, the university began supporting efforts to study early civilizations in the state. Using funding from the WPA (Works Progress Administration), the university started the Laboratory of Archaeology in 1939. Work at the lab was halted during World War II and then revived in 1948 under a new name, Research Laboratories of Anthropology, and with a new director, faculty member Joffre Coe. Lauded as the "Father of Archaeology" in North Carolina, Coe served as director until 1982 and helped build the laboratory into a program of national significance.

In 1997 the name was changed to Research Laboratories of Archaeology. The focus of the department was, and remains, the study of Native American cultures in the Southeast. The North Carolina Archaeology Collection, compiled by students and staff since the founding of the lab, now contains millions of artifacts spanning more than 12,000 years of history and is one of the preeminent resources for the study of Native American life in the region. The collection has had many homes on and off campus—it moved between Alumni and Person Halls in its early years and was housed for many years in Wilson Library. In 2004 the university renovated space in Hamilton Hall to house the collection.

Robertson Scholars. In 2000 alumnus Julian Robertson and his wife, Josephine, gave $24 million to establish an unusual scholarship program that would enable students to enroll jointly at UNC–Chapel Hill and Duke. The Robertson Scholars take classes and participate in extra-curricular activities at both schools. One of the most visible elements of the program is the Robertson Express Bus, which runs regularly between the two campuses.

Rosenau Hall opened in 1962 to serve as the home of the School of Public Health. The additional space was much needed: at the time it opened, public health classes had been offered in fourteen different buildings around campus. In 1965 it was named for Milton Rosenau, founder of the school and a public health pioneer. Rosenau worked in public health positions in the federal government and then went to Harvard, where he established the nation's first school of public health. After retiring from Harvard he came to Chapel Hill and founded the School of Public Health, serving as its dean for several years.

ROTC. The university began a Reserve Officer Training Program on campus in fall 1940, when the U.S. Navy placed a ROTC unit on campus. The new unit came at a time when, faced with the possibility of the United States entering World War II, the university took a more direct role in military preparation, including the establishment of compulsory physical education. The Navy ROTC began with 100 students enrolled and was active through the war. Initially housed in Woollen Gym, the ROTC program moved into the Naval Armory in 1943. ROTC training on campus expanded in 1947, with Air Force ROTC. During Vietnam War protests in the late 1960s and early 1970s, many Carolina students questioned the presence of the military programs on campus, especially after Harvard ended its ROTC programs in 1969. The protests ended after a few years. By 1978 a *Daily Tar Heel* headline proclaimed, "ROTC No Longer Draws Campus Contempt." In 1995 UNC–Chapel Hill added an Army ROTC program, known as the Tar Heel Battalion.

Ruffin Residence Hall was opened in 1922, at the same time as nearby Grimes, Mangum, and Manly dorms. Originally housing only men, Ruffin was converted to a women's dorm by 1976. It is named for two members of the Ruffin family: Thomas Ruffin and Thomas Ruffin Jr. Both were lawyers, served on the state supreme court, and were members of the UNC Board of Trustees. Ruffin Sr. enslaved many people on his plantations in Alamance and Orange Counties and was a partner in a slave-trading business that frequently led to children being taken from their parents and sold. He is probably best remembered for his 1829 ruling in the case *State v. Mann,* which held that people who enslaved African Americans could not be indicted for injuring people they held in bondage. In the opinion he wrote, "The power of the master must be absolute to render the submission of the slave perfect." Ruffin Jr. had a long legal career, interrupted by service in the Confederate army and a stint on the North Carolina Supreme Court.

Ruffin Residence Hall

S

Sangam. UNC–Chapel Hill's South Asian student organization was founded in 1987 with twelve members. The name comes from the Hindi word for togetherness. In 1992 Sangam hosted the first ever National Indian-American Students Conference. The organization has grown significantly, with well over 100 members by the 2010s.

Scuttlebutt. The Scuttlebutt was a snack bar located at the corner of Cameron Avenue and Columbia Street, near Swain Hall. The small building was built as a canteen for U.S. Navy cadets who were on campus for pre-flight school. Given to the university after the war, it was later operated by Student Stores. It was a popular stop for many students on campus, especially for fraternity members living nearby in the houses on Fraternity Court. By the early 1970s the manager said the building was "about to fall down" and the university considered demolition. It lasted a couple of decades longer before being razed in 1996.

Seal. The UNC Board of Trustees first adopted a school seal in 1791. The seal featured the face of the god Apollo and his symbol of the rising sun as being "expressive of the dawn of higher education in our State." It also included the Latin words "Sigil Universitat Carol Septent," translated as "Seal of the University of North Carolina." The Apollo seal was used on official documents for the next century. It was changed slightly in 1895, showing Apollo's face in profile, before being changed more dramatically in 1897. Under the direction of University President Edwin Alderman, the new seal included a shield with a diagonal band and the words "Lux Libertas," Latin for light and liberty, which became the university's motto. This apparently simple design was the subject of controversy due to the direction of the diagonal band on the seal. In what was probably a simple accident, the band crossing the shield was placed in a different direction than those that appear on most standard family crests. This alternate band, known as a "bend sinister," was believed by many to signify illegitimacy. The outcry over the incorrect band was persistent enough that the university formally changed the design of the seal in 1944.

Senior Walk. The path that runs on the north side of the Coker Arboretum behind Spencer Residence Hall and Chapel of the Cross, the Episcopal church on Franklin Street, is what remains of Senior Walk, a popular campus landmark well into the 1960s. It began as an informal path some time in the 1890s and became a formal designation with the Senior Class Gift of 1928, which placed a sandstone tablet designating the path and flowering cherry trees on each side of it. Students for many years lined up on Senior Walk to process to commencement in Memorial Hall. It was also a favorite path for male students to walk their dates home to Spencer and other women's residence halls.

Senior Walk originally extended west from Raleigh Street to the south end of Graham Memorial Hall. Construction of the Morehead Planetarium in the 1940s shifted the path to the north, and with the building expansion in the 1970s, the senior class tablet disappeared from campus. In 2017 the tablet returned to campus from a backyard somewhere in Chatham County, just south of Chapel Hill, and has been reinstalled at the Raleigh Street entrance.

Sexuality and Gender Alliance. Founded in 1974 (initially called the Gay Awareness Rap Group), the Carolina Gay Association was the first recognized student organization for gay and lesbian students on campus. The group was active in its early years, helping host the Southeastern Gay Conference in 1976 and beginning publication of *Lambda*, believed to have been the first LGBTQ student publication in the country. In 1975 the Carolina Gay Association protested local bar He's Not Here after the manager asked two gay men to stop dancing. The organization was at the center of a campus-wide debate in 1991 when the summer student legislature passed a resolution to end funding for the Carolina Gay and Lesbian Association, as it was then called. The attempt to defund the group was ultimately unsuccessful, but that effort, supported by many students, demonstrated that UNC still presented a hostile environment for many LGBTQ students. The organization has changed names multiple times and has been known as the Sexuality and Gender Alliance since 2012. Its members work to foster a strong and supportive LGBTQ community at Carolina.

"Silent Sam." *See* Confederate Monument

Sitterson Hall opened in 1987 to house the Department of Computer Science. In contrast to computer science buildings at other universities, many of which featured a distinctly modern design, Sitterson was built in a more traditional style. A staff member in the department explained to the *Daily Tar Heel* that they didn't want a "Darth Vader building" because "computers are already intimidating." The building is named for former chancellor J. Carlyle Sitterson, who had a long career at Carolina. Beginning as an instructor in 1935, Sitterson was later named a Kenan Professor and served as dean of the College of Arts and Sciences. He was chancellor from 1966 to 1971, a tumultuous period on campus that included the cafeteria workers' strikes, antiracist activism from the Black Student Movement, and large-scale Vietnam protests. Sitterson and other campus administrators were often the focus of the student protests and struggled at times to respond to student demands and activism unlike any that had occurred previously in the university's history.

Slavery. The history of the university is inseparable from the history of slavery in the United States. Most of the early faculty and members of the Board of Trustees were slaveholders. Enslaved people helped build the first buildings and were present all over campus and town as laborers and servants through the end of the Civil War. Students who came from elite slaveholding families in North Carolina and elsewhere brought enslaved personal servants with them until 1845, when the university banned the practice. Instead, students leased enslaved laborers from faculty and townspeople, paying UNC a fee. Students relied on enslaved women and men who cleaned their rooms, did their laundry, and cooked their meals. The university also received income from the sale of enslaved people: because of the state law that awarded unclaimed property (escheats) to UNC, on multiple occasions the university inherited enslaved women, men, and children, who were subsequently sold, with the proceeds going to the university.

Most published histories of the university have failed to fully acknowledge the presence and impact of slavery on the university campus. In 2003 the University Archives put on an exhibit in Wilson Library called *Slavery and the Making of the University*, which helped spark a discussion about early university history. In 2005 the university dedicated the Unsung Founders Memorial, a public commemoration of the enslaved people who, along with free African Americans, helped build and maintain the university. In 2007 the university named a new residence hall for George Moses Horton, an enslaved man from nearby Chatham County who worked on campus and sold poetry to students. The work to understand and explain the university's history with slavery continues. On University Day 2018 Chancellor Carol L. Folt apologized on behalf of the university for its participation in the practice of slavery and called for more work to reconcile its past with its present and future.

Smith Building. Built in 1901 as a men's dormitory with space for sixty-five students, the Mary Ann Smith Building was one of the first to be equipped with heat, lighting, and indoor plumbing. It was designed by architect Frank Milburn, who designed all of the campus buildings from 1901 to 1915, and has a Flemish influence to its style, including rounded gables. It has the distinction of being the first building named for a woman at the university. Smith Building became a men's graduate student residence in 1927 and a women's dormitory from 1945 into the 1960s. Then it became an office and classroom building, which is what it is today, home now for the Department of Women's and Gender Studies.

Mary Ann Smith made a bequest to the university to support a professorship and scholarships in chemistry. The daughter of a wealthy Raleigh merchant, she married James T. Morehead in 1861. The marriage was not a success, and the couple separated. However, Smith retained the rights to her property through a marriage contract and disposed of that property in her will. In the 1870s she was committed to an insane asylum and eventually died still confined to an institution. She left two wills, and by the time legal issues were settled the university desperately needed new student housing, so the trustees committed a portion of it for that purpose.

Soccer. Carolina students began playing soccer during World War I. The first references to it in the *Tar Heel* were in 1917, with the first intramural games played in 1919. The first intercollegiate game was played in 1937, when a group of students organized a scrimmage against Duke

UNC's Mia Hamm (*right*) races down the field ahead of a player from Florida
International University during a game in the 1987 NCAA tournament.
Durham Herald Co. Newspaper Photograph Collection, North
Carolina Collection Photo Archives, Wilson Library.

(the UNC team lost, 2–1). Soccer became a varsity sport in 1947 and
was soon successful, winning the Southern Conference championship
in 1948. In 1963 Edwin Okoroma, from Nigeria, became the first black
varsity athlete at UNC when he joined the soccer team. The men's soccer team won its first Atlantic Coast Conference championship in 1987
and won national championships in 2001 and 2011.

Carolina soccer began a new era in 1977, when Anson Dorrance was hired as coach. Initially hired to coach the men's team, Dorrance also took over as coach of the women's soccer team in 1979, when women's soccer became a varsity sport at Carolina. He would coach both the women and the men through 1988. Women's soccer quickly developed into a successful program. The Tar Heel women won a national championship in 1981, beginning an unparalleled record of success. The team has won twenty-two national championships (as of 2018), including nine in a row between 1986 and 1994. They have had several undefeated seasons, and Dorrance has won national and ACC Soccer Coach of the Year awards multiple times. Many alumnae of the program, including Mia Hamm and Heather O'Reilly, have gone on to successful international careers, leading Olympic and World Cup champion teams. Soccer is without question the most successful athletic program at UNC and is often mentioned as one of the most dominant programs in all of college athletics. The prominence of the program was acknowledged by Dean Smith, who once said of UNC, "This is a women's soccer school. We're just trying to keep up with them."

Social Sciences, Institute for. *See* Odum Institute for Research in Social Science

Social Work, School of. The School of Social Work was founded in 1920 as a professional graduate school, offering master's and doctoral degrees and educating social workers for research and advanced practice. The school, known first as the School of Public Welfare, was created to train professionals for a newly formed state agency to oversee county-level welfare offices. The school's mission also included research on social problems, which led to the creation of the Institute for Social Sciences in 1924. It was the first program of its kind in the country. The school, led by sociologist Howard Odum, adopted a regional approach to its work, looking at the social and economic problems facing the American South, including poverty and race relations. The school has always stressed field research and works closely with public and nonprofit agencies.

The School of Social Work was the first on campus to have an African American faculty member when it hired Hortense McClinton in 1966. The Tate-Turner-Kuralt Building, completed in 1995, is the home of the School of Social Work.

South Building decorated with banners for the 2019 spring commencement.
Photo by Johnny Andrews, UNC–Chapel Hill.

South Building. Construction on South Building, known originally as Main Building, began in 1798, but lack of funds delayed its completion until 1814. Students reportedly built rough cabins inside the unfinished structure to escape crowded conditions in Old East. When it finally opened, South contained dormitory rooms for eighty students, halls for the debating societies, a library space, and a public hall. Unlike Old East, which has remained a dormitory space throughout its history, South Building's configuration changed on a regular basis to fit the university's needs.

In 1926 university leaders committed to a full renovation to house administrative offices. The interior was completely removed, the basement dug out to create another floor, and the large south portico facing Polk Place was added. The northeast corner of the first floor became the president's office and remained so until William Friday moved the Consolidated University offices to the Coates Building on Franklin Street. The South Building office then became the chancellor's office, which it remains today.

South Building still has a bell, which was first installed in the early 1800s and automated in the 1930s. Before that, the building's custodian (known then as a janitor) rang the bell for class changes. It is now rung only for special occasions.

South Campus. While there is no official definition of the area known familiarly as South Campus, students and alumni generally know it as the section of the campus south of Kenan Stadium. The name most often refers to the high-rise dorms that were first constructed in the 1960s. However, as the campus has expanded, the definition of South Campus has shifted. In the 1920s, newspaper reports referred to the area now known as Polk Place as the south campus.

Southern Historical Collection. In the early twentieth century, led by faculty and students in history and social sciences, UNC began to emerge as a center for research on the American South. To support and encourage this work, history professor Joseph Grégoire de Roulhac Hamilton created the Southern Historical Collection in 1930. Hamilton's legendary collecting trips took him around the Southeast as he gathered family papers, plantation records, and more, bringing it all back to Chapel Hill. His work earned him the nickname "Ransack" Hamilton from people who were both amused and angered by his relentless collecting. The work of Hamilton and his successors helped build the collection into the largest repository of manuscript materials about the American South. As part of the Wilson Special Collections Library, the Southern Historical Collection has provided research materials for generations of historians, helping inform many popular and influential works on southern history.

Southern Oral History Program. Founded in 1973, the Southern Oral History Program (SOHP) conducts oral histories and provides training for future oral historians. Under the leadership of history professor Jacquelyn Dowd Hall, it grew into a nationally recognized program. While the program interviewed some prominent and well-known people, a major focus was on capturing voices that would otherwise be marginalized or simply absent from the historical record. In 1987 Hall and several of her colleagues published *Like a Family: The Making of a Southern Cotton Mill World*, an influential work that drew on oral histories to explore the lives of mill workers in the early twentieth-century South.

The SOHP has been recognized as a national leader in oral history practice and education. In 1999 Hall was awarded a National Humanities Medal by President Bill Clinton in recognition of her work and that of the SOHP. After Hall's retirement from the program in 2011, subsequent directors have continued to expand the work, engaging under-graduate and graduate students in the active practice of oral history. Its collection of more than 6,000 interviews is housed in the Southern Historical Collection at Wilson Library and available online. Originally based in the Department of History, the program is now part of the Center for the Study of the American South.

"Southern Part of Heaven" is often used as a nickname for Chapel Hill. The term comes from William Meade Prince's fond memoir of growing up in Chapel Hill, *The Southern Part of Heaven*, first published in 1950. In the book Prince recalls a local resident who, on his deathbed, asked the minister what he thought heaven was like. After a moment of re-flection, the minister said, "I believe Heaven must be a lot like Chapel Hill in the spring."

Speaker Ban Law. In 1963 the North Carolina General Assembly passed the Act to Regulate Visiting Speakers, which prohibited from speaking at a state-supported college campus anyone who was a known member of the Communist Party, had advocated the overthrow of the state or federal constitution, or had ever invoked the Fifth Amendment before any judicial tribunal with respect to subversive activities. Passed with-out warning in the last hours of the legislative session in June, the bill seemed to be about anticommunism but was in fact a sharp rebuke to student activists for their participation in racial integration and civil rights protests. It quickly became known as the Speaker Ban Law, and administrators, faculty, and students organized to oppose it.

Administrators and trustees worked within the system to challenge it. This resulted in a compromise in 1965, in which the General As-sembly amended the law to give college boards of trustees power over the approval of campus speakers. This occurred primarily because the Southern Association of Colleges and Schools declared that the Speaker Ban Law, a violation of academic freedom and free speech, threatened university accreditation.

Students undertook a series of protests that coalesced with the elec-tion of student body president Paul Dickson III (UNC–Chapel Hill class of 1966), who won election on a platform of defense of free speech. In March 1966 Dickson and other student leaders invited Frank Wil-kinson (who had invoked the Fifth Amendment before a congressional committee) and Herbert Aptheker (a Communist) to appear on cam-

Frank Wilkinson (*left*) speaks to UNC students gathered on Franklin Street. Photo by Charles Cooper. Durham Herald Co. Newspaper Photograph Collection, North Carolina Collection Photo Archives, Wilson Library.

pus. Prevented from speaking by Chancellor J. Carlyle Sitterson, both of them spoke from the sidewalk on the town side of the stone wall on McCorkle Place. Wilkinson's and Aptheker's appearances formed the basis for a lawsuit brought by the student leaders, *Dickson v. Sitterson*, which overturned the law in 1968.

In 2011, encouraged by former UNC System president William C. Friday, the university installed a plaque on one of the stone walls commemorating the students who advocated for the repeal of the Speaker Ban Law.

Spencer Residence Hall. Located at the southwest corner of East Franklin Street and Raleigh Street, Spencer opened in 1924 as the first residence hall for women at Carolina. The building included parlors and a dining room and kitchen facilities. In 1930 the third floor was finished, adding nine rooms. In 1958 an addition provided room for an additional seventy students. In the 1960s the kitchen and dining room were replaced with a study room and an apartment for the residence director. Spencer is now a residence hall for women and men and, because of its prime location on Franklin Street, a popular choice for Carolina students.

The building was named in 1927 for Cornelia Phillips Spencer, the first woman to receive an honorary degree from the university, in 1895. Spencer was a writer and journalist and the daughter and sister of UNC professors. She is best known for chronicling university and village life during the Civil War and Reconstruction. During Reconstruction, Spencer sided with the Democratic Party, composed mainly of former Confederates, against Republicans on the question of racial equality. Spencer was best known in Carolina history for being the "woman who rang the bell." This was a reference to the legislature announcing that the university would reopen in 1876, after Democrats had regained control of state government. Reportedly, when news of the reopening reached Chapel Hill, Spencer led a small group to campus, where they rang the bell in South Building to mark the occasion. Even though as a woman Spencer did not have an official role at Carolina, she was very much part of the community. She wrote hymns for special occasions, organized events, and helped keep alumni records. Despite her conservative stance on race, Spencer supported public education and increased opportunities—if not coeducation—for white women.

When the university created an award to honor women in the 1990s, they named it the Cornelia Phillips Spencer Bell Award, in homage to the popular story. In 2002, galvanized by graduate student and activist Yonni Chapman, scholars began to talk about Spencer's outspoken support of white supremacy. After a campus seminar on the subject, then-chancellor James Moeser abolished the award in 2005. It has been replaced by the University Award for the Advancement of Women.

Springfest. Following the cancellation of the annual Jubilee concerts, UNC–Chapel Hill students started a new tradition in 1974 known as Springfest. Originally envisioned as a multiday arts and music festival, Springfest turned into a day-long concert by local bands on "Connor Beach," the lawn in front of Connor dorm. By the mid-1980s Springfest crowds ranged from 3,000 to 5,000 people. Students brought kegs and coolers to the increasingly alcohol-fueled event. The size of the crowds and the amount of beer consumed began to concern campus officials, especially after the legal drinking age was raised to twenty-one in 1986. In 1990 alcohol was banned from the event, and in 1991 the campus housing department denied a permit for the concert, citing concerns over liability.

Stacy Residence Hall was completed as a men's dormitory in 1938, one of several new dorms built at the time using funds from the Public Works Administration. It is named for Marvin Hendrix Stacy, a math professor at Carolina who served briefly as acting president of the school after the death of Edward Kidder Graham in 1918, until he too succumbed to the flu epidemic.

St. Anthony Hall. The Xi Chapter of Delta Psi, known as St. Anthony Hall, was active for a few years before the Civil War and then returned in the 1920s. Like the other chapters around the country, St. Anthony Hall at Carolina has a distinctive literary focus. The chapter has long hosted readings and a regular "Pancakes and Poetry" event. St. Anthony Hall has been a trailblazer among campus fraternities: in 1967 it was the first social fraternity to accept an African American member, when basketball star Charles Scott joined, and in 1971 it became the first to go coed, admitting women as members on an equal basis.

Steele Building. Opened in 1921 as a dormitory, Steele housed students until the late 1950s, when it was renovated and converted to office space. Beginning in 1951, Steele was the home of UNC's first African American students. After court rulings forced the university to admit African American graduate students in 1951 and undergraduates in 1955, these pioneering students found a campus that was still largely segregated. In an arrangement that continued for several years, all African American students were assigned dorms on the third floor of Steele. Even though many empty rooms were left on the floor, no other students lived there.

Steele was also home in the 1950s and 1960s to the university-run Book Exchange (at one point called the Booketeria), which sold textbooks and school supplies. The rest of the building was converted to office space in 1958 and has since housed many different campus offices.

The building is named for alumnus Walter Leake Steele (class of 1844). Steele served several terms in the state legislature and was a member of the state secession convention prior to the Civil War. After the war he was elected to the U.S. House of Representatives and later worked in the textile industry in his native Richmond County. He was a longtime member of the UNC Board of Trustees.

Steward's Hall. Constructed for the care and boarding of students, this wooden structure was located just north of present-day Carr Building where Cameron Avenue now runs, facing west. Completed in 1795, it was the second building completed on campus. For many years the trustees fixed the price of board and hired a steward to run the operation. There are multiple accounts of student complaints about bad food and poor care throughout the early 1800s, such as the charge of "invariable service of mutton and of bacon too fat to be eaten." The steward soon came to be in charge of the general care of buildings and grounds, eventually leading to an official position of superintendent. In 1847 the university razed the building and filled in the nearby well. University president David Swain used the wings of the building to construct houses for enslaved workers on his nearby property, and the structure was sold to become the village schoolhouse.

Stone Center. The Sonja Haynes Stone Center for Black Culture and History is home to Carolina's research, outreach, cultural, and service programs related to the study of the African American, diaspora, and African experiences. Designed by award-winning African American architect Philip Freelon, the building, which opened in 2004, is situated in a wooded area near the bell tower. It includes a gallery and museum exhibit space, a library, and an auditorium, as well as office and seminar spaces. Its existence is a testament to the determination of a coalition of students, alumni, faculty, and staff who urged the university to build the center and who supported it with private gifts. The majority of the $10 million needed to complete the building came from private donations from alumni and other supporters.

The Stone Center was established in 1988 as the Black Cultural Center, housed in the Graham Student Union. As it grew in popularity, so did calls for a freestanding building, especially after Dr. Stone's death in 1991. The university's chancellor initially opposed the idea, which sparked large student protests. Critical to the protest was the Black Awareness Council, a group of African American student athletes who brought more attention to the cause. After reading about the protests

Sonja Haynes Stone Center for Black Culture and History, 2018.
Photo by Johnny Andrews, UNC–Chapel Hill.

in the *New York Times*, filmmaker Spike Lee came to UNC, where he addressed a crowd of more than 7,000 people in the Dean Smith Center. The chancellor and board eventually agreed to support a freestanding center and in 1993 selected the location. The center's name was changed in 2002 to the Sonja Haynes Stone Center for Black Culture and History to mark its newly expanded mission and to emphasize its campus-wide mandate to explore, research, and support African American and diaspora arts, cultures, and histories.

Dr. Sonja Haynes Stone came to Chapel Hill in 1974 to direct the Curriculum in African and Afro-American Studies as an assistant professor and became associate professor in 1984. She was the founder of the Southeastern Black Press Institute and was an advocate for the African American rights movement. At Carolina she also was the adviser to the Black Student Movement and was active in expanding the Afro-American studies curriculum. She was the first recipient of the Alumni Association's Outstanding Black Faculty Award.

Stone walls. Geology professor Elisha Mitchell is credited with bringing the distinctive stone walls to the university campus. Serving double

This view of Franklin Street, ca. 1892, shows the stone walls along McCorkle Place, then much higher than they are now. Kemp Battle Photograph Album, North Carolina Collection Photo Archives, Wilson Library.

duty as faculty member and university bursar, Mitchell was charged with enclosing the campus, partly as a means of defining the boundaries of the university, but also to keep neighboring livestock from straying onto the college grounds. He was inspired by the long-lasting rock walls in his native Connecticut. Mitchell was also trying to save the university money by using the many rocks excavated during campus and town construction. Mitchell used enslaved laborers to build the walls, for which he was later reimbursed by the UNC Board of Trustees.

The original rock walls were dry stacked, relying on the artistry of the masons to find ways to fit the irregular rocks into a solid and sturdy pattern. Later walls, including those built today, use mortar to hold the rocks in place. As the university and town grew, a number of Chapel Hill African American masons built and maintained the walls, including brothers Alfred David and Willis Barbee and brothers Thomas and Lewis Booth. Examples of some of the original walls can still be found along Raleigh Street near the Coker Arboretum and the President's House.

Streaking. In the mid-1970s streaking (running naked through campus buildings and grounds) was more than just a way of letting off steam on campus: it was a source of pride. UNC students founded the American Streaker Society (ASS), and competed with other schools to see who could have the largest group streak. The fad peaked in the spring of 1974 as groups of naked students streaked across campuses around the country. On the night of March 7 of that year, 924 UNC–Chapel Hill students (including 65 women) streaked through campus for about ten minutes, passing through South Building and the House Undergraduate Library along the way. The Carolina students thought they set a record, but it was eclipsed that same night by over 1,500 streakers at the University of Georgia. The tradition remains on campus, though on a smaller scale: each semester, on or around the last day of class, a group of students shed their clothes and streak through Davis Library.

Student Body **sculpture.** The *Student Body* sculpture was installed in front of Davis Library in October 1990. A gift of the UNC–Chapel Hill class of 1985, the collection of seven bronze statues by artist Julia Balk was said to represent different aspects of student life. The sculpture was controversial immediately after it was installed. It was criticized as portraying stereotypical images of students, particularly a figure of an African American student spinning a basketball on his finger. Other statues drew criticism as well, including an African American woman with books balanced on top of her head and an Asian American woman carrying a violin case. The statues were repeatedly vandalized, and at one point the basketball player was tipped over and the basketball stolen. The university canceled its planned dedication ceremony. In June 1991 the statues were relocated to a less prominent location in a small courtyard behind Manning Hall. At some point after the move, the statues of the students with the basketball and the violin were removed.

Student government is the mechanism for self-governance that Carolina students have managed in one form or another for the university's entire history. Today it consists of an undergraduate division and a graduate and professional student division, both of which have executive, legislative, and honor system branches. All students pledge to follow the Honor Code, which includes ideals of academic honesty, personal integrity, and responsible citizenship. Members of both honor systems are responsible for hearing and adjudicating alleged Honor Code violations. The respective legislative branches oversee the management and disposition of student fees to approved organizations. By state law, since 1972 the undergraduate student body president serves as a full voting member on the UNC Board of Trustees.

For the first 100 years or so the Dialectic and Philanthropic Societies made laws governing the conduct of their members on and off campus. In 1875 the university required every student to join one of the societies, so that they would all come under a governing policy. Student government got its start in 1904, when class representatives organized a committee—later the Student Council—to preside over cases of hazing, cheating, and other violations of the Honor Code. The first student body constitution, adopted in 1946, established a Student Council, a Men's Social Council, a Women's Social Council, an Interdenominational Council, and the Women's Council. In the 1960s the student body grew more diverse and administrators became more involved in adjudicating student conduct, especially over the issues of dorm visitation rules, participation in protests, and drug use. In 1969 a committee appointed jointly by the chancellor and the student body president considered the issue of reform. Their work resulted in the creation of the Instrument of Student Judicial Governance, passed in 1974. The instrument has been amended since then but is the basis for the current governing system. The Graduate and Professional Student Federation was founded in 1971 to represent those students' interests within student government and university administration. In 2017 students voted to separate the two, creating the dual system that exists today.

Student Recreation Center. In 1989 students voted to increase fees in order to support construction of a new gym on campus. In contrast to Woollen and Fetzer Gyms, which were controlled by the athletic department, the Student Recreation Center would be managed by student-led organizations. The new facility, located adjacent to Fetzer, opened in 1993.

Student Television. In 1983 a small group of UNC–Chapel Hill students interested in television production formed Student Television. They received a loan from the university and borrowed equipment from the Department of Radio, Television, and Motion Pictures to get started.

The initial shows were feature stories broadcast on a local cable channel and were viewable only by students living in Granville Towers or in fraternity and sorority houses, as the dorms did not yet have cable. Within a year Student Television membership had grown to more than 150 students. The best-known program is the long-running soap opera *General College*, which debuted in January 1987 and continues today. The network offers a variety of other programs, including *Off the Cuff*, a sketch comedy show that also premiered in 1987. Many former Student Television members have gone on to careers in the TV or movie industry, including actors Billy Crudup and Dan Cortese and ESPN anchor Stuart Scott.

Study abroad. One of the earliest study abroad opportunities for students was a UNC System "Year at Lyon" program, which enabled a select group of students from UNC–Chapel Hill, North Carolina State University, and UNC-Greensboro to spend their junior year at the University of Lyon in France. Sponsored by the French department, the program began in 1964 and was repeated annually through the early 1970s. The Romance language departments continued to be the primary sponsors of study abroad programs through the 1970s and 1980s. In 1989 the *Daily Tar Heel* reported low participation in study abroad among students not majoring in one of the Romance languages. The university did not always make it easy—to study at another university in the 1970s, students had to withdraw from UNC and then reapply when they returned to the country. The numbers continued to rise as the university provided more support and more opportunities for students. In 1997 the UNC System began the UNC Exchange Program, which focuses on providing low-cost study abroad opportunities for students. A 2000 *Daily Tar Heel* story, "Study Abroad No Longer Just for Rich Kids," suggested that study abroad was becoming more accessible to all students. By the mid-2010s UNC–Chapel Hill reported that more than 30 percent of undergraduates participated in a study abroad program.

Summer Reading Program. This annual project, directed by the New Student and Family Programs office, introduces incoming students to intellectual life at Carolina. On the day before the fall semester begins, new students join small-group discussions on a selected book that they read during the summer. The late chancellor Michael Hooker introduced the Summer Reading Program in 1999 to add more intellectual content to orientation. It has proved to be a popular and sometimes controversial addition.

In 2002 the book selection committee chose *Approaching the Qur'an: The Early Revelations*, by Michael Sells, inspired by what they saw as the need for Americans to better understand Islam after the attacks of September 11, 2001. Conservative journalists publicized the selection and helped encourage public criticism of Carolina for its choice. The Family Policy Network (FPN) filed suit against the university (*Yacovelli v. Moeser*) on behalf of several students, claiming that the requirement violated the Establishment Clause of the First Amendment. FPN lost in court and on appeal, but the university offered students who did not wish to take part in discussions the option of writing a paper instead.

Summer school. In 1877 UNC began offering classes during the summer. The Summer Normal School was not an extension of the regular curriculum but a new program to provide education for teachers in North Carolina. The courses were designed for primary school teachers in North Carolina and were immediately popular, drawing close to 2,500 students in its first eight years. However, the program struggled to maintain support and was suspended twice before being revived in 1907. These early summer school programs were among the first at the university that women were able to attend. Women made up nearly half of the class at the first summer school, and in 1878 Emily Coe became the first woman to teach on campus when she joined the summer school faculty. The success of the program and the demand for teacher education led the university to establish the Department of Normal Instruction in 1885 and a graduate program in education in 1896. By 1916 the university began offering regular courses during the summer.

Sutton's Drug Store opened on Franklin Street in 1923 and quickly became a vital part of student life. It is now one of the few remaining links to the past in the rapidly changing downtown. In its early days, when the store was known as Sutton and Alderman's, students went to the drugstore to buy a wide variety of goods and services beyond the traditional medicines and soda fountain drinks: clothing, concert tickets, record players—students could even get their yearbook photos taken there. Pharmacist John Woodward purchased the store in 1977 and began a new tradition a few years later when he began photographing customers. These photos now lining the wall show generations of students and community members eating at Sutton's, with a large number of Tar Heel athletes represented. Facing increased competition from national chain drugstores in the 2010s, Sutton's shut down its prescription service in 2014. The store was sold at that time to longtime grill manager Don Pinney, who ensured that the lunch counter remained, continuing to draw crowds for the store's well-known grilled cheese sandwiches, hot dogs, and milkshakes.

Swain Hall was opened in 1914 for use as a cafeteria. Built on the former site of the university president's house, Swain provided a much-needed expansion of dining space for the campus, which had long outgrown the limited seating capacity in Commons Hall. The novelty of the new space appeared to wear off quickly, for only a few years after it opened students were routinely referring to it as "Swine Hall," in reference to the quality of food served there.

The building is named for David Lowry Swain, university president from 1835 to 1868. A native of Buncombe County, Swain was a lawyer and politician, serving as governor of North Carolina from 1832 to 1835. After leaving office he was selected to replace Joseph Caldwell as president of the university. Swain presided over the university during a period of expanding enrollment followed by a struggle to keep the campus open during the Civil War as the student population dwindled. Swain also had a strong interest in state history and helped found the North Carolina Historical Society at the university, a predecessor to the North Carolina Collection and Southern Historical Collection in Wilson Library.

Swain was one of the wealthiest men in Chapel Hill, profiting from the work of a large number of laborers he had enslaved. He supplemented his income by leasing enslaved servants to the university. One of these people was Wilson Caldwell, who would later serve in local government and help found and operate schools following the Civil War.

Swain is often credited with his role in negotiating the surrender of Chapel Hill and the university at the end of the Civil War in 1865, helping save the town and campus from destruction. His household was at the center of a local scandal when Swain's daughter became engaged to marry a Union officer from Illinois who was stationed in Chapel Hill at the end of the war. At odds with the newly elected state government in 1868, Swain left the university presidency and died shortly thereafter.

Swim test. When the United States entered World War II, there was widespread concern that the physical fitness of young Americans was poor compared to that of their German counterparts. Schools and colleges across the country began more intensive physical education programs as a result. Inspired in part by the demanding fitness regime of the navy pre-flight trainees on campus during the war, the university, joining other colleges around the country, decided to institute a requirement that students learn how to swim before they graduated. The original swim test required students to demonstrate three different strokes over four laps in the pool. The test evolved to focus simply on survival: students had to swim one lap and then tread water for five minutes. Students were frequently reluctant to take the test, with many putting it off until just before graduation. The best-known procrastinator was future chancellor Michael Hooker (class of 1969), who waited until the last possible opportunity to take the test. He failed, was unable to graduate with the rest of his class, and had to enroll in a swimming class in summer school. Increasingly unpopular and seen as an outdated requirement, the swim test was finally eliminated in the fall of 2006.

T

Tar Babies was an unofficial nickname given to the freshman (or junior varsity) basketball and football teams. It was used primarily by journalists (including those at the *Daily Tar Heel*) roughly from the 1920s through the 1970s. Similar to the "White Phantoms" nickname used in newspaper coverage for the men's basketball team during the same era, "Tar Babies" does not appear to have been used in official university publications or announcements.

Tar Heels. UNC–Chapel Hill's unique "Tar Heels" nickname is also the nickname for a resident of the state, as well as for the state itself. The term traces back to the eighteenth century, when North Carolina, with its plentiful pine trees, was a major producer of tar and turpentine for the naval industry. "Tar Heel" emerged as a derogatory term for the enslaved people and other poor, barefoot North Carolinians who made the products and thus had pine resin or tar stuck to the bottoms of their feet ("rosin heels" was an earlier version of the term). The nickname became popular after the Civil War to represent North Carolina people and products. When students started the university's first student newspaper, in 1893, they called it the *Tar Heel*.

It is not clear when Carolina athletic teams began officially using the Tar Heels nickname. Early newspaper coverage referred to the team as the Tar Heels only when they played teams from other states, suggesting that the formal nickname was not yet used. In fact, some newspaper articles referred to other college teams in the state as Tar Heels when they played teams outside of North Carolina. By the 1910s and 1920s the nickname was used more frequently in reference to the UNC teams, even when they played other teams from North Carolina. As the reputation of UNC's basketball and football teams grew through the twentieth century, the Tar Heels nickname became more firmly associated with the university. When UNC–Chapel Hill entered its first licensing agreement in the 1980s, "Tar Heels" was one of the phrases registered by the university, and it remains an official word mark of the university.

Tarrson Hall. Adjacent to Brauer Hall, Tarrson opened in 2000 to serve as a teaching facility for the School of Dentistry. The building is named for E. B. "Bud" Tarrson, an executive in a Chicago company that sold dental hygiene products. Tarrson donated to dental schools around the country. Even though he did not attend Carolina, he gave $2 million to support dental education at the university.

Tate-Turner-Kuralt Building. Opened in 1995 to house the School of Social Work, the Tate-Turner-Kuralt Building is named for three different people. Jack Tate was an early supporter of the school and was effective in gaining state support for teaching social work at Carolina. John Turner had a long career in social work, was hired as Kenan Professor in 1974, and became the first African American dean at Carolina in 1981. And journalist Charles Kuralt, whose father was a social worker in Charlotte, was a longtime supporter of the school. The new building enabled the social work programs at UNC to operate in the same location for the first time since the founding of the school in 1920.

Taylor Campus Health Services Building. The student infirmary is named for James A. Taylor (class of 1939), a member of the student health service staff beginning in 1949. When Taylor took over as director of student health in 1971, he began advocating for a new facility, as well as the expansion of student health services. Under Taylor's leadership, UNC–Chapel Hill established its first sports medicine program and greatly expanded women's health services. The new Campus Health Services Building was completed in 1980 and was named for Taylor in 1988.

Taylor Hall. When it first opened in 1969, this building was known as Swing Building. It housed classrooms, a lecture hall, and labs for the School of Medicine. In 1989 the building was renamed for Isaac M. Taylor, an alumnus (class of 1942) who joined the faculty of the School of Medicine in 1952 and served as dean from 1964 to 1971. In his brief tenure leading the school, Taylor oversaw a period of growth and expansion, spearheading the construction of several new buildings. He also brought a renewed emphasis on primary health care, helping establish teaching units in hospitals across the state and laying the foundation for the establishment of the Area Health Education Centers in 1972. Despite his long career on campus, Taylor may now be best known as the father of popular singer-songwriter James Taylor.

Taylor Residence Hall. Opened in 2006, the new apartment-style dorm is part of the Ram Village Community on South Campus. The building is named for former chancellor Nelson Ferebee Taylor (class of 1942), who joined the School of Law faculty in 1968, soon moved into administration, and was named chancellor in 1972. It was a challenging era as UNC, along with many universities nationwide, was still reeling from widespread protests over the Vietnam War and struggling to adapt to an increasingly vocal and diverse student body. During Taylor's time as chancellor (1972–80), the diversity of the student body increased significantly, especially the number of women students at UNC. He was also a successful fund-raiser, most notably in his efforts to expand the university's library system. He was instrumental in securing approval and resources for a new main library, now the Walter Royal Davis Library, completed in 1984, as well as a major renovation of Wilson Library and expansion of the Health Sciences Library.

Teague Residence Hall opened on Stadium Drive as a men's dormitory in 1958, around the same time as nearby Parker and Avery dorms. In the 1970s and 1980s Teague was one of the most notorious dorms on campus. With a strong focus on fellowship and tradition, Teague was often compared to a fraternity. Teague residents were known for their rowdy behavior and for their emphasis on intramural sports (teams from Teague were frequent winners of intramural sports championships). In 1983 Teague residents entered a candidate for homecoming queen: Scott Latham, who ran under the name "Yure Nmomma" and won, becoming the first male homecoming queen at UNC. Latham's pseudonym was in reference to the phrase "Your Mamma Sleeps in Teague," which appeared on aerial banners flown over Kenan Stadium during football games in the early 1980s. In 1988, shortly after Teague residents were accused of sexual and racial harassment directed at a campus housing employee, university officials decided to turn Teague into a coed dorm.

The building is named for Claude Edward Teague, class of 1912, and a longtime educator. He served as UNC business manager from 1943 to 1957.

Thurston-Bowles Building. Opened in 1995, these two adjoining buildings house research centers at the School of Medicine. They are named in recognition of D. Jones "Doc" Thurston Jr. and Hargrove "Skipper" Bowles Jr. Thurston was a graduate of UNC's School of Engineering in the 1930s (before the program closed) and built a successful trucking company. He donated funds in support of arthritis research at Carolina. "Skipper" Bowles was a prominent business leader and politician and was the father of UNC System president Erskine Bowles. Skipper Bowles was a leading fund-raiser for the university, helping secure private donations toward the Dean Smith Center and funding research on alcoholism.

Tin Can. As Carolina expanded in the 1920s, and as interest picked up in college sports, including the still relatively new basketball team, the campus needed a new indoor athletic facility (basketball games were previously held in the small gym in Bynum Hall). The new building was completed in 1923. It was big enough for multiple basketball courts and an indoor track and had enough seats to hold 4,000 spectators. Before the university had a chance to give the structure a proper name, students took to calling it the "Tin Can" after the galvanized tin covering the walls and roof. The Tin Can was at the heart of Carolina life for decades. In addition to basketball games (played in the Tin Can until Woollen Gym opened in 1938) and intramural sports, the building hosted concerts and dances. In the 1940s and 1950s some of the biggest names in jazz played in the Tin Can, including Louis Armstrong, Duke Ellington, and Benny Goodman. When enrollment swelled after World War II, nearly 200 students were forced to make the Tin Can their temporary home. The building was torn down in 1977 to make way for Fetzer Gym.

Title IX. In 1972 the U.S. government passed Title IX of the Education Amendments Act—laws that govern various educational policies—to prohibit discrimination on the basis of sex in any federally funded education program or activity. Its enactment struck down the last of UNC's rules that restricted the admission of women. Even though UNC had begun accepting white women in the 1890s, the university always controlled their numbers through various policies. At first women could enroll only as upper-class or graduate students. By the 1940s women could enroll as freshmen or sophomores only if they lived in Chapel Hill with family members. The trustees removed these restrictions in 1963, but scarce housing continued to limit the number of women who were able to enroll. The passage of Title IX also led to the hiring of more women faculty and the creation of the Association for Women Faculty and Professionals, founded in 1978 to help advance the status of women on campus. Five years after the passage of Title IX, women outnumbered men in the student body. Progress toward equity for women students and faculty members was slow at best, and they sometimes used Title IX as the basis for a suit against the university.

Title IX also brought dramatic changes to athletics. Carolina women set up the Women's Athletic Association in 1934 to support intramural teams and provide athletic opportunities. Carolina women athletes were instrumental in founding the Association for Intercollegiate Athletics for Women in 1970, which hosted national championships until it merged with the NCAA in the 1980s. The university consolidated the administration of women's and men's teams then, and women received their first athletic scholarships. The 1981 soccer team won Carolina's first NCAA championship in a women's team sport.

Toronto Exchange. One of the university's earliest exchange programs, the Toronto Exchange ran for more than thirty years. In the program, a group of Carolina students spent a week at the University of Toronto, and the Toronto students paid a return visit. The program began in 1959 and was organized and sponsored by the student governments at the two universities. By the 1980s as many as forty students from each school participated. As more study abroad programs became available, there was less interest in the Toronto Exchange. Funding for the program was cut by the student government in 1992.

Town Girls Association. For many years women at the university were required to live on campus. The only exceptions made were for students who were from Chapel Hill or the surrounding area who could live at home. These students were known informally as "town girls." In an era when social activity and intramural sports were often concentrated around dorms, the Chapel Hill students started the Town Girls Association. Active from the 1930s through the early 1960s, the group met regularly, fielded intramural sports teams, and sponsored dances and other events.

Trademarks and licensing. UNC–Chapel Hill signed its first trademark licensing agreement in 1982, not long after the men's basketball team won the NCAA championship. The licensing agreement enables the university to control the use of the school name, logos, and symbols in merchandise and to collect royalties from authorized uses. The original trademarks included the university seal, the Old Well, the Tar Heel foot, Rameses, and the interlocking NC design. Licensing has become a lucrative operation for the university: in the 2012–13 academic year the school earned close to $4 million from licensing, money that would be used for student aid and scholarships.

Tuition has been a complicated and controversial topic at the university since its founding. The initial cost to attend the university when it opened in 1795 was $15 per year (roughly equivalent to $300 in 2015). In North Carolina's Constitution of 1868, the article on education said that "the General Assembly shall provide that the benefits of the university, as far as practicable, be extended to the youth of the State free of expense for tuition." While the wording changed slightly through subsequent revisions, the mandate for free education has remained, and the clause "as far as practicable" has remained a source of debate.

Even as the university grew through the twentieth century, tuition increases remained fairly modest. Tuition did not top $100 until the 1920s and remained below $1,000 for in-state residents until the 1990s. The university began charging a higher rate for out-of-state residents in the 1920s, briefly exploring a model that would charge different amounts for students from different parts of the country, adjusted for how much universities in those areas charged for out-of-state tuition.

Costs for attending UNC–Chapel Hill rose more rapidly in the 2000s due to a number of factors, most notably a decline in direct support from the state following a series of budget cuts. The university sought to offset rising tuition through increased financial aid opportunities. In 2003 the university announced the creation of the Carolina Covenant, a new program that would ensure that qualifying students who could not afford tuition were able to graduate debt-free.

U

UNC System presidents. UNC–Chapel Hill is part of the University of North Carolina System, along with sixteen other institutions. The leader of the UNC System is a president, a title that has been in place since the first consolidation of three universities (UNC, UNC-Greensboro, and North Carolina State University) took place in 1932, and continued when the current system was created in 1971. There have been eight system presidents since then. The longest-serving UNC president thus far is William C. Friday. Friday's thirty-year tenure spanned great social change, including racial desegregation and the evolution of UNC into the system it is today.

UNC System Presidents
Frank Porter Graham: 1930–49
Gordon Gray: 1950–55
William C. Friday: 1956–86
C. D. Spangler: 1986–97
Molly Corbett Broad: 1997–2006
Erskine Bowles: 2006–11
Thomas W. Ross: 2011–16
Margaret Spellings: 2016–19
William Roper (interim): 2019–

UNC-TV. The University of North Carolina Center for Public Television, established by the UNC System Board of Governors in 1979, began as a single station that began broadcasting from the Chapel Hill campus in 1955. This early foray into educational television was promoted by successive university leaders, the state legislature, individual donors, and thousands of volunteers. Their efforts eventually placed North Carolina in the forefront of public television. WUNC-TV was the tenth educational television station in the country, and the first south of Washington, D.C. The studio at Carolina was in Swain Hall, with additional studios at UNC-Greensboro (then Woman's College) and North Carolina State College of Agriculture and Engineering in Raleigh. The station, which is now a statewide public media system with four channels, operates from the Joseph and Kathleen Bryan Communications Center in Research Triangle Park, which opened in 1989.

Both UNC-TV and WUNC radio originated in the early 1940s at Carolina from courses developed by Earl Wynn (1911–1986), professor of drama and radio. Wynn coordinated the interests of a number of faculty and staff interested in broadcasting to establish the Department of Radio, Television, and Motion Pictures (RTVMP) and an allied Communication Center in Swain Hall to house equipment, studio, and broadcasting facilities.

University Day, celebrated annually on October 12, commemorates the laying of the cornerstone of Old East on that date in 1793. University Day was first held in 1877 and featured a Glee Club performance and a lecture from university president Kemp Plummer Battle on the charter and establishment of the university. Music and speeches have been a part of the ceremonies ever since. In 1906 the university first awarded honorary degrees during the ceremony, and in 1907 it began the tradition of a procession through campus to Memorial Hall. Two U.S. presidents have spoken at University Day celebrations, both held in Kenan Stadium: John F. Kennedy, in 1961, and Bill Clinton, as part of the UNC bicentennial celebration in 1993.

University Laundry. *See* Cheek/Clark Building

University of North Carolina Press. In 1922 a group of faculty established UNC Press, primarily with the goal of publishing faculty research, under the direction of university librarian Louis Round Wilson. The first title published, in 1923, was *The Saprolegniaceae, with Notes on Other Water Molds,* by William Chambers Coker. UNC Press initially served as a printing operation. The staff did not comment on editorial content, especially if it came from a UNC faculty member. In 1932 William T. Couch took over as director. The work began to reach beyond

President John F. Kennedy speaking at the University Day celebration in Kenan Stadium, October 12, 1961. UNC Photo Lab Collection, North Carolina Collection Photo Archives, Wilson Library.

the campus, and the Press took on a more traditional editorial role, with staff involved in selecting and editing manuscripts.

Inspired in part by Howard Odum and the Institute for Social Sciences, the Press specialized in southern studies, a growing area of research and study at the university. It also published work by African American scholars, which was unusual for a southern university at that time. In fact, UNC Press was publishing works by African American authors at the same time that state and university leaders were fighting to prevent African American students from enrolling at Carolina. The scope of the publications offered by the Press gradually expanded to include literary studies, African American history, and natural history, among other topics. By the 1950s and 1960s UNC Press was widely recognized as one of the leading university presses in the country and acknowledged for its work in regional studies.

UNC Press is part of the UNC System, not the Chapel Hill campus. It has always operated as an independent publisher with a separate board of governors that approves publications. It is supported primarily by income from sales, foundation and grant support, and donations. Originally located in the basement of Alumni Hall, the Press moved to renovated Bynum Hall in 1939 after the gymnasium was removed. The offices remained in Bynum until 1980, when they moved to the new Brooks Hall.

University Railroad. The eighteenth-century choice to locate UNC in a relatively sparsely populated area left the university and town stranded in the 1840s when railroad lines began to crisscross the state. The east-west line between Goldsboro and Greensboro bypassed Chapel Hill some eight miles to the north, which encouraged the later growth of Durham but isolated Chapel Hill. In 1873, while the university was closed, local iron mine owner Robert F. Hoke obtained a charter for the Chapel Hill Iron Mountain Railroad Company. When the university re-opened two years later, trustees worked with Hoke to make the project happen. Renamed the State University Railroad, the project gained state support through the use of convict labor, and additional support through an agreement with the Richmond and Danville Railroad Company to provide iron and rolling stock. The line opened in 1881.

The Chapel Hill terminus was located two miles away from campus, at a spot known as West End, later to become the town of Carrboro. The line met the main line at a point midway between Durham and Hillsborough, marked now by University Station Road. Hoke never found it profitable to ship his iron ore by rail, but the West End depot quickly became a hub for new industry. In 1898 Thomas Lloyd built textile mills there, which Julian Carr bought in 1904.

Passenger service on the University Railroad line ended in 1940. About the same time, UNC purchased property at the west end of Cameron Avenue to build a power plant on the rail line. The current plant there, the Gore Cogeneration Facility, was completed in the early 1990s. Today the only rail traffic on the University Railroad line comes from the freight cars that deliver coal to the power plant.

Unsung Founders Memorial. The Unsung Founders Memorial is an art installation located on McCorkle Place, dedicated to the African American people who helped build the university. The piece, created by artist Do Ho Suh, features bronze figures holding up a black stone table, surround by five stone seats. Inscribed on the top is, "The Class of 2002 honors the university's unsung founders, the people of color bond and

Unsung Founders Memorial, 2005.
Photograph by Sarah Arneson / Carolina Alumni Review.

free, who helped build the Carolina that we cherish today." The senior gift of the class of 2002, it was installed and dedicated on November 5, 2005. Descendants of enslaved university workers attended the dedication, along with university leaders and students. Suh designed the piece to be accessible and interactive, noting that, "when you touch it and sit on it, and use it, . . . you become part of it." He also noted that the seats were inspired by the rocks that mark some of the graves in the African American section of the Old Chapel Hill Cemetery.

While its installation represented a landmark moment for a predominantly white institution to acknowledge its debt to enslaved people, the memorial has been criticized for its appearance. The low profile of the piece and the implicit encouragement to sit at a table being held up by the depicted enslaved people seems to convey their oppressed condition and to diminish their achievements. The monument has also been criticized for its proximity to the much larger and more prominent Confederate Monument that stood nearby on McCorkle Place until 2019.

Upendo Lounge. In 1972 the Black Student Movement (BSM) was allocated a meeting and event space on the first floor of Chase Hall. They named it the Upendo Lounge, after the Swahili word for love. Upendo quickly became a hub for African American students on campus. It was used for meetings, practices, lectures, and church services and as a general gathering space and community center. It was the first space on the campus dedicated to and controlled by African American students. The location and use of Upendo were often a source of contention. When the space was taken over by dining services in 1976, Upendo was moved upstairs. In 1983 the space was unavailable during renovation and was again relocated. The BSM often clashed with university administrators who repeatedly challenged the group's control of the space and discussed making it available to other student groups. Even after the opening of the Black Cultural Center in the student union in 1988 and the Stone Center in 2004, Upendo remained the center of BSM activities and an important part of student life. After Chase was torn down in 2005, space was allocated for a new Upendo in the Student and Academic Services Building North. The new Upendo was renovated in 2016, and the university confirmed that the BSM would have priority use of the space.

U.S. presidents. The only UNC alumnus to go on to become president of the United States was James K. Polk, from Mecklenburg County, an 1818 graduate. One other future president briefly attended UNC: Gerald Ford enrolled for summer classes at the law school in 1938. Future president George H. W. Bush did not take classes at UNC but was on campus in 1942 to attend the navy pre-flight school there, as did Gerald Ford. Seven presidents have visited UNC while in office: James K. Polk, James Buchanan, Andrew Johnson, Franklin D. Roosevelt, John F. Kennedy, Bill Clinton, and Barack Obama.

Utilities. A major theme for the early twentieth-century history of the university and Chapel Hill—as it was for much of the United States—was the development of utilities. Both university and village grew steadily from the 1880s to 1930, adding students, faculty, and staff, a new railroad line, and new residences and businesses. UNC made the transition from a liberal arts college focused on undergraduate education to a multipurpose university by adding graduate and professional study, research, publications, extension, and service to its mission. The population of Chapel Hill more than doubled, and the mill village that became Carrboro came into existence.

These new enterprises demanded new infrastructure: more buildings to house more students, new research labs, and new ways to move water and wastewater and to provide heat and light. UNC physics professor Joshua W. Gore built the first water plant in 1893. A steam pump moved water from a well south of Memorial Hall to storage tanks in the attic of South Building and then through underground pipes to showers, tubs, and toilets in the basement of Smith Hall (now historic Playmakers Theatre). Two years later Gore added a small electric lighting plant, and in 1901 he designed a new power plant built on the future site of Phillips Hall. For the first time steam heat and hot water were piped to campus buildings and sewage was piped away. Gore also installed and became co-owner of Chapel Hill's first telephone system.

In 1921 the university began to purchase land at the west end of Cameron Avenue, which eventually became the site of a power plant and laundry building. The laundry (now the Cheek/Clark Building) opened in 1921 and provided laundry and dry-cleaning services to students and town residents. The first power plant on the site opened in 1940.

As the university continued to expand campus utilities, it also extended service to the town of Chapel Hill. That ended in 1977, when Carolina sold all of its public utilities. Under an agreement with the state legislature negotiated by trustee Walter Royal Davis, the Chapel Hill campus kept most of the funds from the $40 million sale. This funded the construction of Davis Library and renovations to Wilson and Health Sciences Libraries. It also helped fund the plans for the cogeneration facility completed in 1986.

Today multiple systems handle utilities for the campus and UNC hospitals. The cogeneration facility produces steam for heating and hot water, while the electricity produced as a by-product helps to power electrical systems. Although it is powered by coal, the facility uses the latest technologies to minimize emissions and waste. The electric network consists of 820 electric and telecommunications manholes, tied together with 39 miles of duct bank, containing 68 miles of underground cable. Steam is distributed through an extensive network of underground steam and condensate return piping in excess of fifty miles. In partnership with Orange Water and Sewer Authority, the university operates a water reclamation and reuse system and a storm water system comprised of thousands of catch basins and inlets, miles of piping, and outfalls that discharge water into nearby creeks.

V

Vance Hall was built in 1912 as part of a three-part dormitory for men students, along with Battle and Pettigrew. It is on the northwest corner of McCorkle Place on Franklin Street. The buildings were converted to offices in the 1960s. In excavations related to building construction near the Pettigrew and Vance Hall sites, UNC Research Laboratories of Archaeology staff have uncovered artifacts from prehistoric American Indian occupation.

Vance was named in honor of Zebulon Baird Vance, who studied law at Carolina. Vance was in the U.S. Congress in 1861 when North Carolina seceded. He resigned his seat and entered the Confederate army. He served as North Carolina governor from 1862 to 1865. After the war and the conservatives regained political power, Vance served again as governor from 1876 to 1878, and then in the U.S. Senate until his death.

Vandermint Auditorium. In the 1984 movie *This Is Spinal Tap*, the British metal band Spinal Tap played a concert in Chapel Hill at the fictional Vandermint Auditorium. Despite problems with the food backstage—guitarist Nigel Tufnel was upset by the "miniature bread"—the band delivered a rousing performance of their song "Hell Hole."

Van Hecke–Wettach Hall, the current home of the UNC School of Law, sits on Ridge Road on the eastern edge of campus. The building was completed in 1968 to give more space for the law school, which had outgrown its home in Manning Hall. The building is named for two law school deans, Maurice Taylor Van Hecke and Robert H. Wettach, both of whom joined the law school faculty in 1921.

The building also houses the Kathrine R. Everett Law Library, named in 1993 in recognition of Everett's support for the school and

One of the landmark features of old Venable Hall was the huge periodic table in the chemistry classroom, shown here during a class in fall 1957. UNC Photo Lab Collection, North Carolina Collection Photo Archives, Wilson Library.

her career. Everett was the only woman in the law school class of 1920. She graduated first in her class, was one of the first women admitted to the state bar, and was the first woman to argue—and win—a case before the North Carolina Supreme Court. She was also one of the first two women to win a seat on the Durham City Council (1951), a seat she held for twenty years.

Venable and Murray Halls are home to the Departments of Chemistry and Marine Science. The conjoined buildings opened in 2010 as the final phase of the Carolina Physical Science Complex, the largest construction project in university history. From 2004 to 2010 the university completed Chapman Hall, Caudill Labs, the Brooks Computer Science Building, and then Venable and Murray Halls to complete the complex.

Venable and Murray Halls replaced the first Venable Hall, built in 1925 as a home for the Department of Chemistry. For a time in the late 1980s the pharmaceutical firm Glaxo leased lab space in Venable until its facilities in Research Triangle Park were constructed.

Venable Halls old and new were named in honor of Francis Preston Venable, professor of chemistry and university president from 1900 to 1914. He was the first faculty member to hold a Ph.D., and both as faculty member and as president he helped begin the transformation of Carolina into a research institution.

Murray Hall is named in honor of professor emeritus Royce Murray, who began his career at Carolina in 1960. He is an internationally recognized scientist in electrochemistry and the chemistry of new materials, who led the committee that guided the design of lab facilities in the new buildings.

The **Victory Bell** is the prize awarded to the winner of the UNC-Duke football game each year. Cheerleaders from UNC and Duke came up with the idea in 1948, most likely inspired by the tradition of traveling trophies exchanged by other college rivals. The large bell was obtained from an old railroad engine and mounted on a wheeled platform. In the 2000s, the players began spray-painting the platform in the school color of the winning team. The spray-painting ended in 2016, when the schools agreed to a professional paint job for the platform that featured the logos of both teams.

Victory Village. After World War II the university experienced a rapid increase in enrollment, especially among married students attending college on the GI Bill. Faced with a housing shortage, the university obtained former army barracks that were no longer needed by the military. These metal, prefabricated houses, installed in 1946, were intended as a temporary solution but would remain on campus for more than twenty years. The new housing community was named Victory Village. Future UNC System president William C. Friday and future chancellor William B. Aycock were among the many students who lived at one point in Victory Village. While they served a necessary purpose, they were unpopular. The *Daily Tar Heel* referred to the buildings as "architect's nightmares" and reported that they had been called, at various times, "egg-crate construction, fire traps, and bandboxes." After the last ones were finally demolished in the early 1970s, the name Victory Village continued to be used by a university-sponsored daycare center.

Whitehead Hall. Located next to the Carolina Inn, Whitehead was completed in 1938 as a dormitory for students in the medical school. Funded in part by money from the Public Works Administration, the dorm was part of a major expansion of on-campus housing for students. It is named for Richard Henry Whitehead, dean of the medical school and a professor of anatomy.

White Phantoms. From the 1920s through the early 1950s the men's basketball team was known informally as the "White Phantoms." They were still the Tar Heels; this was an unofficial nickname used often by journalists, similar to how University of Virginia sports teams were sometimes referred to as "Wahoos," a term still used by fans of the University of Virginia and journalists. The nickname was probably first used by a journalist in Atlanta watching the team during the 1925 Southern Conference championship. At the time the basketball players wore white uniforms with a blue "NC" logo on the chest. The name is also said to refer to the fast, fluid play of the team. UNC was not the only team with an unofficial nickname. A 1927 newspaper headline, "Red Terrors and White Phantoms Meet Tonight," referred to a basketball game between Carolina and N.C. State.

Wilson Hall. Opened in 1940, Wilson is located on a hill near the corner of South Road and Columbia Street, described as "one of the most beautiful natural grounds for a building" on campus. It was built to house classrooms, laboratories, and offices for the Department of Biology and was expanded in 1965. The building is named for Henry Van Peters Wilson, hired in 1891 as the first biology professor at UNC, who later became chair of the Department of Zoology. He taught until his retirement in 1936. The proximity of Wilson Hall to Wilson Library has been an ongoing source of frustration to the first-year students seen every year on the first day of class wandering the halls of the library looking for their biology classroom.

Wilson Library. The Carnegie Library (now Hill Hall) had been in use for only a couple of decades before university officials began talking about the need for a new library building. University president Harry Woodburn Chase described the Carnegie Library as built to serve the needs of a small college. As the university continued on a path of ambitious growth and transformation into a major research university, it would need a new library. The new building would be not just a home for the library collections but a symbol of the university's aspirations. The building was designed by architect Arthur Nash, who had worked on other campus buildings. The library was completed in 1929 and dedicated on October 19, 1929, just a few days before the stock market crash. At the dedication ceremony, Governor O. Max Gardner said, "The heart of a true university is its library."

In addition to housing the library collections and reading rooms, the new library was also the home of the School of Library Science and for many years housed the Bull's Head Bookshop on the ground floor. Even with the much larger space available, the library collections eventually outgrew its stack space. New stack additions were added in 1952 and 1977. Once Davis Library opened as the main university library in 1984, the building was renovated to serve as the home for Wilson Library's Special Collections: the North Carolina Collection, Rare Book Collection, Southern Historical Collection, Southern Folklife Collection, and University Archives.

Originally known simply as the University Library, it was renamed Wilson Library in 1956 after librarian Louis Round Wilson. Wilson graduated from UNC in 1899 and was hired soon after as university librarian. Under his direction the library greatly expanded its collections, staff, and services. Wilson was also instrumental in founding the School of Library Science (now the School of Information and Library Science). His work on campus extended beyond the library: he was involved in establishing the university's Extension Division and the University of North Carolina Press and wrote about university history. In 1932 Wilson left to lead the library school at the University of Chicago.

Wilson Library, 1929. Photo by Bayard Wootten. Bayard Wootten Photo Collection, North Carolina Collection Photo Archives, Wilson Library.

He returned to Chapel Hill in the 1940s and remained active as a library consultant, author, and special assistant to university leaders.

Winston House. The location of the Honors Carolina Center for European Study in London, Winston House is an eighteenth-century townhouse located on Bedford Square, near the British Museum, the University of London, and the London School of Economics. Purchased with private donations, Winston House is a hub for UNC's study abroad programs and research initiatives across Europe. It is available to University of North Carolina students, faculty, staff, and alumni and is used by other educational institutions in London and the United States.

James Horner Winston, class of 1955, contributed the lead gift. He was an involved alumnus who served at various times on the UNC Board of Visitors, the General Alumni Association board, and the board of the Arts and Sciences Foundation. At his request, the name on Winston House reflects the family's involvement with the university, which goes back six generations to the 1840s.

Winston Residence Hall, along with Connor and Joyner, opened in 1948 as a dormitory for men students. It is named in honor of UNC president George Tayloe Winston. In the late 1960s the hall was renovated for women students. In 1973 the dorm became the first room-by-room coed residence hall at UNC, and it was the location for a sleepover by then chancellor Nelson Ferebee Taylor and other administrators who wanted to bring attention to overcrowded conditions in student housing.

George Tayloe Winston attended UNC from 1866 to 1868, completing his education at the U.S. Naval Academy and Columbia University. When the university reopened in 1875, Winston returned to teach Latin and German. He became UNC president in 1891 and became known for expanding enrollment and programs and fiercely defending the need for state support for the university. He left in 1896 to be president of the University of Texas, returning to North Carolina in 1899 to assume the presidency of the North Carolina College of Agriculture and Mechanic Arts (now North Carolina State University) — that campus has a building named in his honor as well, originally built in 1910 for the engineering program. While a proponent for public education and other progressive ideas, Winston was also an avowed white supremacist. His 1901 article, "The Relation of the Whites to the Negroes," argued for a hierarchical view of society, with whites inherently superior to African Americans.

Women's rules. Soon after the first women students entered the university in the 1890s, administrators began to devise separate rules to manage their behavior. Inez Koonce Stacy was the first adviser for women students. Largely due to her lobbying efforts, the first women's dormitory, Spencer Residence Hall, opened in 1925. She was succeeded by Katherine Kennedy Carmichael, who became the first dean of women at UNC. With a separate honor system and student council and different admission standards, housing regulations, and rules, women generally operated as a separate college within the university until the late 1960s.

Women's rules, detailed in the *Women's Handbook*, required that dormitories have a housemother, a sign-out system, and curfews. Visits to fraternity houses were at first banned, but the rules were later amended to permit them with a chaperone. Any parties in women's dorms had to be chaperoned and approved in advance by the dean of women. Women students had to wear skirts or dresses for everyday wear, and suits for football games. The rules applied off campus as well. Women students could spend the night in town only with parents. They had to register a full itinerary with the university before traveling and were expected to adhere to all of the university rules wherever they visited. Except for the overall Honor Code, no similar additional rules applied to male students.

In the middle of the century women began to push back against the rules. In 1963 the Women's Council declared it would no longer enforce the "apartment rule," which banned women students from visiting a man's apartment unless another couple was present. Dean Carmichael vetoed the council's vote but eventually eased the rule in the face of massive opposition. Perhaps the most notorious example of the double standard occurred in 1965. The student body president and his girlfriend were sanctioned for spending the night together in his fraternity room. The male student received an official reprimand through the men's honor court, while the female student was expelled through the separate women's honor court.

The uproar against this wildly uneven standard eventually led to changes. The dress code was eliminated in 1967, as were curfews and dorm visitation regulations a year later. Still, it took the passage of Title IX in 1972, one outcome of the women's movement, to completely do away with separate systems and regulations. The honors courts were combined in 1974, as well as the student government.

Women students. The University of North Carolina was for white men only for the first 100 years of the institution's existence. In 1877 the university allowed women to enroll in its summer school for teachers. This annual program soon had nearly as many female students as men. Not until 1896 did the trustees vote to admit white women as regular students, and then only under tightly controlled circumstances. Full acceptance as students, faculty, and staff took nearly the next 100 years, until the passage of Title IX of the federal Education Amendments Act in 1972 banned any restrictions on enrollment or hiring in institutions receiving federal funds.

When the first women registered in 1897, they had to be juniors, seniors, or graduate students. An average of 25 women out of a total student body of 800 were enrolled in the first decades of their admission at Carolina. Women were not widely welcomed on campus, often sitting alone in class and barred from public commencement ceremonies. They were also barred from most student organizations and had a separate honors committee and student council.

Mary MacRae, the daughter of a law school professor, was the first full-time student. A graduate of St. Mary's College in Raleigh, MacRae did well at the university and became literary editor of the *Tar Heel*. Joining MacRae in the first group of official students were four others— Lulie Watkins, Cecye Roanne Dodd, Dixie Lee Bryant, and Sallie Walker Stockard, who became the first woman to graduate in 1898. Stockard came to Chapel Hill in 1897 from Guilford College, went on to receive a master's degree in 1900, and then pursued graduate study at Columbia University.

In graduate programs, Margaret Berry was the first woman to graduate from the law school, in 1915. That same year, Cora Zeta Corpening became the first woman student in the medical school. The male students voted not to admit her, but she came to classes anyway.

The first dormitory for women, Spencer Residence Hall, was built in 1925, thanks largely to the determined lobbying of Inez Koonce Stacy, the first adviser for women students. She faced stiff opposition from male students. Weekly articles in the student newspaper opposing the residence hall had titles like "Women Not Wanted Here" and "Shaves and Shines, but No Rats and Rouge." Katherine Kennedy Carmichael followed Stacy and became the first dean of women. She carried on the fight for more dormitories as enrollment grew. In 1946 the number of women students topped 1,000 for the first time. A coeducational residence hall named for Carmichael opened in 1986.

In 1974 the separate honor courts for men and women merged into a single body. The student government organizations also consolidated and wrote a single standard of conduct for both sexes. In 1979 women outnumbered men in UNC's first-year undergraduate class for the first time. In 1985 the student body elected the first woman, Patricia Wallace, as its president.

Woollen Gym opened in March 1938 to serve as a replacement for Bynum Gymnasium, which the university had long outgrown. In addition to more space for games and exercises, the most exciting feature of the new gym was the Bowman Gray Memorial Pool, which was said to be the largest pool in the South when it opened. In December 1938 the gym hosted a speech by President Franklin D. Roosevelt. The men's

Students Charles Kuralt (*left*) and Kent Jackson read at a performance during the dedication ceremony for WUNC radio, March 1953. UNC Photo Lab Collection, North Carolina Collection Photo Archives, Wilson Library.

basketball team began playing its home games in Woollen in 1939; their first game there was a victory over Atlantic Christian College.

Basketball games moved to the larger Carmichael Auditorium after it opened in 1965, but Woollen remained a center for student activities. The gym celebrated its fiftieth anniversary in 1988 with a series of events, including a mass aerobics class that drew approximately 300 people.

The building is named for Charles Woollen, an administrator at UNC for several decades. Woollen began working on campus as an assistant to the university president in the early 1900s. He held a series of jobs, including registrar, business manager, and comptroller. He was an early advocate for the new gym and helped oversee its construction. Woollen was also the first director of the UNC band. Under his leadership the band became a regular feature at home football games.

WUNC 91.5 is a National Public Radio (NPR) affiliate station at UNC–Chapel Hill. The station made its first broadcast in the early 1940s on AM and in 1952 began broadcasting on FM. Charles Kuralt and Carl Kasell, both of whom would have long and prominent careers in broadcasting, were involved with the station as students in the early 1950s.

Staffed by students and volunteers, the station lasted until the early 1970s, when equipment problems forced it off the air.

WUNC returned to the air in 1976 as an NPR affiliate. The station operated from Swain Hall, which housed the university's Communication Center, a centralized location for all of the radio and television projects. In 1999 the radio station moved into a new facility, the James F. Goodmon Building, near the Friday Center. The Goodmon Building is named for James Fletcher Goodmon, president and CEO of Capitol Broadcasting Company and president of his family's foundation, the A. J. Fletcher Foundation. In addition to the Goodmon Building, WUNC has a broadcast facility on the American Tobacco Campus in Durham, North Carolina. One of WUNC's most popular local programs is *Back Porch Music*, showcasing folk and acoustic music for more than forty years. Another longtime popular program is *The People's Pharmacy*, which focuses on health education.

WXYC. Student-run FM radio station WXYC began broadcasting in March 1977 at 89.3 FM. WXYC was preceded by WCAR and other smaller stations, many of them based in dorms. Beginning in the early 1970s, Carolina students began the process of applying for an FM license, which would enable them to broadcast over the air (earlier efforts were "carrier current" stations, which used low-power signals transmitted through electric wires and were typically available only in small areas). The university initially supported the application but then later withdrew its support over concerns about assuming liability for student media. The students then helped establish a nonprofit organization, Student Educational Broadcasting, to apply for an FCC license and oversee the station. They were ultimately successful in early 1977. WXYC has always presented an eclectic musical selection in a wide variety of styles. In 1994, by working with the university's SunSITE (a predecessor of the iBiblio digital library at UNC), WXYC became the first radio station in the world to stream its live signal over the internet.

Y

Yackety Yack. The university's first yearbook, *The Hellenian*, was published in 1890. As reflected in the name, the yearbook was published by the campus fraternities. It included photos of students, engravings, and information about the classes. In 1901 the Dialectic and Philanthropic Societies joined as copublishers and the name was changed to *Yackety Yack*, drawing from a popular school cheer. The yearbook grew with the university. In addition to photos of students and groups, it was also a source of creativity, with some early issues including poetry and humorous class histories and always serving as a showcase for student photographers.

The 1920s marked an especially creative series of yearbooks, perhaps inspired in part by future novelist Thomas Wolfe, editor of the 1920 *Yackety Yack*. Many of the yearbooks from that era included a great deal of information about members of the senior class, including short biographies, caricatures, and their height and weight. The yearbook editors in those days also showed a cruel sense of humor as the page of senior superlatives included not just positive ones (like Best Orator and Best Athlete) but negative ones as well, including Ugliest and Laziest.

The period of robust and creative yearbooks continued through the mid-twentieth century, with the 1972 *Yackety Yack* named the best in the country by the Printing Industry of America. By the 1990s and 2000s it became harder to represent a much larger and more diverse student body in a single yearbook. Fewer students had their pictures taken for the *Yackety Yack* or purchased the yearbook. In the 2010s the *Yackety Yack* finally ended its run of annual publication, with no yearbooks appearing in 2013 and 2014 before resuming publication in 2015.

Z

Zoo. The university had an often contentious relationship with Jesse Helms, and it began long before he was first elected to the U.S. Senate in 1972. As a commentator for Raleigh TV station WRAL, Helms often criticized Carolina students who were involved in protests and was a frequent critic of the *Daily Tar Heel*. In the late 1960s, when the state of North Carolina was discussing the creation of a state zoo, Helms is reported to have said that instead of building a zoo they could just put a fence around Chapel Hill. However, there is no evidence that he ever made the comment. It does not appear in the transcripts of his WRAL editorials, and Helms later denied making it.

Acknowledgments

We are grateful to the many librarians and archivists in Wilson Library, past and present, whose work to collect, preserve, and provide access to official records, manuscript collections, publications, photographs, and recordings makes it possible to study the history of UNC–Chapel Hill. We are especially grateful for the help and contributions of staff members Jennifer Coggins, Sarah Carrier, Jason Tomberlin, Matt Turi, John Blythe, Bob Anthony, Stephen Fletcher, Patrick Cullom, Kerry Bannen, Biff Hollingsworth, and Linda Jacobson.

Throughout the writing of this book we sought information and feedback from some of the many people on campus and in the community who are deeply knowledgeable about university history. Thank you to Bill Burlingame, Doug Dibbert, Sarah Geer, Reg Hildebrand, Joseph Jordan, Missy Julian-Fox, Jim Leloudis, Malinda Maynor Lowery, Aaron Nelson, Rachel Seidman, and others for their ideas and corrections. Thanks also to the anonymous peer reviewers whose detailed suggestions helped to make this a better book. And finally, and most importantly, a thank you to our families—Tuck, Jackie, Lois, and Natalie—for their encouragement and support and for their patience with the many anecdotes about Carolina history that we were always eager to share.

Sources

In doing research for *UNC A to Z*, we relied on a wide variety of sources, which are listed below. However, we owe our biggest debt to the generations of student journalists and editors from the *Daily Tar Heel*. With the majority of the paper's archives now available online through the North Carolina Digital Heritage Center, we nearly always turned to it as our first source and frequently found stories and editorials that shed new light on historic events. We also turned regularly to the *Carolina Alumni Review*, which has often written about UNC history, and we especially want to acknowledge the work of David Brown in the *Review*. For coverage of more recent events, the *University Gazette* is always reliable. While they are not listed individually, numerous dissertations, theses, and undergraduate honors papers in the North Carolina Collection in Wilson Library cover UNC subjects. We relied heavily on many of the publications and unpublished memos by former Institute of Government director and administrator John L. Sanders, who has written extensively on the history of university governance. The wealth of online sources has made research into campus history easier than ever. We are especially grateful to the many sources available through the UNC–Chapel Hill Libraries, including Documenting the American South and the many online exhibits and blog entries that address UNC history. We relied often on the Carolina Story website, the earlier effort to provide a comprehensive, encyclopedia-style history of the university, and we also regularly used the excellent histories of campus buildings from Names in Brick and Stone, the terrific website from students in Dr. Anne Mitchell Whisnant's public history courses. For additional information on buildings, we were appreciative of the wealth of information provided by the UNC Facilities Services through the Plan Room website.

PERIODICALS

Carolina Alumni Review. General Alumni Association of the University of North Carolina at Chapel Hill, 1912–2018.

Daily Tar Heel. Chapel Hill, 1893–2018.

University Gazette. University of North Carolina at Chapel Hill, 1973–2018.

University Magazine. Dialectic and Philanthropic Societies at the University of North Carolina, 1844–1948.

BOOKS AND ARTICLES

Allcott, John V. *The Campus at Chapel Hill: Two Hundred Years of Architecture.* Chapel Hill, N.C.: Chapel Hill Historical Society, 1986.

Baker, Bruce. "Why North Carolinians Are Called Tar Heels." *Southern Cultures* 21, no. 4 (2015): 81–94.

Battle, Kemp Plummer. *History of the University of North Carolina.* 2 vols. Raleigh, N.C.: Edwards and Broughton, 1907–12.

Berryhill, W. Reece, William B. Blythe, and Isaac H. Manning. *Medical Education at Chapel Hill: The First Hundred Years.* Chapel Hill: UNC School of Medicine, 1979.

Bowers, Tom. *Making News: One Hundred Years of Journalism and Mass Communication at Carolina.* Chapel Hill: UNC School of Journalism and Mass Communication, 2009.

Bullock, J. Marshall. "A Brief History of Battle Park." Chapel Hill, N.C.: J. M. Bullock, 1990.

Bursey, Maurice M. *Carolina Chemists: Sketches from Chapel Hill.* Chapel Hill: UNC Department of Chemistry, 1982.

Chapman, John Kenyon. "Black Freedom and the University of North Carolina, 1793–1960." Ph.D. diss., UNC–Chapel Hill, 2006.

Cherry, Kevin. "'And They Talked. Always They Talked': 215 Years of the Dialectic and Philanthropic Societies." Gladys Coates Hall University History Lecture. Chapel Hill: UNC–Chapel Hill, 2011.

Coates, Albert, and Gladys Hall Coates. *The Story of Student Government in the University of North Carolina at Chapel Hill.* Chapel Hill, N.C.: Professor Emeritus Fund, 1985.

Connor, R. D. W. *A Documentary History of the University of North Carolina, 1776–1799.* Chapel Hill: University of North Carolina Press, 1953.

[Davis, Morris]. "History of Astronomy at the University of North Carolina at Chapel Hill 1792–1975." Chapel Hill: UNC Department of Physics and Astronomy, 1975.

Dean, Pamela. *Women on the Hill: A History of Women at the University of North Carolina at Chapel Hill.* Chapel Hill: UNC Division of Student Affairs, 1987.

Fryar, Charlotte Taylor. "Reclaiming the University of the People: Racial Justice Movements at the University of North Carolina at Chapel Hill, 1951–

2018." Ph.D. diss., UNC–Chapel Hill, 2019. Documentary website: https://
uncofthepeople.com.

Godschalk, David R., and Jonathan B. Howes. *The Dynamic Decade: Creating
the Sustainable Campus for the University of North Carolina at Chapel Hill,
2001–2011.* Chapel Hill: University of North Carolina Press, 2012.

Hall, Jacquelyn Dowd, and Kathryn Nasstrom. "Case Study: The Southern
Oral History Program." In *The Oxford Handbook of Oral History,* edited by
Donald A. Ritchie, 409–16. Oxford: Oxford University Press, 2010.

Henderson, Archibald. *The Campus of the First State University.* Chapel Hill:
University of North Carolina Press, 1949.

Herman, G. Nicholas. *The Order of the Golden Fleece at Chapel Hill, 1904–
2004: America's First Honor Society for University Leaders.* Chapel Hill: UNC
Library, 2005.

Holden, Charles J. *The New Southern University: Academic Freedom and
Liberalism at UNC.* Lexington: University Press of Kentucky, 2012.

House, Robert B. *The Light That Shines: Chapel Hill—1912–1916.* Chapel Hill:
University of North Carolina Press, 1964.

Jackson, Victoria. "Title IX and the Big Time: Women's Intercollegiate
Athletics at the University of North Carolina at Chapel Hill, 1950–1992."
Ph.D. diss., Arizona State University, 2015.

Kain, Thomas R. "The History of Required Physical Education and Intramural
Athletics at the University of North Carolina." Master's thesis, University of
North Carolina, 1950.

Knudson, Kermit, and Clifton E. Crandell. *From Quonset Hut to Number One
and Beyond: A History of the UNC School of Dentistry.* Chapel Hill: University
of North Carolina Dental Alumni Association, 1982.

Lamontagne, Nancy D., ed. *Ahead of Our Time: Chapel Hill's First Nightingales.*
Alexandria, Va.: Nightingales, 1955, 2014.

Link, William A. *William Friday: Power, Purpose, and American Higher
Education.* Chapel Hill: University of North Carolina Press, 2014.

Little, Ruth M. *The Town and Gown Architecture of Chapel Hill, North Carolina:
1795–1975.* Chapel Hill, N.C.: Preservation Society of Chapel Hill, 2006.

Long, Rachael. *Building Notes, University of North Carolina at Chapel Hill.*
Chapel Hill: UNC Facilities Planning and Design, 1993.

Lucas, Adam. *Carolina Basketball: A Century of Excellence.* Chapel Hill:
University of North Carolina Press, 2010.

Madry, Sarah Brandes. *Well Worth a Shindy: The Architectural and Philosophical
History of the Old Well at the University of North Carolina at Chapel Hill.*
Lincoln, Neb.: iUniverse, 2004.

Powell, Adam. *University of North Carolina Football.* Charleston, S.C.: Arcadia,
2006.

Powell, William S. *Dictionary of North Carolina Biography.* Chapel Hill:
University of North Carolina Press, 1979–96.

———. *The First State University: A Pictorial History of the University of North
Carolina.* Chapel Hill: University of North Carolina Press, 1992.

245

Sources

————. *The North Carolina Gazetteer*. Chapel Hill: University of North Carolina Press, 1968.

Powell, William S., ed., and Jay Mazzocchi, associate ed., *The Encyclopedia of North Carolina*. Chapel Hill: University of North Carolina Press, 2006.

Prince, William Meade. *The Southern Part of Heaven*. New York: Rinehart, 1950.

Puaca, Laura Micheletti. *Pioneer to Powerhouse: The History of Graduate Education at Carolina*. Chapel Hill: UNC Graduate School, 2003.

Rogoff, Leonard. *Homelands: Southern Jewish Identity in Durham and Chapel Hill, North Carolina*. Tuscaloosa: University of Alabama Press, 2001.

Sanders, John L. *The University Campus and Purposeful Growth*. Chapel Hill: General Alumni Association, 1993.

Schumann, Marguerite. *The First State University: A Walking Guide*. Rev. ed. Chapel Hill: University of North Carolina Press, 1985.

Smith, Dean. *A Coach's Life*. New York: Random House, 1999.

Snider, William D. *Light on the Hill: A History of the University of North Carolina at Chapel Hill*. Chapel Hill: University of North Carolina Press, 1992.

Tepper, Steven J. *The Chronicles of the Bicentennial Observance of the University of North Carolina at Chapel Hill*. Chapel Hill: University of North Carolina at Chapel Hill, 1998.

UNC School of Information and Library Science. *Illuminating the Past: A History of the First 75 Years of the University of North Carolina's School of Information and Library Science*. Minneapolis, Minn.: PhotoBook Press, 2007.

————. *1931–2011: 80 Years: The UNC School of Information and Library Science*. Chapel Hill: UNC School of Information and Library Science, 2011.

Wilson, Louis Round. *Louis Round Wilson's Historical Sketches*. Durham, N.C.: Moore Publishing, 1976.

————. *The University of North Carolina, 1900–1930*. Chapel Hill: University of North Carolina Press, 1957.

Zogry, Kenneth Joel. *Print News and Raise Hell: The "Daily Tar Heel" and the Evolution of a Modern University*. Chapel Hill: University of North Carolina Press, 2018.

————. *The University's Living Room: A History of the Carolina Inn*. Chapel Hill: University of North Carolina at Chapel Hill, 1999.

ONLINE SOURCES

Calingaert, Peter. "Growth of a Department: A Personal History of Computer Science at UNC–Chapel Hill." Department of Computer Science, UNC–Chapel Hill, January 25, 2002. http://www.cs.unc.edu/History/.

The Carolina Hall Story. Chancellor's Task Force on UNC–Chapel Hill History, 2017. https://carolinahallstory.unc.edu/.

The Carolina Story: A Virtual Museum of University History. UNC Libraries and UNC Center for the Study of the American South, ca. 2006–15. http://museum.unc.edu/.

DigitalNC, which includes digitized archives of the *Daily Tar Heel*, *Black Ink*, *University Magazine*, and many other campus and student publications. North Carolina Digital Heritage Center. http://digitalnc.org.

"The First Century of the First State University." Documenting the American South, UNC Libraries, 2006. http://docsouth.unc.edu/unc/.

Haisley, Waldo E. "Section I: Physics and Astronomy at Chapel Hill (1795–1946)." Department History, Department of Physics and Astronomy, UNC–Chapel Hill, 1989. http://physics.unc.edu/department-history/.

I Raised My Hand to Volunteer. UNC Libraries, 2007. https://exhibits.lib.unc .edu/exhibits/show/protest.

Muller, Eric L. "Judging Thomas Ruffin and the Hindsight Defense." UNC Legal Studies Research Paper 1186524, July 30, 2008. https://ssrn.com /abstract=1186524.

Names in Brick and Stone: Histories from UNC's Built Landscape. History/ American Studies 671: Introduction to Public History, UNC–Chapel Hill, 2015 and 2017. http://unchistory.web.unc.edu/.

Plan Room. Engineering Information Services, Facilities Services, UNC–Chapel Hill. https://planroom.unc.edu/.

Slavery and the Making of the University. UNC Libraries, 2006. https://exhibits .lib.unc.edu/exhibits/show/slavery/introduction.

Abernethy, Dr. Eric, 1, 130
Abernethy, Milton "Ab," 72, 134
Abernethy Hall, 1, 9, 130, 147
Abu-Salha, Razan Mohammad, 4–5
Abu-Salha, Yusor Mohammed, 4–5
academic freedom, 14, 58, 68, 183,
    202
a cappella groups, 1–2, 27, 48
Ackland, William Hayes, 2
Ackland Art Museum, 2
activism, 42, 58, 99, 108, 119, 168;
    in 1960s, 2–5, *3*, 75, 132, 196, 202;
    of African Americans, 26–28, 56;
    boycotts, 132, 189; Confederate
    Monument and, 70–71, *71*;
    petitions by students as, 63, 85;
    Saunders Hall and, 46–47, *47. See
    also* protests, rallies, and marches
Adams, Claude, III, 4
Adams, Claude A., Jr., 4
Adams, Grace Phillips, 4
Adams School of Dentistry, 4–5, 31,
    146, 216
African, African American, and
    Diaspora Studies, Department of,
    5, 206–7
African Americans, 30, 97, 99, 102,
    114, 122, 123, 131, 134, 144–45,
    172, 197, 198, 208, 209, 217, 224;
    activism of, 26–28, 56; admittance
    of, 14, 84, 128, 131–32, 205, 223;
    advocacy for, 3, 26, 27, 119, 189,

207; as athletes, 19, 99, 134,
    206; Black Alumni Reunion, 123;
    cadavers of used in early medical
    school courses, 156; cultural
    center for, 3, 119, 206–7, 226; as
    employees and staff, 32, 37, 39,
    40, 48, 58; equality and, 103, 204;
    on faculty, 90, 134, 137, 199, 216;
    in fraternities and sororities, 102,
    163–64, 205; in Knapp-Sanders
    murals, 145; in Old Chapel Hill
    Cemetery, 172; Upendo Lounge
    and, 225–26; in U.S. Navy, 166,
    166; violence against, 70, 143, 161.
    See also Black Student Movement;
    segregation
Agriculture, Department of, 151
Air Force ROTC, 165, 192
Airport Road, 33, 126
Akers, Susan Grey, 131
Alamance County, 53, 192
alcohol and alcoholism, 44, 106, 114–
    15, 119, 188, 204–5, 218
Alderman, Edwin Anderson, 5, 151,
    173–74, 183, 194
Alderman Residence Hall, 5
Alexander, Eben, 6, 110, 175
Alexander Residence Hall, 6, 71
Allman Brothers, 139
alma mater ("Hark the Sound"), 6–7,
    67, 98, 110
Alpha Chi Sigma, 102

Alpha Kappa Alpha Sorority, Inc., 163
Alpha Phi Alpha Fraternity, Inc., 163
Alpha Pi Omega, 102, *102*
Alpha Tau Omega, 101
Alumni Center, 8, 55, 106; *The Circus Parade* in, 63
Alumni Hall, 5, 8, 141, 191
Alumni Review, 8, 36, 106
Amber Alley, 188
American Idol, 2
American Indian Center, 1
American Streaker Society (ASS), 209
anatomy classes, 156, 231
Anderson, Eugene A., 9
Anderson Stadium, 9
Anesthesiology, Department of, 35
animals, 35; circus, 63; dogs, 123; horses, 88; lab, 35, 38, 79; livestock, 65, 208; mascots, 38–39, 186–88, *188*
Anthropology, Department of, 8
Anthropology, Research Laboratories of, 191
antiwar activism, 2–3
Apollo, 64, 194–95
Apollo moon missions, 10, 161
APPLES Service-Learning program, 46
Applied Science: Department of, 111; School of, 66
Aptheker, Herbert, 202–3
ARA and Aramark, 85
Archaeology, Research Laboratories of, 8, 88–89, 117, 191, 228
architects, 55, 79, 81, 110, 128, 167, 181, 197, 206, 230; Arthur Nash, 48, 143, 182, 232; William Nichols, 107, 174
architecture, 8, 41, 172; styles of, 26, 55, 88, 113, 142, 158, 161, 178, 196, 197
archives, archivists, 71, 150, 232
Area Health Education Center (AHEC), 9, 9–10, 99, 125, 156, 217

Armstrong, Louis, 107, 218
Armstrong, Neil, 10
Army ROTC, 165, 192
art, arts, 67, 103, 129, 142, 145, 224; museums and galleries for, 2, 177. *See also* sculptures
Art and Art History, Department of, 2, 118, 177
Arts and Sciences, College of, 61, 66–67, 118, 124, 186, 196
Arts and Sciences Foundation, 118, 233
Asian Americans, 10, 209; Student Association, 10
Asian Studies, Department of, 168
Association for Intercollegiate Athletics for Women, 12, 95, 219
Association for Women Faculty and Professionals, 219
Association of American Universities, 115
Association of American University Students, 134
astronauts, 10, *11*
astronomy, 11–12; department of, 56
Athletic Association, 75, 98
athletic conferences: ACC, 13–14, 18; Southern, 6, 13, 17, 18
athletic facilities, 9, 30, 42–43, 89–91, 95, 98, 124–25, 144–46, 165, 179, 210, 218, 236–37. *See also* Smith Student Activities Center; gymnasiums; Kenan Stadium; pools; *and names of specific facilities*
athletics, athletes, 1, 41, 60, 84, 132; academics and, 13, 143; athletics department and, 95, 168, 179, 210; concerns over, 18, 103–4; intercollegiate, 17, 44, 67, 95, 103–4; Monogram Club and, 137, 159; scholarships for, 86, 99, 134, 219; Tar Heels name and, 215–16; team uniforms and, 10, 139–40; Title IX and, 218–19; women, 9, 12, 14, 19, 21, 43, 60, 94, 95, 96, 135, 147, 175,

218–19. *See also* NCAA; sports; *and names of specific sports*

Atlantic Coast Conference (ACC), 13–14; basketball championships in, 19, 21; fencing championships in, 94; field hockey championships in, 95; football and, 99; founding members of, 18; Pride of, 154

Atwood and Nash, 143

auditoriums, 15, 42, 43, 94, 106, 115, 121, 146, 154, 206, 228, 237

automobiles, 22, 23, 129, 178

Avery, William Waightstill, 14

Avery Residence Hall, 14, 217

aviation and space travel, 217; astronaut training and, 10, 11; Horace Williams Airport and, 9, 9–10, 50, 125–26; U.S. Navy pre-flight school, 30, 39, 125–26, 137, 144, 158, 159

Aycock, Charles Brantley, 14–15, 78, 137

Aycock, William Brantley, 14, 55, 230

Aycock Family Medicine Center, 14

Aycock Residence Hall, 14–15, 113, 149

Ayr Mountaineers, 56

Back Porch Music (radio program), 238

Baity, Elizabeth Chesley, 16

Baity, Herman G., 16

Baity Hill Graduate and Family Housing, 16, 171

Baker, Claiborne, 32

Baldwin, Brooke, 156

Balk, Julia, 209

Bank of America, 97, 154

Barakat, Deah Shaddy, 4–5

Barbee, Alfred David, 208

Barbee, Willis, 208

Barnes and Noble, 78

baseball, 6, 12, 16–18, 17, 29–30, 90–91, 154, 165, 166

basketball, 17, 18–21, 42–43, 136, 187, 215, 218; African Americans and, 19, 134, 209; women's, 12, 13, 19, 21, 43

basketball, men's, 18–19, 82, 125, 147, 168, 175, 231, 237; bribery scandal and, 14, 86; Dixie Classic and, 85–86; as NCAA champions, 42, 76, 100, 101, 140, 220; team uniforms of, 10, 44, 139–40. *See also* Smith, Dean; Smith Student Activities Center

Battle, Kemp Plummer, 12, 21, 92, 179, 183, 222

Battle, William Horn, 148

Battle Hall, 5, 21, 86, 100–101, 228

Battle Park, 21–22, 99, 110, 169, 179

Battle-Vance-Pettigrew building, 177, 178

B Dorm, 71

Beard, John Grover, 92

Beard Hall, 22, 92, 128

Beat Dook Parade, 22, 23, 60, 123

Beaumont, Arthur, 136

Beech, Harvey, 30, 131, 133

Belk, Irwin, 95

Belk Track, 95

Bell (Cornelia Phillips Spencer) Award, 204

bells, 200; bell tower and, 22–24, 23, 65, 87, 120, 206; "woman who rang the bell," 204

benefactors and donors, 24–26, 40, 48, 52–53, 55, 62, 82, 96, 108, 121, 142, 154, 181, 197, 216, 221; alumni as, 54, 56, 89, 90, 92, 95, 106, 112, 124, 129, 143, 144, 146, 160, 206, 218, 233; buildings named after, 33–34, 177

Ben Folds Five, 56

Bennington College, 124

Berlin Olympics (1936), 175

Berry, Chuck, 139

Berry, Margaret, 236

Berryhill, W. Reece, 26

Index

Berryhill Hall, 26
Bertie County, 172
Betts, Doris, 74
Bicentennial Celebration (1993), 81, 88, 119, 222
Bingham, Mary Lily Kenan Flagler, 25, 141–43
Bingham, Robert Hall, 26
Bingham Hall, 26, 115, 141
Biochemistry, Department of, 105
Biology, Department of, 66, 167, 231
Biophysics, Department of, 105
Biostatistics, Department of, 155
Birdsong, Gary, 180
Black Awareness Council, 206
Black Ink, 27
Black Student Movement (BSM), 1, 3, 5, 26–28, 27, 37, 47, 149, 162, 172, 196, 207, 225–26
Blackwell, W. T., 53
Blood on the Old Well (Emery, 1963), 28
Blue Jeans Day, 28
boarding houses, 48, 68, 85, 88, 134, 206
Board of Governors, 28, 29, 54, 55
Board of Trustees, 11, 14, 25, 28, 33, 40, 46, 54, 55, 63, 72, 77, 81, 84, 88, 107, 121, 177, 227; admittance of women by, 235; alumni on, 116, 152, 206; approves demolition of Odum Village, 171; approves seal, 151; botanical garden and, 168; campus speakers and, 202; chair of, 149; committees of, 65, 116; Confederate Monument and, 70; Consolidation and, 91; former Confederate officers on, 115; founding and, 154, 177; fraternities and, 102; members of, 46, 78, 81, 93, 113, 118, 149, 152, 153, 162, 163, 176, 192; minutes of, 115; railroad and, 224; selects names of buildings, 34, 47; slavery and, 196; stone walls and, 208;

undergraduate seat on, 210; women on, 29
Board of Visitors, 233
Boettcher, Carl, 63
Bondurant, Stuart, 29
Bondurant Hall, 29
Book Exchange ("Book-Ex"), 29, 77, 205
bookstores, 29, 32, 34, 41, 77, 134–35, 205, 232
Booth, Lewis, 208
Booth, Thomas, 208
Boshamer, Cary C., 29–30; scholarship and professorship, 30
Boshamer Stadium, 18, 29–30, 165
Botany, Department of, 65, 66, 79, 169
Boundary Street, 33
Bowles, Erskine, 218, 221
Bowles, Hargrove "Skipper," Jr., 218
bowling, 114, 135
Bowman Gray Memorial Pool, 30, 146, 236
boxing, 30–31, 136
Brandon, John Lewis, 132
Brauer, John C., 4, 31
Brauer Hall, 4, 31, 216
bricks, 31, 32, 184
Brinkhous, Kenneth M., 32
Brinkhous-Bullitt Building, 31–32
Broad, Molly Corbett, 221
Bromo-Seltzer, 91
Brookings Institution, 72
Brooks, Aubrey Lee, 33
Brooks, Frederick P., Jr., 32, 68
Brooks, James T., 33
Brooks, Thornton H., 33
Brooks Computer Science Building, 32, 229
Brooks Hall, 33, 224
Brooks Scholarship Fund, 33
Browder, Earl, 51
Brown v. Board of Education, 132
Bryan Communications Center, 222
Bryant, Dixie Lee, 236

Bryant, Paul "Bear," 125
Bryson, Nancy, 30
Bryson, Vaughn, 30
Buchanan, James, visits campus, 226
Buckley Public Service Scholars, 46
Buddhism, 191
buildings: biblical quotes on, 107; Board of Trustees Building Committee and, 65; demolition of, 68, 163, 165, 171, 194, 206, 218, 226, 230; environmentally friendly, 106, 146; first, 24; largest, 105, 229; named for living persons, 21; names of, 33–34; renaming of, 46–47; second, 206; slavery and, 196; temporary, 4; for U.S. Navy, 165. *See also* dormitories and residence halls; libraries; *and names of specific buildings*
Bull Durham tobacco, 53
Bullitt, James B., 32
Bull's Head Bookshop, 34, 35, 77, 78, 232
Buncombe County, 213
Bureau of Extension, 121
Burke County, 14
Burnett, Dr. Charles H., 35
Burnett, Ellington, 172
Burnett-Womack Clinical Sciences Building, 34–36
Bush, George H. W., 125, 165, 226
Business School. *See* Kenan-Flagler Business School
Buttitta, Anthony, 72, 134
Bynum, William Preston, Jr., 36
Bynum Hall, 18, 30, 36, 64, 67, 155, 216, 224, 236

cadets, naval, 163, 165, 184, 194
Caduceus book store, 32
cafeterias and dining halls, 63, 67–68, 115, 148–49, 213; strikes by workers of, 27, 37, 38, 85, 149, 153, 196
Cain, Gordon and Mary, Foundation, 160

Cake Race, 37–38
Caldwell, Helen Hooper, 39
Caldwell, Joseph, 150, 183, 190, 213; as first president, 11, 38, 39; memorial to, 7, 39–40, 154
Caldwell, Wilson Swain, 39, 40, 213
Caldwell Hall, 38–39, 152, 156
Caldwell monuments, 7, 39–40, 154
Cameron, Paul C., 21, 40–41
Cameron Associates, 128
Cameron Avenue, 40–41, 65, 102, 107, 121, 154, 194, 206, 224, 227
Camp Butner, 165, 184
Campus Health Services Building, 216
Campus Recreation, Department of, 136
Campus Y, 29, 34, 47, 84, 93, 107, 112, 120, 178, 190
Cancer Hospital, North Carolina, 127
cancer research, 108, 157
Canterbury, Archbishop of, 177
Capitol Broadcasting Company, 238
Cardboard Club, 42, 60
Cardiology Division, 35
career services, 41, 118
carillon, 23–24, 24. *See also* bells
Carmichael, Katherine Kennedy, 43–44, 234, 237
Carmichael, William D., Jr., 43
Carmichael Arena, 42–43, 82, 237
Carmichael Residence Hall, 43–44, 237
Carnegie, Andrew, 25, 121
Carnegie Corporation, 181
Carnegie Foundation, 131
Carnegie Library Building (Hill Hall), 102, 121–22, 150, 232
Carolina blue, 44–45, 95, 98, 139–40, 186
Carolina Buccaneer, 45, 50
Carolina Center for Genome Sciences, 106
Carolina Center for Public Service, 45–46

Carolina Cheerios, 60

Carolina Chocolate Drops, 56

Carolina Club, 106

Carolina Coffee Shop, 46, 100, 139

Carolina Computing Initiative, 69

"Carolina Cool," 10

Carolina Covenant, 122, 220

Carolina First fund-raising campaign, 122

Carolina for the Kids, 77

Carolina Gay and Lesbian Association, 28, 74, 195

Carolina Hall, 34, 46–47. *See also* Saunders Hall

Carolina Hispanic Association (CHispA), 158, 159

Carolina Indian Circle, 48

Carolina Inn, 48–49, 49, 55, 59, 63, 106, 158, 121, 163, 169, 231

Carolina Jewish Society, 120

Carolina Latino/a Collaborative, 147

Carolina Magazine, 52, 73

Carolina North, 50, 125

Carolina Performing Arts, 158

Carolina Physical Science Complex, 56, 229

Carolina Play-Book, 50

Carolina Playmakers, 50, 51, 73, 99

Carolina Political Union, 50–51

Carolina Population Center, 51–52, 108

Carolina Vaccine Institute, 35

Carolina Women's Center, 52

Carr, Julian Shakespeare, 52–53, 70, 78, 177, 224

Carrboro, 53, 224, 226

Carr Building, 52–53, 64, 206

Carrington, Elizabeth Scott, 53

Carrington Hall, 53, 170

Carroll, Dudley Dewitt, 54

Carroll Hall, 54, 105, 118, 141, 155, 176

Carson, Eve, 93

Carter, June, 139

Carter, Vince, 19

Carter-Finley Stadium, 96

Case, Everett, 85–86

Cash, Johnny, 139

Cassell, Sam, 82

Castle, Hippol, *109*, 110, 120

Catawba Nation, 164

Caudill, Susan S., 54

Caudill, W. Lowry, 54

Caudill Labs, 54, 229

Cellar Door, 154

cemeteries and graveyards, 39, 108, 124, 172

Centennial celebration (1889), 7

Center for Civil Rights, 148

Center for European Study in London, 233

Center for Integrative Chemical Biology and Drug Discovery, 105

Center for International Studies, 65

Center for Media Law and Policy, 148

Center for Nanotechnology in Drug Delivery, 105

Center for Public Television, 221

Center for the Study of the American South, 151, 202

Center for Urban and Regional Studies, 119–20

Center on Poverty, Work and Opportunity, 148

Chambers, Julius LeVonne, 148

championships, conference: ACC, 14, 19, 21, 94, 95, 198; Southern, 198, 231

championships, national: field hockey, 13, 95; Franklin Street celebrations of, 100, *101*; men's basketball, 10, 13, 18, 19, 42–43, 76, 100, *101*, 140, 220; men's lacrosse, 13, 147; men's soccer, 13, 198; men's tennis, 13, 70; women's basketball, 13, 21; women's lacrosse, 13, 147; women's soccer, 13, 199, 219; women's tennis, 13, 70

chancellors, 5, 14, 26, 27, 33, 54, 56, 70, 99, 119, 121, 124–25, 128, 142,

169, 197, 203, 204, 206–7, 211–12, 214, 217, 234; list of, 55; offices of, 200; residence of, 55; student government and, 210. *See also names of specific chancellors*

chapel, chapels, 55, 107, 177, 190, 195. *See also* churches; religion

Chapel Hill, 53, 58, 72, 74, 114, 117, 125, 152; African Americans in, 27, 132, 208; boarding in, 48, 68, 85, 219; businesses in, 46, 97, 100, 126, 134–35, 139–40, 212–13; cemeteries in, 39, 172; grit of, 31, 56; history and prehistory of, 25, 55–56, 64, 128, 130, 132, 164, 184; mosque planned for, 162; neighborhoods of, 22, 33, 59, 166, 212; *Patch Adams* and, 176; population of, 226; railroads and, 224; relations with, 33, 50, 227, 235; residents of, 28, 108; restaurants and bars in, 96, 119, 188; as Southern Part of Heaven, 202; taverns and hotels in, 88, 96; Town Girls and, 219–20. *See also specific names of businesses*

Chapel Hill Flying Club, 125

Chapel Hill High School, 114

Chapel Hill Iron Mountain Railroad, 224

Chapel Hill Preservation Society, 33

Chapel Hill Tire Company, 100

Chapel of the Cross, 195

Chapman, Max C., Jr., 56

Chapman, Robert Hett, 183

Chapman, John K. "Yonni," 204

Chapman Hall, 56, 229

Charlotte, 8, 10, 26, 119, 128, 154, 216

charter, 74, 97

Chase, Harry Woodburn, 57, 93, 171, 183, 232

Chase Hall, 57, 57–58, 85, 225–26

Chatham County, 25, 58, 59, 74, 126, 153, 195, 197

Cheek, Kennon, 33, 34, 58–59

Cheek/Clark Building (University Laundry), 58–59, 59, 227

cheerleading, cheerleaders, 42, 59–60, 159, 186; cheers of, 60–61, 61, 239; Victory Bell and, 230

chemical engineering, 91, 160

chemistry, 54, 91, 102, 178, 181, 230

Chemistry, Department of, 61–62, 128, 141–42, 177, 229

Chemistry Building, 128

Cherokees, 164

cherry trees, 62

Chickasaws, 25, 164

Children's Hospital, North Carolina, 127

Chi Omega, 102

Christianity, Christians, 180, 190, 191

churches, 55, 195. *See also* chapel, chapels; religion

Circus Room, 63, 63, 137, 159–60

City and Regional Planning, Department of, 8, 167

civil rights, 103, 114, 148, 202; activism for, 42, 75

Civil Rights Act (1964), 127, 132

Civil War, 2, 16, 21, 63–64, 70, 73, 88, 101, 177–78, 196, 204–6, 213, 215; slavery and, 25, 126. *See also* Confederacy; Confederate Monument; Confederate veterans and officers; secession

Clark, Rebecca, 34, 58, 59

Clarke, George, 172

class gifts, 64–65, 195, 225

Classics, Department of, 162

classrooms, 26, 29, 53, 66, 73, 95, 115, 229

Clef Hangers, 1–2

Cleveland, Grover, 6

Clinton, Bill, 144, 201, 222; visits campus, 226

closing of university (1870), 17, 101, 189–90, 224

coaches: baseball, 17; basketball, 18, 19, 21, 82, 85–86, 134, 147; boxing,

30; fencing, 94; field hockey, 95; soccer, 199; tennis, 69–70

coal, 111, 224, 227

Coates, Albert, 65, 112, 145

Coates, Gladys Hall, 65, 112

Coates Building, 65, 200

Cobb, Collier, Jr., 65

Cobb, Collier, Sr., 65

Cobb, George, 95

Cobb Residence Hall, 65

Coe, Emily, 212

Coe, Joffre, 191

coed dorms, 43, 146, 217, 234, 236

Coffin, Oscar J., 155

Cogen Facility, 111, 224, 227

Coker, William Chambers, 65, 66, 157, 222

Coker Arboretum, 56, 65–66, 169, 195, 208

Coker Hall, 66

Coker Pinetum, 157

Cole, Genevieve Lowry, 164

College Avenue, 40

College Chapel, 177

College Graveyard, 172

College of William and Mary, 43, 96

College World Series of baseball, 17

Colonial Drug Store, 132

Colonial Revival style, 158

Colonial Williamsburg, 31

colors, school, 44–45, 67, 98. *See also* Carolina blue

Columbia Street, 53, 102, 194, 231

Columbia University, 234, 236

Commencement, 6, 8, 44–45, 88, 107, 110, 144, 147, 158, 189, 200; alumni at, 7, 123; graduation gowns at, 139–40; traditions of, 190, 195; women and, 236

Commencement Ball, 106

Commerce, Department of, 46

Commerce, School of, 141

Committee on LGBTQ Life, 149

Commons Hall, 67–68, 85, 179

Communication, Department of, 26, 186

Communism, 68; accusations of, 28, 171; anti-, 75

Communist Party, 51, 68, 75; Speaker Ban Law and, 202

comparative literature, 115

Computation Center, 68, *69*, 178

computers, 68–69, 128, 134, 169, 178; libraries and, 150–51. *See also* technology

Computer Science, Department of, 32, 68, 168, 196

concerts, 43, 82, 139, 144, 218. *See also* Springfest music festival

Cone, Ceasar, II, 69

Cone-Kenfield Tennis Center, 69–70

Confederacy, 70; alumni in Congress of, 14, 73; apologists for, 118; defeat of, 189; draft exemption from, 64; flags of, 99; memorializing of, 71, 101; North Carolina joins, 73

Confederate Monument ("Silent Sam"), 71, 154, 225; efforts to remove, 4, 70–71

Confederate veterans and officers, 193, 228; on faculty, 64, 152, 153; monument to, 4, 70–71, *71*, 154, 225; as students and alumni, 14, 46, 53, 64, 113, 115, 153, 158

Connor, Robert Digges Wimberly, 71–72

Connor Beach, 71, 204

Connor Community, 71

Connor Residence Hall, 71–72, 204, 234

Connorstock, 71

conservatives, 75, 148, 190, 212, 228

Consolidation, 72, 91, 103, 105, 114, 128, 183, 221

Contempo, 72, 134

continuing education, 103–4

controversy: over *Approaching the Qur'an* summer reading

requirement, 191, 212; over
Confederate Monument, 4, 70–71,
154, 225; over Cornelia Phillips
Spencer Bell Award, 204; over
funding of Carolina Gay and
Lesbian Association, 195; over
naming of buildings, 94, 115–16;
over Nike as supplier, 168; over
ROTC, 192; over seal, 194–95;
over *Student Body* sculpture, 209;
over tuition, 220; over Unsung
Founders Memorial, 224–25;
religion and, 190–91
Conversation, 129
Converse, 168
Cooper, Roy, 112
Cooper, Willie, 19
Corpening, Cora Zeta, 236
Cortese, Dan, 211
Couch, William T., 222
Country Club Road, 55, 99, 108, 145,
172
Craig, Locke, 70
Craige, Francis Burton, 73
Craige North Residence Hall, 73, 119,
126, 146
Craige Residence Hall, 73, 86, 161
Crucible, The (Arthur Miller), 181
Crudup, Billy, 211
Cube, the, 74
Cullen, Countee, 49
Currituck County, 145
Curtis, Nathaniel Cortlandt, 110
Cyprett's Bridge, 74

Daily Tar Heel, 19, 22, 30, 31, 73,
75–78, 76, 90, 98; debates in,
113; editorials in, 28, 29; editors
of, 155; on fencing, 94; on Jesse
Helms, 240; on High Noon, 120;
on lacrosse, 147; on Lenoir Hall,
148–49; on Mangum haunted
house, 153; offices of, 112, 155; on
the Pit, 180; POWs mentioned in,

184; on ROTC, 192; Confederate
Monument and, 71; on Sitterson
Hall, 196; on study abroad
programs, 211; on Tar Babies, 215;
on Victory Village units, 230
dance, dances, 106–7, 150, 158, 218,
220; Dance Marathon, 77
Daniels, Josephus, 78
Daniels Building, 29, 34, 77–78
Danziger, Edward C., 78–79
Danziger's, 78–79
Davidson College, 38, 143
Davie, William Richardson, 91, 154,
179; as father of university, 79, 81
Davie Hall, 79
Davie Poplar, 79–81, 80, 154
Davis, Alexander Jackson, 172, 174,
181
Davis, Walter Royal, 81–82, 227
Davis Library, 81–82, 91, 150, 209,
217, 227, 232
DEAH DAY (Directing Efforts and
Honoring Deah and Yusor), 5
"Dean Dome." *See* Smith Student
Activities Center
deans, 14, 16, 31, 33, 54, 103, 115,
128, 131, 155, 196, 216–17, 228; of
administration, 54, 72, 128; African
Americans as, 216; of School of
Medicine, 26, 29, 99, 152, 156,
190, 231; of School of Pharmacy,
22, 92; of School of Public Health,
155, 192; of women, 43–44, 234,
235, 236; women as, 131
debating societies, 67, 83–84, 98,
167, 200
Deberry, Martha Decker, 62
DeLillo, Don, 52
Delta Kappa Epsilon, 101, 103
Delta Psi, 101, 205
Delta Sigma Theta, 102, 163
Democratic Party, 15, 53, 78, 183, 189,
190, 204
demolition: of buildings, 163, 165,

194, 206, 218, 226; of Old Well, 174; of Victory Village units, 171, 230

Dental Education Building, 31

Dental Foundation of North Carolina, 4, 31

Dental School. *See* Adams School of Dentistry

departments. *See names of specific departments*

Dermatology, Department of, 35

Desai, Anoop, 1–2

Dey, William Morton, 83

Dey Hall, 83, 162

Dialectic Society, 44, 67, 83–84, 168, 210, 239; library of, 121, 150

Diamond, Neil, 139

Dickson, Paul, III, 202–3

Dickson v. Sitterson, 203

Dick Taylor Track, 89

Diggs, Edward Oscar, 131

Dillard, Annie, 52

dining, 84–85, 165, 166, 184, 213; complaints about food, 2, 257, 206. *See also* cafeterias and dining halls

DiPhi. *See* Dialectic Society; Philanthropic Society

diplomas, 44, 67

diseases, 36, 130, 205

dissecting hall, 156

Divine Nine, 163

diving, 12, 146

Division of Academic Affairs, 137

Dixie Classic, 85–86; gambling scandal involving, 13, 18, 86, 103

Dobbins, Preston, 26

Documenting the American South, 150–51

Dodd, Cecye Roanne, 236

Domino, Fats, 107

donors. *See* benefactors and donors

dormitories and residence halls, 34, 86–87; apartment-style, 217; community in, 119; coed, 43, 146;

217, 234, 237; computers in, 69; directors of, 204; intramural sports teams and, 136; private dorms, 114–15; on South Campus, 201; visitation rules in, 210;. *See also* student life; *and names of specific dormitories and residence halls*

Dorrance, Anson, 199

Dramatic Art, Department of, 108, 113, 180

dress code for women, 44, 234–35

Drew University, 119

Dromgoole, Order of, 109. *See also* Order of the Gimghoul

Dromgoole, Peter, 109

drugs, 97, 210; marijuana, 120

Duke University, 2, 13, 15, 22, 40, 82, 125, 134, 169, 197–98; mascot of, *188*; rivalry with, 7, 18, 22, 82, 86, 230; Robertson Scholars and, 191–92. *See also* Beat Dook Parade

dunce cap, 87

Durham, N.C., 4, 25, 41, 43, 53, 55, 56, 106, 121, 130–31, 224, 229, 238. *See also* Duke University

Eagle Hotel, 88–89, *89*

Ebony Readers/Onyx Theatre, 27

Economics, Department of, 46, 105

Eddie Smith Field House, 89

Education Amendments Act (1972). *See* Title IX

Education, Department of, 90

Education, School of, 89–90, 177

Ehringhaus, John Christoph Blucher, 90

Ehringhaus Residence Hall, 90, 157, 161

Ehringhaus South Residence Hall, 146

Elder-in-Residence program, 9

electricity and electrification, 64, 111, 227

Ellington, Duke, 218

Emerson, Isaac, 90

Emerson Field, 29, 77, 90–91, 98, 143, 179–80

Emery, Sarah Watson: *Blood on the Old Well*, 28

employees and staff, 33, 34, 62, 63, 106; African Americans as, 32, 32, 37, 38, 39, 40, 48, 58; buildings named after, 126; e-mail and, 134; harassment of, 217; LGBTQ, 150; protests by, 71; public service and, 45. *See also* cafeteria workers, strikes by

Endocrinology Division, 35

endowments, 4, 26, 33, 62, 64–65, 142, 160

Engineering, Department of, 178

Engineering, School of, 91, 218

England, 155

English Collegiate style, 178

English, Department of, 26, 73, 112–13, 115, 137, 155, 162

Eno River, 179

Eno Indians, 164

Environmental Sciences and Engineering, Department of, 72

Episcopalians, 190, 195

escheats, 91–92, 196

Escheats Act, 91

Eshelman, Fred, 92

Eshelman School of Pharmacy, 92, 105

ESPN, 156, 168, 211

Evans, Hiram Wesley, 51

Eve Carson Memorial Garden, 93

Evening College, 1

Everett, Katherine Robinson, 148, 228–29

Everett, William Nash, 93

Everett Law Library, 228

Everett Residence Hall, 93

Evergreen House, 103

evolution, teaching of, 58, 161–62

Extension Division, 186, 232

faculty, 14, 21, 33, 39, 66, 91, 106; academic freedom of, 14, 58, 68, 183, 202; African Americans on, 137, 207, 216; alumni on, 62, 119, 216; athletics and, 13, 42, 129; during Civil War, 64; club for, 137; Confederate veterans on, 64, 152, 153–54; criticize naming of FedEx center, 94; distinguished and endowed professorships and, 8, 21, 25, 30, 72, 83, 115; e-mail and, 134; first African American on, 134, 199; former presidents on, 39; German model of, 121; Golden Fleece and, 110; golf and, 95–96; governance of, 5, 52; housing for, 33, 151; Jews on, 190; as members of Gimghoul, 109; as Nobel prize winners, 168; presiding professors, 183; protest segregation, 132; public service and, 45; salaries of, 142, 189; slavery and, 196; support cafeteria workers' strike, 37; as target of Klan, 189; teaching awards and, 64; as too liberal, 28; training of, 129; as UNC Press authors, 222; wives and partners of, 28, 126; women on, 16, 90, 212, 219

Family Medicine, Department of, 14

Family Policy Network (FPN), 191, 212

Faulkner, William, 72

Fazio, Tom, 96

FBI (Federal Bureau of Investigation), 75

FCC (Federal Communications Commission), 238

FedEx Global Education Center, 94

fencing, 12, 13, 94

Festifall, 100

Fetzer, Robert, 95

Fetzer Field, 91, 95, 165

Fetzer Gymnasium, 95, 210, 218

field hockey, 12, 13, 95, 96, 165

Field of Dreams, 18

financial aid, 177, 220. *See also* scholarships

Finley, Albert Earle "A.E.," 96

Finley Golf Course, 69, 96–97

fires, 33, 88, 102, 135, 177

First Nations Graduate Circle, 48

Flagler, Henry Morrison, 141

Flat River, 179

Flatt and Scruggs, 139

Fletcher, Louise, 50

Flirtation Knoll, 21

Florida International University, *198*

Florida State University, 82

flower ladies, 97, *97*

Folt, Carol L., 55, 70, 197

football, 12, 17, 30, 98, *98*–100, 105, 132, 143; African Americans and, 99; "Carolina Victory" and, 24; cheering for, 42; faculty team members, 129; field for, 90–91; freshmen or junior varsity, 215; halftime performances, 154; Homecoming and, 123–24, 217; in Kenan Stadium, 217; marching band and, 237; postseason ban on, 13; practice for, 89, 165; rams and, 186–88, *188*; rivalry with Duke in, 22, 230; uniforms, 166, *167*

Ford, Gerald, 125, 161, 165, 226

Ford, Phil, 19

Ford Foundation, 51

Fordham, Christopher C., III, 55, 99

Fordham Court, 64

Fordham Hall, 99

Foreign Languages, Department of, 83

Forest Theatre (Koch Memorial Theatre), 21, 99–100, *100*

foundations, 4, 31, 33, 51, 118, 145, 160, 171, 233, 238

Four Preps, 139

France, 83, 211

Frank, Nyle, 136

Franklin, Benjamin, 100

Franklin and Armfield, 2

Franklin Street, 21, 45, 46, 48, 55, 65, 100–101, *101*, 114, 119, 132, 154, 177, 200, 203, 204, 228; businesses on, 78, 120, 134, 139–40, 212–13; churches on, 195; flower ladies on, 97, *97*; Halloween on, 117; as parade route, 22, *23*; peace vigils on, 3; stone walls along, 62, *208*

Frank Porter Graham Child Development Institute, 101

Frank Porter Graham Student Union, 112, *135*

Frasier, LeRoy, 132

Frasier, Ralph, 132

fraternities and sororities, 22, 101–3, *102*, 106, 194, 205, 217, 234; African Americans and, 205; Beat Dook Parade and, 22; cable television in, 211; *The Hellenian* and, 239; intramural sports teams of, 136; National Pan-Hellenic Council and, 163–64. *See also* Greek Life; *and names of specific fraternities and sororities*

Fraternity Court, 1, 102–3, 194

Fraternity Row, 102

Freelon, Philip, 206

Freemasons, 79

freshmen, 90, 124, 211, 215, 231; orientation for, 41, 212; women as, 170, 219

Friday, Ida Howell, 103

Friday, William C., 13, 49, 68, 86, 103, 114, 200, 203, 230; and desegregation, 221

Friday Center, 69, 103–4, 238

fund-raising, 25, 39, 43, 65, 122, 143, 206, 217; for basketball arena, 82, 218; by students, 77, 153

Furchgott, Robert, 168

gardens, 93, 129, 163, 169, 173–74. *See also* North Carolina Botanical Garden

Gardner, O. Max, 105, 232
Gardner Hall, 54, 105, 118
gargoyles, 177
Gay Awareness Rap Group, 195
Gay Awareness Week, 28
gays and lesbians, 28, 74, 195–96
Gemini, *11*
gender equity, 52
gender ratio, 237
General Alumni Association, 7–8,
 90, 106, 123, 172, 207, 233
General College, 66
General College (soap opera), 211
Genetic Medicine Building, 92, 105
Genetics, Department of, 105
Genome Sciences Building, 106
Geography, Department of, 47, 65
Geology, Department of, 65, 158–59,
 167
German Club, 106–7
German, Department of, 162
Germans, 214; as POWs, 165, 184
Gerrard, Charles, 25, 107
Gerrard Hall, 25, 64, 107, 157, 176
Gettysburg, Battle of, 178
GI Bill, 230
Gilbert, Jane Tenney, 172
Gillespie, James S., 183
Gillings, Dennis, 108
Gillings, Joan H., 108
Gillings Center for Dramatic Art,
 108, 181
Gillings School of Global Public
 Health, 16, 72, 108–9, 155
Gimghoul Castle, 179
Gimghoul Road, 110, 120
Giurgola, Aldo, 81
Glaxo, 229
Glee Club, 110, 222
Glenn, John, 10
Golden Fleece, Order of, 110–11
Goldsboro, 5, 224
golf, 12, 13, 95–96
Goodman, Benny, 218
Goodmon, James Fletcher, 238

Goodmon Building, 238
Gore, Joshua W., 111, 227
Gore Cogeneration Facility, 111, 224,
 227
Gorgon's Head, 110
Government, School of, 111–12, 145
Graduate and Professional Student
 Federation, 210
graduate programs, 21, 108, 112, 131,
 141, 170, 178, 191, 199; African
 Americans in, 132
graduate students, 16, 48, 57, 66, 115,
 119, 136, 209; African Americans
 as, 114, 205; women as, 5, 219, 236
graduate women's dormitory. *See*
 Alderman Residence Hall
graduation ceremony. *See*
 Commencement
graduation requirement, swim test
 as, 124, 214
graffiti, 24, 74
Graham, Archibald "Moonlight,"
 17–18
Graham, Billy, 43
Graham, Edward Kidder, 57, 77, 110,
 112, 183; death of, 112, 130, 205
Graham, Frank Porter, 13, 17, 23, 43,
 54, 59, 60, 68, 75, 77, 101, 114, 176,
 183, 190, 221; Consolidation and,
 91; controversies under, 120
Graham, John Washington, 113
Graham, Martha, 161
Graham, William A., 113
Graham Kenan Professorship, 142
Graham Memorial Hall/Graham
 Memorial Student Union, 62, 64,
 74, 77, 81, 88, 89, 91, 112–13, 121,
 124, 139, 195
Graham Plan, 13
Graham Residence Hall, 14, 113, 149
Graham Student Union, 64, 74, 77,
 81, 91, 113–14, 128, 179–80, 206
grants, 35, 131, 224
Granville County, 184
Granville Towers, 114–15, 211

Grateful Dead, 82
Gray, Bowman, Sr., 30, 156
Gray, Gordon, 221
Great Depression, 72, 90, 95, 105, 114, 128
Greece, 6, 175, 191
Greek, Department of, 162
Greek life, 101–3, *102*. *See also* fraternities and sororities
Green, Danny, 19
Green, Elizabeth Lay, 50
Green, Paul, 49, 50, 108
Green Theatre. *See* Gillings Center for Dramatic Art
Greenberg, Bernard George, 155
Greenlaw, Edwin A., 115
Greenlaw Hall, 115, 162
Greensboro, University of North Carolina at, 15, 29, 54, 72, 105, 137, 155, 211, 221, 222
Griffith, Andy, 50
Grimes, Bryan, 115–16
Grimes, J. Bryan, 115
Grimes Residence Hall, 34, 115–16, 152, 153, 192
Guskiewicz, Kevin, 55
gymnasiums, 36, 67, 85, 95, 179, 192, 210, 218, 236–37
gymnastics, 12, 13, 43

Hackney's Educational and Industrial School, 59
Halifax County, 128
Hall, Jacquelyn Dowd, 201
Halloween, 100, 117, 152–53
Hamilton, Joseph Grégoire de Roulhac "Ransack," 117–18, 191, 201
Hamilton, Mary Cornelia, 117–18
Hamilton Hall, 12, 117–18, 191
Hamm, Mia, *198*, 199
Hanes, Barbara Lasater, 118
Hanes, Frank Borden, 118
Hanes, Robert March, 118
Hanes Art Center, 118

Hanes Hall, 54, 105, 118
Hansborough, Tyler, 19
Hardin, Paul, 55, 119
Hardin Residence Hall, 73, 118–19, 126, 146
"Hark the Sound," 6–7, 67, 98, 110
Harmonyx, 1, 27
Harris, Bernice Kelly, 50
Harris, Charles W., 183
Harvard University, 11, 16, 91, 96, 160, 178, 192
Hatchell, Sylvia, 19, 21
hate speech, 74, 162
HAVEN (Helping Advocates for Violence Ending Now), 52
Hawkins, Reggie, 26
hazing, 111
health sciences, 32, 156
Health Sciences Library, 10, 119, 217, 227
Hearn, Bunn, 17
Hedrick, Benjamin S., 62
Heeley, Desmond, 108
Heisman Trophy, 99
Hellenian, The, 101, 239
Helms, Jesse, 240
Henderson, Archibald, 178
Hentz, Caroline, 126
heraldry, 194–95
Herbarium, 169
Herman, Woody, 107
Herman G. Baity Environmental Laboratory, 16
He's Not Here (bar), 119, 195
Hickerson, Thomas Felix, 119–20
Hickerson House, 119–20
High Noon, 120
Hill, Anne Gibson, 55
Hill, George Watts, 55, 106
Hill, John Sprunt, 48, 55, 106, 121, 169
Hillard, Ann Segur "Miss Nancy," 88
Hillard Hotel, 88
Hillel, 120–21, 162

Hill Hall, 102, 103, 150
Hill Hall Annex, 103
Hill Hall Library, 121–22, 232
Hillsborough, 26, 163, 224
Hinduism, 191, 194
Hindu YUVA, 122–23
Hinton James North, 126
Hinton James Residence Hall, 36, 86, 122
hippies, 97
Hippol Castle, 21, *109*, 109–10
Hispanic students, 158, *159*
historical archaeology, 88–89, 191
history: exhibits of, 47, 197; graduate studies in, 21; sources of, 201–2, 204; Southern, 151; of University, 21, 65, 92, 96–97
History, Department of, 46, 117, 202
HIV/AIDS research, 108
Hogan family, 186
HoJo. *See* Hinton James Residence Hall
Hoke, Robert F., 224
Holden, William Woods, 46, 113, 189
Holi Moli, 122–23
Holloway-Reeves architectural firm, 79
Homecoming, 123–24, 217
honorary degrees, 53, 161, 204, 222
Honor Code and honor system, 111, 132, 209–10, 234–35
Honors Carolina, 67, 113, 124, 233
Hooker, Michael, 27, 55, 124–25, 211–12, 214
Hooker Fields, 123, 124–25
Hooper, William, 39
Hooper Lane, 33
Hoover, Herbert, 176
Hoover, J. Edgar, 75
Horace Williams Airport, 9, *9*, 50, 125–26; closing of, 125, 126
Horney, Giles Foushee, 126
Horney Building, 126
Horton, George Moses, 34, 126, 197

Horton Residence Hall, 73, 119, 126, 146, 197
hospitals and clinics, 103, 111, 126–27, 130, 164, 217, 227
hotels and taverns, 88–89, *89*
House, Robert Burton, 55, 56, 128
House Undergraduate Library, 77, 113, 127–28, 150, 180, 209
housing: off campus, 4; overcrowded, 234; temporary, 218, 230
Howell, Edward Vernon, 92, 128–29
Howell Hall, 62, 92, 128–29, 155
Huggins, Vic, 60, 186
Hughes, Langston, 49, 72
Hunt, James, 148
Hurston, Zora Neale, 47
Hurston Hall, 47, *47*
Hussman School of Journalism and Media, 148, 155–56, 186
Hutchins, James A., Jr., 151
Hutchins Forum, 151
Hyde, Barbara Rosser, 129
Hyde, J. R. "Pitt," 129
Hyde Hall, 129

iBiblio digital library, 238
IBM, 32, 68
Indigenous Peoples Day, 48
infirmary, 1, 59, 130, 216
influenza, 130, 205
Information and Library Science, School of, 131, 232
Information Science, Department of, 68
information technology, 68–69
infrastructure, 227
Innovate Carolina program, 43
Institute for Arts and Humanities, 129
Institute for Social Sciences, 171, 199, 223
Institute of Government, 65, 112, 145
Institute of Marine Sciences, 131
Institute of Pharmacogenomics and Individualized Therapy, 105

Institute on Human Relations, 42

institutes, 42, 65, 105, 112, 129, 145, 199, 207, 223; research, 67, 131, 171

Instrument of Student Judicial Governance (1974), 210

integration, 14, 131–34, 132, 202

intercollegiate athletics, 13, 60, 123, 197; women and, 19, 219. *See also* NCAA

interdisciplinary programs, 67

international studies, 94

internet, 134, 238

Intimate Bookshop, 134–35

intramural sports, 124–25, 135, 135–36, 146, 197, 217, 218; women and, 219, 220

Invisible University, 136

Islam, 190–91, 212

Italians, as POWs, 165

Jackson, Blyden, 137

Jackson, Kent, 237

Jackson, Roberta, 90, 137

Jackson Hall, 137, 160

James, Hinton, 36, 86; as first student, 34, 122

Jamison, Antawn, 19

Janitors Association, 58

jazz, 218

Jefferson Davis Highway, 101

Jim Crow, 70, 84, 118, 131

Johnson, Andrew, 226

Johnson, Gerald W., 155

Johnston, James M., 53, 124

Johnston, James M., Center for Undergraduate Excellence, 124

Johnston Charitable Trust, 124

jokes and pranks, 75, 123, 217

Jones, Clifton, 32

Jones, Howard Mumford, 34

Jordan, Michael, 10, 19, 209

Jordan Lake, 74

Journalism, Department of, 155

Journalism, School of, 36, 54, 75, 128. *See also* Hussman School of Journalism and Media

journalists, 215, 231

Joyner, James Y., 137

Joyner Residence Hall, 137, 234

Jubilee, 138, 139, 204

Judaism and Jews, 102, 120–21, 190, 191

judges and justices, 148, 153, 163, 176, 192–93

Julian, Alexander, 10, 44–45, 139–40

Julian, Maurice, 120, 139

Julian, Milton, 139

Julian's, 100, 120, 139–40

juniors, 109, 211, 235

junior varsity sports, 215

Justice, Charlie "Choo Choo," 98–99

Kappa Alpha Psi Fraternity, Inc., 163

Kappa Sigma, 103

Karen Shelton Stadium, 95

Kasell, Carl, 237

Kenan, Mary Hargrave, 143

Kenan, Randall, 74

Kenan, William Rand, Jr., 62, 98, 141, 143

Kenan, William Rand, Sr., 143

Kenan Charitable Trust, 142

Kenan family, 25, 141

Kenan-Flagler Business School, 16, 105, 118, 141, 142, 146, 154

Kenan Laboratories, 62, 141–42

Kenan Music Building, 142

Kenan Professorships, 25, 72, 83, 115, 141, 142, 143, 196, 216

Kenan Residence Hall, 142–43, 155

Kenan Stadium, 23, 57, 86, 98, 98, 141, 143–44, 144, 157, 217; football team and, 91; Jubilee in, 139; Marching Tar Heels in, 154; seating capacity of, 143; segregation in, 132; South Campus and, 201; University Day celebrations in, 222, 223

Kenan Theatre, 181

Kenfield, John, 69–70
Kennedy, John F., 51, 144, 222, *223*
Ker, David, 183
Kernersville, 22
Kerr, Banks, 144
Kerr Drug stores, 144
Kerr Hall, 92, 144
Kessing, Oliver Owen, 144
Kessing Pool, 144–45
kickball, 136
King, B. B., 139
King, Martin Luther, Jr., 48, *71*
Kinsella, W. P.: *Shoeless Joe*, 18
Knapp, Joseph Palmer, 145
Knapp, Margaret Rutledge, 145
Knapp Foundation, 145
Knapp-Sanders Building, 111, 145–46
Knight, Phil, 168
Knight Commission on Intercollegiate Athletics, 13, 104
Koch, Frederick Henry "Proff," 50, 73, 99
Koch Memorial Theatre (Forest Theatre), 99
Koury, Maurice J., 146
Koury Natatorium, 16, 146
Koury Oral Health Sciences Building, 4, 146
Koury Residence Hall, 73, 119, 126, 146
Krasny, Morris, 190
Kresge, W. K., Foundation, 33
Kughle, Frances Vandeveer, 145
Ku Klux Klan, 46, 51, 113, 116, 118, 132, 189
Kuralt, Brenda, 135
Kuralt, Charles, 77, 216, 237, *237*
Kuralt, Wallace, 135
Kyser, Kay, 60

laboratories, 16, 66, 99, 128, 141, 157, 229; archaeological, 88, 117; chemistry, 54, 62, 160, 177, 181; computer, 128; foreign language, 83; genomic research, 106; for nursing students, 53; pharmaceutical, 168; for School of Medicine, 26; underground, 79
labor organization, 59, 114, 176
lacrosse, 12, 13, 147, 165
Lambda, 195
land-grant colleges, 189
Langton, Stephen, 177
Lanier, Ricky, 99
Lassiter, James, 131
Late Night with Roy, 147
Latham, Steve "Yure Nmomma," 123, 217
Latin, 151, 194
Latin, Department of, 162
Latinos, 1, 158, *159*
Latinx Center, 147–48
laundry, 58–59, *59*, 227
Law, School of, 50, 78, 90, 148, 153, 155, 181, *181*, 226, 228–29; African Americans and, 30, 131, *133*; alumni of, 33, 103, 105; deans of, 14; faculty of, 217; Kenan Professorships in, 142
lawsuits against university, 191, 203, 212
lawyers, 90, 105, 113, 148, 153, 176, 178, 192, 193, 213, 229
League of Resident Theatres in the United States (LORT), 180
Lee, Howard, 56
Lee, J. Kenneth, 131, *133*
Lee, Spike, 207
LEED (Leadership in Energy and Environmental Design), 53, 146
Legion of Honor, 83
Lenoir, William, 149
Lenoir Hall, 37, 85, 148–49, 153, 184
lesbians. *See* gays and lesbians
Lewis, Richard Henry, 149
Lewis Residence Hall, 14, 113, 149
LGBTQ Center, 149–50
LGBTQ organizations, 195–96

Liberal Arts, College of, 66, 113
liberalism, 28, 68, 75, 171
librarians, 10, 112, 131; university librarian, 222, 232–33
libraries, 150–51, 191; acquisitions for, 26; computers in, 69; funding of, 64, 106, 217; special collections, 21, 232. *See also names of specific libraries*
Library Science, School of, 131, 153, 232
licensing and trademarks, 166, 174, 187, 216, 220
Lineberger Comprehensive Cancer Center, 127
Lineberger family, 25
Linville, 160
literary magazines, 134
literary studies, 223
Little River, 179
Lloyd, Thomas, 224
lobbyists, 105
logo, 166, *167*, 220, 230, 231
London, Winston House in, 233
Look Homeward Angel (Thomas Wolfe, 1929), 184
Loreleis, 1
Lost Cause, 118
Loudermilk Center for Excellence, 143
Love, James Lee, 151
Love, Julia Spencer, 151
Love family, 25
Love House and Hutchins Forum, 151
Lover's Loop Trail, 179
Lowry, Cecil B., 132
Lowry, Genevieve, 132
Lowry, Otis M., 132
Lumbee Indians, 132
Lumberton, 89
"Lux Libertas," 151, 194
lynching, 116
lyrics: "Hark the Sound," 6–7; "Tar Heels Born and Tar Heels Bred," 7

MacNelly, Jeff, 156
MacNider, William de Berniere, 152
MacNider Hall, 29, 152
MacRae, Mary, 236
Major League Baseball, 17
makerspace, 43
malaria, 16
Mangum, Adolphus Williamson, 152
Mangum, William Preston, 152
Mangum, Willie Person, 152
Mangum Residence Hall, 34, 115, 152–53, 192
Manly, Charles, 153
Manly, Matthias, 153
Manly Residence Hall, 34, 115, 152, 153, 192
Manning, Isaac, 190
Manning, John, 153–54
Manning Drive, 14
Manning Hall, 12, 34, 37, 105, 131, 133, 153–54, 209; Law School in, 148, 153, 228
marching band, 154, 237
marijuana, 120
Marine Sciences, Department of, 56, 229
Marks, Sallie, 90
Marsico, Thomas F., 154
Marsico Hall, 154
mascots, 186–88, *188*
Mason Farm Biological Reserve, 169
Massey, Elaine, *71*
mathematics, 67
Mathematics, Department of, 56, 159, 178
Maverick House, 73
McCauley Street, 94, 163
McClinton, Hortense, 134, 199
McColl, Hugh, 154
McColl Building, 141, 154
McCorkle, Jill, 54, 74
McCorkle, Samuel Eusebius, 154–55; "Plan of Education" (1792), 11
McCorkle Place, 8, 17, 21, 65, 88, 154–55, 177, 182, 203, *203*, 228;

cherry trees on, 62; monuments on, 39, 64, 154, 225; as oldest part of campus, 129, 154

McCoy, William O., 55

McDivitt, James Alton, *11*

McFee, Michael, 54

McGavran, Edward G., 155

McGavran-Greenberg Hall, 16, 155

McGuire, Frank, 18, 86

McIver, Charles Duncan, 155

McIver Residence Hall, 142, 155

McKim, Mead and White, 182

McKissick, Floyd, 131, 144–45

McKissick v. Carmichael, 131

mechanical engineering, 91

Mecklenburg County, 226

Media and Journalism, School of. *See* Hussman School of Journalism and Media

Medical Air Service, 9

Medical Drive, 53

Medical Sciences Research Building, 29

medicine and health sciences, 9–10, 16, 26, 29, 91

Medicine, Department of, 34, 35

Medicine, School of, 26, 53, 92, 99, 108, 131, 149, 152, 156–57, 177; buildings of, 29, 38; deans of, 190; dormitories for, 231; expansion of, 25; facilities of, 105, 154; research centers in, 218; Sarah Graham Kenan Professorships in, 142

Meeting of the Waters Creek, 143, 157

Memorial Grove, 172

Memorial Hall, 2–3, 23, 40, 72, 94, 111, 157, 157–58, 227; Commencement Day and, 8, 195

memorials and monuments: to Confederates, 4, 53, 70–71, 71, 101, 154; to Joseph Caldwell, 7, 39–40, 154; in Memorial Hall, 158; on McCorkle Place, 154; to Unsung Founders, 64, 154, 197, 224–25, 225

Menorah Society, 120

Men's Residence Council, 93

menswear stores, 139

Meredith College, 103

Merge Records, 56

Merritt, Jack "Battering Ram," 186

Merritt, Tift, 54

Merritt Mill Road, 111

Methodism, 152

Michael D. Green Lecture in American Indian Studies, 8–9

Milburn, Frank, 41, 197

military science, 91

Miller, Andrew, 17

Miller, Ron, 94

Miller, William, 112, 158

Miller Hall, 158

Milton's Clothing Cupboard, 139

Minerva, 64

Mines, School of, 111

mining, 91

Mi Pueblo, 158, *159*

Mississippi, 41, 75

Mitchell, Elisha, 11, 159, 183, 207–8

Mitchell, Joseph, 49

Mitchell Hall, 99, 158–59

Moeser, James C., 55, 121–22, 142, 204

Moeser, Susan, 121, 122

Moeser Auditorium, 121

Monogram Club, 63, 85, 137, 159–60

Morehead, James T., 197

Morehead, John Motley, III, 7, 11–12, 62, 87, 160; bell tower and, 22, 23

Morehead-Cain Foundation, 160

Morehead Chemistry Laboratory, 160

Morehead City, Institute of Marine Sciences in, 131

Morehead family, 25

Morehead Laboratories, 62, 142

Morehead-Patterson Bell Tower. *See* bell tower

Morehead Planetarium and Science Center, 11–12, 160–61, 195; astronaut training in, 10, *11*, 161

Morgan, Robert, 52

Morgan Creek, 157

Morrill Act (1862), 189

Morrison, Cameron, 161–62

Morrison Residence Hall, 73, 86, 119, 161–62

Morrison South Residence Hall, 119

motto, 151, 194

Mount Mitchell, 159

movies, 176, 186

murals, 145

murders, 4–5, 66, 93, 116

Murphey, Archibald DeBow, 162

Murphey Hall, 26, 34, 64, 105

Murray, Pauli, 114

Murray, Royce, 230

Murray Hall, 62, 229–30

museums, 2, 206, 233

Music, Department of, 110, 121, 168, 177

music, musicians, 56, 82, 122, 123, 142, 217, 218; festivals of, 71, *138*, *139*

music groups: B-1 Band, 166, *166*; barbershop quartets, 1–2; a capella, 1–2; Glee Club, 6, 110; Gospel Choir, 27; Harmonyx, 27; Marching Band, 154

Muslim Student Association, 162

Myers, Walter Starr, 6, 67

myths and legends, 122, 178

NAACP (National Association for the Advancement of Colored People), 26, 176

Naismith Memorial Basketball Hall of Fame, 21

naming and renaming of buildings, 33–34, 46–47; after women, 197; controversies over, 94, 115–16

Nash, Arthur C., 8, 48, 182, 232

Nash, Frederick, 163

Nash Hall, 163

National Humanities Medal, 201

National Indian-American Studies Conference, 194

National Institutes of Health, 35

National Pan-Hellenic Council, 163–64

National Public Radio (NPR), WUNC 91.5 FM and, *237*, 237–38

National Register of Historic Places, 22, 154, 172

National Science Foundation, 68

Native Americans, 164; admittance of, 132; American Indian Center and, 1, 8–9; archaeology and, 191; Carolina Indian Circle and, 48; as graduates, 164; in sororities, 102, *102*; prehistoric, 228; segregation of, 131; treaties with, 25

Native Leaders Symposium, 48

natural gas, 111

natural history, 223

natural philosophy, 11

natural sciences, 67, 159

Naval Armory, 165, 192

naval stores industry, 215

Navy, U.S., pre-flight school, 165–66, 184, 194; B-1 band of, 166, *166*; buildings for, 163, 165; U.S. presidents at, 226; swimming and, 214

Navy Field, 139, 165

Navy ROTC, 165

NBA (National Basketball Association), 18, 19

NCAA (National Collegiate Athletic Association), 13, 14, 219; field hockey championships in, 95; men's basketball champions, 18, 42–43, *76*, *101*, 140, 220; men's basketball Final Four, 19; women's basketball champions, 21; women's soccer champions, *198*, 199

NC logo, 166, *167*

N.C. State. *See* North Carolina State University

neoclassical style, 8

Nephrology Division, 35

Neurology, Department of, 35

neuroscience, 128

Neurosciences Hospital, 127
New Bern, 150
New Chapel (Gerrard Hall), 107
New Deal, 177
New East Building, 156, 166–67
New Hope Chapel Hill, 55
New Hope Creek, 74
News and Observer (Raleigh), 78
New Students and Family Programs
  office, 211
New West, 39, 86, 92, 167–68
New York Giants (MLB), 18
New York Times, 156, 207
New York University, 58
New York Yankees (MLB), 18
Nichols, William, 107, 172, 174
nicknames, 215–16, 231
Nigeria, 134, 198
Nike, 10, 45, 168
Nixon, Richard, visit by, 69
Nobel Prize, 168
nonprofits, 77, 199, 238
Normal Instruction, Department of,
  89–90, 212
North Carolina: Bureau of Exchange,
  113; in Confederacy, 73; counties
  of, 81, 125; Good Health Plan of,
  53; health and hospitals in, 9, 108,
  217; history, 145; industrialists in,
  25; local government in, 111; Native
  American population of, 8, 9,
  164; public education in, 131, 162;
  secession of, 63; secretary of state
  of, 46, 93, 116; segregation in, 131;
  State Board of Education, 29, 189;
  State Board of Health, 108, 149;
  state constitutions, 29, 46, 96–97,
  145, 189, 220; State Laboratory of
  Public Health, 164; state sales tax
  of, 90, 118; state song of, 110; Tar
  Heel Bus Tour through, 45–46; as
  Tar Heel State, 215; textile industry
  in, 30; western, 159, 164
North Carolina A&T University
  (Greensboro), 132

North Carolina Archaeology
  Collection, 191
North Carolina Botanical Garden, 22,
  66, 99, 157, 168–69
North Carolina Central University, 131
North Carolina Children's Hospital,
  77
North Carolina Collection, 48, 121,
  169, 213, 232
North Carolina College for Women,
  29, 72, 105
North Carolina College of Agriculture
  and Mechanic Arts. *See* North
  Carolina State University
North Carolina Digital Heritage
  Center, 169
North Carolina Equipment Company,
  96
North Carolina governors, 33; alumni
  as, 15, 90, 112, 148, 153, 158, 228;
  during Civil War, 64; as presidents
  of Board of Trustees, 28; send state
  troopers to campus, 37, 149, 153
North Carolina Higher Education
  Improvement Bonds Referendum,
  94
North Carolina High School Athletic
  Association, 1
North Carolina Historical Society,
  169, 174, 213
North Carolina Memorial Hospital,
  126–27, 127, 132, 156
North Carolina People (UNC-TV), 104
North Carolina Poverty Research
  Fund, 148
North Carolina Science Festival, 161
North Carolina State Archives, 72
North Carolina State College of
  Agriculture and Engineering. *See*
  North Carolina State University
North Carolina State Fair, 98
North Carolina state legislature, 33,
  81–82, 113, 189, 221; alumni as
  members of, 93, 118, 122, 154, 205;
  appropriates money, 14, 24–26, 35,

62, 128, 141, 145, 154, 160; Board of Trustees and, 28, 29; charter from, 74, 97; creates UNC Health Care System, 127; cuts financial support, 220; Escheats Act of, 91; establishes school of dentistry, 4; establishes UNC System, 54; evolution and, 58; health care improvement by, 169–70; medical education and, 156; members of, 149, 162; public utilities sale and, 227; Speaker Ban Law of, 3, 14, 68, 75, 103, 121, 202–3; supports Area Health Education Centers, 9

North Carolina State Literary and Historical Association, 116

North Carolina State University, 4–5, 13, 29, 54, 72, 91, 103, 105, 180, 221, 234; Centennial Campus of, 50; in Dixie Classic, 86; donors to, 96; engineering program transferred to, 16; Red Terrors of, 231; rivalry with, 7, 18, 42; Triangle University Computation Center and, 134; Year at Lyons program and, 211

North Carolina Supreme Court, 163, 192–93, 229

North Carolina Zoo, 240

Notre Dame, University of, 99

nurses, 59

Nursing, School of, 53, 169–70

Nye, Kemp, 66

Oates, Joyce Carol, 52

Obama, Barack, 2; visit by, 226

Occaneechi Indians, 164

Odum, Howard W., 171, 199, 223

Odum Institute for Research in Social Science, 171

Odum Village, 16, 171

Office of Scholarships and Student Aid, 177

Office of Undergraduate Admissions, 63, 137

oil industry, 82, 141

Okoroma, Edwin, 134, 198

Old Chapel Hill Cemetery, 39, 108, 124, 172; African Americans in, 225

Old East, 33, 39, 84, 154, 172–74, 177, 200, 222; as first building, 24, 86, 122, 172

"Old North State, The," 110

Old South, 48

Old Students Club, 172–73

Old Well, 1, 32, 107, 154, 172–74, 174, 184, 220

Old West, 39, 107, 148, 157, 173–75; restoration of, 172, 175

Oliver Smithies Nobel Symposium, 168

Olmstead, Denison, 61

Olympics, 6, 19, 146, 175, 199

Omega Psi Phi, 102, 163

Opeyo! Dance Company, 27

Ophthalmology, Department of, 35

Orange County, 25, 40, 58, 189, 192

Orange Water and Sewer Authority, 227

Order of Dromgoole, 109

Order of the Gimghoul, 21–22, 109–10, 120; Hippol Castle of, 21, 109, 110, 179

Oregon State University, 17

O'Reilly, Heather, 199

origins, 96; Cyprett's Bridge and, 74; escheats and, 91–92; first campus, 154; first state university, 96–97; first student, 122; Franklin Street and, 100; McCorkle and, 11

Owl, Henry, 164

Oxford University, 160

Pancakes and Poetry event, 205

Pantone 542, 45

Papermail, 134

parades, 22, 100, 123; Beat Dook, 23, 60, 123; Homecoming, 123

Parker, John J., 176

Parker Residence Hall, 14, 176, 217

parking lots, 81, 158, 163

Parks, Sheri, 123

Pasquotank County, 82, 90

Patch Adams filmed on campus, 176

Patterson, James, 172

Patterson, Rufus Lenoir, II, 23

Peabody, George, 25, 177

Peabody Education Fund, 90, 177

Peabody Hall, 90, 177

Pediatrics, Department of, 35

Pender County, 122

People's Pharmacy, The (radio programs), 238

pep rallies, 22, 123

Percival, William, 167

Percy, Walker, 49

performing arts, 108, 157, 180–81

Person, Thomas, 25, 33, 177, 191

Person Hall, 2, 25, 33, 39, 62, 92, 107, 128, 156, 177, 191

petitions by students, 2, 63, 85

Pettigrew, Gen. James Johnston, 177–78

Pettigrew, John, 173

Pettigrew Hall, 21, 86, 177–78, 228

pharmacogenomics, 105

Pharmacology, Department of, 105, 152

Pharmacy, School of, 22, 92, 105, 128, 144, 177

Phi Beta Sigma Fraternity, Inc., 164

Phi Gamma Delta, 101

Philanthropic Society, 44, 67, 83–84, 98, 167, 168, 210, 239; library of, 121, 150, 172, 200

Phillips, Charles, 91, 110, 178, 183

Phillips, James, 178

Phillips, William Battle, 178

Phillips Annex, 68, 178

Phillips Hall, 67, 85, 134, 178, 227

Philosophy, Department of, 28, 39

physical education, 179, 192, 214

Physical Education, Exercise, and Sport Science, Department of, 95, 179

physical plant and facilities support, 126

Physics, Department of, 8, 12, 56, 177, 178

Physics and Astronomy, Department of, 12

Pi Beta Phi, 102

Piedmont, Indigenous peoples of, 164

Pi Kappa Alpha, 22

Pine Rock College, 184

Pine Room, 85

Pines Restaurant, 96

Piney Prospect, 179

Pink Floyd, 82

Pinney, Don, 213

Pioneer Team (baseball), 17

Pit, the, 74, 77, 136, 179–80

Pitt County, 149

Pittsboro, 74, 188

Pittsboro Street, 94, 163

plantations, 2, 25, 41, 79, 192

PlayMakers Repertory Company, 50, 180–81

Playmakers Theatre, 1, 25, 33, 50, 62, 64, 148, 150, 181, *181*, 227

poetry, 126, 197, 205, 239

Pogue, Joseph Ezekiel, 26

police, campus, 136, 180

Political Science, Department of, 117

politics, 113; conservative, 116; faculty and, 62; newspapers and, 78; progressive, 114; of Reconstruction, 183, 189, 204, 228; of state election of 1898, 161

Polk, James K., 107, 182; as alumnus, 88, 226; visits campus, 226

Polk, Leonidas, 115

Polk, William, 107

Polk Place, 57, 85, 93, 99, 105, 116, 182, *182*, 200, 201; construction of, 8; flagpole in, 23; Holi Moli on, 123; Manning Hall on, 153; in *Patch Adams*, 176

Pool, Solomon, 183, 189

pools, 36, 237

Porthole Alley, 102

Pound, Ezra, 72

power plant, 224, 227

Preclinical Education Building, 31

Presbyterianism, 154, 190

presidents, UNC, 25, 33, 77, 182–83, 189, 190, 237; acting, 113, 159, 178, 183, 205; Alderman, 5, 151, 173–74, 183, 194; Battle, 12, 21, 92, 179, 183, 222; Caldwell, 7, 11, 38, 150, 213; Chase, 57, 93, 171, 183, 232; deaths of, 130, 205; E. K. Graham, 57, 77, 110, 112–13, 130, 183, 205; faculty members as, 183, 230; first, 38; F. P. Graham, 13, 17, 23, 43, 54, 59, 60, 68, 75, 77, 91, 101, 114, 120, 165, 176, 190, 221; house for, 5, 208, 213; list of, 183; offices of, 8, 200; Swain, 63–65, 157–58, 169, 206, 213; Venable, 61–62, 70, 113, 183, 230; Winston, 183, 234

presidents, U.S., 51, 72, 78, 105, 165, 176, 201, 226; alumni as, 88, 107, 182; as Commencement speakers, 107, 144; trained as Navy pilots at UNC, 125, 165, 226; at University Day celebrations, 222, 223; as visitors, 161, 226, 236

President's House, 5, 208, 213

Prince, William Meade, 63; *The Southern Part of Heaven* (1950), 202

Princeton University, 79

printing, 168, 222

Printing Industry of America, 239

printing press, 134

prisoners of war (POWs), 165, 184

private clubs, 110–11

programs, 156, 211, 216, 233; interdisciplinary, 67, 99, 115

Project RETCH (Refuse to Eat Trash in Chase Hall), 57

Prospect Point, 179

protests, rallies, and marches, 132, 196, 210, 240; against apartheid, 27, 99; by blacks, 27, 206–7; by cafeteria workers, 3, 27, 37, 38, 85, 149, 153; on Franklin Street, 100; at He's Not Here, 195; in Memorial Hall, 2–3, 158; against N.C. Speaker Ban Law, 3, 202–3, 203; against Nike, 168; against ROTC, 192; for South Africa divestment, 3, 3; against Vietnam War, 217. *See also* activism

Psychology, Department of, 79, 103, 168

Psychology and Neuroscience, Department of, 128

public administration, 112

publications, 44, 112, 130; *Alumni Review*, 57, 106; *Black Ink*, 27; *Carolina Buccaneer*, 45, 50; *Carolina Magazine*, 49–50, 52, 73; *Carolina Quarterly*, 52; *Cellar Door*, 54; *Contempo*, 72, 134; *Daily Tar Heel*, 19, 22, 28–31, 71, 73, 75–78, 76, 90, 94, 98, 112, 113, 120, 147, 148, 153, 155, 180, 184, 192, 196, 211, 215, 230, 240; *The Hellenian*, 101, 239; *Lambda*, 195; *Tar Heel*, 6, 17, 36, 45, 67, 68, 75, 95, 98, 106, 130, 141, 178, 197, 215, 236; *Tarnation*, 50; *White and Blue*, 67, 75; *Yackety Yack*, 27, 38, 60, 102, 112, 239; yearbooks, 109, 239

public education, 81, 204, 234

Public Health, School of, 103, 108–9, 152, 155, 169, 192

public policy, 101

Public Policy, Department of, 1

public relations, 155

public service, 45–46, 53

Public Service Roundtable, 45

Public Welfare, School of, 199

Public Works Administration, 6, 148, 152, 205, 231

Pulitzer Prizes, 77, 108, 156

Pulpit Hill, 184

Purdue University, 68

Quail Hill, 55, 185
Queen, Anne, 42
queen and king, homecoming, 123
Quonset huts, 86

rabbis, 120–21
race relations, 199, 234
radio, 99, 186, 222, 237, 237–38
Radio, Television, and Motion
  Pictures (RTVMP), Department of,
  186, 210, 222
railroad, railroads, 53, 141, 182, 224,
  230
Raleigh, 16, 17, 64, 72, 79, 84, 128,
  144, 149, 164, 197, 236, 240;
  Medical Department in, 156;
  newspapers in, 78; Research
  Triangle and, 55
Raleigh, Sir Walter, 99
Raleigh-Durham International
  Airport (RDU), 9, 125
Raleigh Road, 9, 55, 145
Raleigh Street, 91, 203, 208
Rameses (mascots), 38–39, 187–88,
  188; trademarked, 220
Ram's Head Plaza, 57
Ram's Head Rathskeller ("The Rat"),
  79, 188
Ram Village Community, 217
Rare Book Collection, 232
Rathskeller. See Ram's Head
  Rathskeller ("The Rat")
Rayburn, Sam, 51
Real Silent Sam Coalition, 47
Reconstruction, 56, 113, 183, 204,
  228; closing and, 189–90
Red Clay Ramblers, 56
Red Shirts, 161
Rehder, Jessie, 73
religion, 41, 42, 107, 120–23, 162;
  Anglicans, 55; Buddhism, 191;
  Christianity, 180, 190, 191;
  clergy, 132; College Chapel,
  177; Episcopalians, 190, 195;
  evangelicals, 180; Hinduism,
  191, 194; Judaism and Jews, 102,
  120–21, 190, 191; Methodism,
  152; Presbyterianism, 154, 190;
  presidents and, 190–91; required
  chapel attendance, 190. See also
  chapel, chapels; religion
Religious Studies, Department of, 191
reopening (1875), 7, 21, 40, 62, 183,
  204, 234
Republican Party, 62, 189
requirements: for physical exercise,
  179; swim test, 124, 214
research, 34, 53, 57, 62, 92, 99,
  191; on arthritis, 218; on cancer,
  92, 108, 157; centers for, 119,
  218; for children, 101; clinical,
  35; computer science, 32, 68;
  dental, 31; endowments for, 26;
  expansion of, 25, 106; facilities for,
  12; fieldwork, 46, 199; genomic,
  106; on HIV/AIDS, 108; institutes
  of, 67; laboratories, 8, 88–89, 117,
  191, 228; library for, 150; medical,
  29, 31; in neuroscience, 128;
  population, 51–52; publication of,
  222; public service and, 45; on
  social problems, 199; on South,
  201; technology and, 22; by
  undergraduates, 67
Research Day, 36
Research Triangle Park, 55, 92, 118,
  134, 222, 229
residences. See dormitories and
  residence halls
Revolutionary War, veterans and
  officers of, 24, 34, 79, 107, 149,
  177
Reynolds Coliseum, Raleigh, 85
Rhodes Scholarships, 160
Richmond, Va., 98
Richmond and Danville Railroad
  Company, 224
Richmond County, 93, 161, 206
Ridge Road, 165, 228
rituals and ceremonies, 110–11, 122–

23, 136. *See also* events; tradition, traditions
rivalries, sports, 7, 18, 22, 98, 230
R. J. Reynolds Tobacco Company, 30
Roanoke Island, 99
Roberts, Brian, 17
Robertson, Julian, 191–92
Robertson Express Bus, 192
Robertson Scholars, 191–92
Rockefeller family, 25
Rocky and Bullwinkle, 139
Romance Languages, Department of, 162, 211
Roosevelt, Franklin D., 51, 72, 78, 105, 165; visits campus, 226, 236
Roper, William, 221
Rosemary Street, 56, 119, 121
Rosenau, Milton, 192
Rosenau Hall, 192
Rosenbluth, Lennie, 19
Ross, Thomas W., 221
ROTC (Reserve Officers Training Corps), 74, 165, 192
RTVMP. *See* Radio, Television, and Motion Pictures, Department of
Ruffin, Thomas, Jr., 192, 193
Ruffin, Thomas, Sr., 192–93
Ruffin Hall, 34
Ruffin Residence Hall, 115, 152, 153, 192–93

SafeZone, 150
Saga Corporation, 37, *38*, 85
Sancar, Aziz, 168
Sanders, John Lassiter, 145–46
Sanford, 125
Sanford, Terry, 114, 148, 153
Sangam, 194
sanitation, 130
Saponi Confederation, 164
Saunders, William L., 46–47
Saunders Hall, 26, 34, 105, 141; protests over name of, 3, 46–47, 47
Sayre, Thomas, 129
Scales, Junius, 68

scandals: alleged in *Blood on the Old Well*, 28; athletics and, 13, 18, 86, 103; *Carolina Buccaneer's* "Sex Issue," 45; president's daughter engaged to Union officer, 213
scholarships, 31, 33, 36, 46, 53, 64, 92, 124, 142, 160, 177, 191; athletic, 86, 99, 134, 219; endowments for, 26, 30; licensing earnings goes toward, 220; need-based, 25
Scott, Bob, 37, 149, 153
Scott, Charles, 19, 134, 205
Scott, Stuart, 156, 211
sculptures, 70, 103, 129; as senior class gifts, 64, 209; statues, 64, 177
Scuttlebutt, 194
seal, 151, 194–95, 220
Sears Cup, 13
Secession, 73, 178, 189, 206, 228
secret societies, 109–10
segregation, 15, 70, 84, 118; administration and, 132; in campus housing, 205; in Chapel Hill, 56, 132; of fraternities and sororities, 163; in hospital, 127; Native Americans and, 164; in Old Chapel Hill Cemetery, 172; in public education, 131–32; of swimming pools, 144–45; during World War II, 166, *166*
Sells, Michael, 190, 212
seniors: class gifts from, 64–65; in Golden Fleece, 110; as members of Gimghoul, 109; Senior Walk and, 195; women as, 235; yearbook and, 239
September 11, 2001, terrorist attacks, 190, 212
Servomation, 85
Sexuality and Gender Alliance, 195–96
Shakori Indians, 164
Shapley, Harlow, 11–12
Sharp, Paul F., 55

Sharp, Susie Marshall, 148
Shelton, Karen, 95
Sherman, Gen. William T., 64
sidewalks and walkways, 31, 32, 56, 65, 66, 126, 203, 203
Sigma Alpha Epsilon, 101
Sigma Gamma Rho Sorority, Inc., 164
"Silent Sam." See Confederate Monument
Simmons, Floyd "Chunk," 175
Simpson, Bland, 74
Sissipahaw Indians, 164
sit-ins, 132
Sitterson, J. Carlyle, 26, 55, 196, 203
Sitterson Hall, 32, 196
Skull and Bones, 109
slavery, 34, 39, 79, 84, 88, 115–16, 149, 177, 192–93, 196–97, 213; construction by, 107, 172, 174, 208; defense of, 159; escheats and, 92; opposition to, 62; Three-Fifths Compromise and, 79; trade, 2
Sloane, Art Library, 118
Smith, Benjamin, 25, 33–34, 181
Smith, Dean: championship seasons of, 42–43, 76; fund-raising and, 82; hiring and promotion of, 14, 18, 86; men's basketball team uniforms and, 10; recruits African Americans, 134; reverence for, 19; on women's soccer, 199
Smith, Eddie, Jr., 89
Smith, Eddie, Sr., 89
Smith Building, 197
Smith, Mary Ruffin, 25
Smith, Willis, 114
Smith Building, 170, 178, 197
Smith Hall, 25, 33, 50, 148, 150, 181, 181, 227
Smith Student Activities Center, 16, 19, 43, 82, 83, 141, 146, 154, 207, 218
Smithies, Oliver, 168
soap opera, 211
soccer, 12, 95, 134, 197–98

soccer, women's, 13, 95, 198, 199; as NCAA champions, 219; Olympics and, 175
Soccer and Lacrosse Stadium, 95
Social Work, School of, 134, 199, 216
sociologists, 171, 199
Sociology, Department of, 8, 117
soda fountains, 41, 46, 63, 63, 137, 159–60, 188, 212
softball, 9, 136
Sonja Haynes Stone Center for Black Culture and History, 3, 52, 162, 206–7, 207, 226
sororities. See fraternities and sororities
Soul Food cafeteria, 153
South, American, 171, 199; research on, 201, 223
South Africa, 3, 3, 56
South Asian students, 102, 122–23, 194
South Building, 8, 39, 41, 62, 86, 87, 107, 148, 157, 173, 182, 182, 200, 200; attic of, 227; bell in, 204; bell tower rejected for, 23; streaking through, 209
South Campus, 14, 54, 57, 73, 85, 86, 87, 122, 126, 141, 146, 171, 201, 217; Medical School on, 152, 157
South Carolina, 66, 79, 178
Southeastern Black Press Institute, 207
Southeastern Gay Conference, 195
Southern Association of Colleges and Schools, 202
Southern Conference, 6, 13, 198; basketball in, 18, 231
Southern Folklife Collection, 232
Southern Historical Collection, 118, 201, 202, 213, 232
Southern Methodist University, 119
Southern Oral History Program (SOHP), 201–2
South Merritt Mill Road, 59
South Road, 43, 124, 172, 231

Spangler, C. D., 221
Speaker Ban Law (1963), 3, 14, 68, 75, 103, 121, 202–3
speakers and lecturers, 42, 43, 51, 72; U.S. presidents as, 107. *See also* Speaker Ban Law; visitors
Speech, Department of, 26
Speech Communication, Department of, 186
Spellings, Margaret, 221
Spencer, Cornelia Phillips, 81, 151, 189, 204
Spencer Residence Hall, 86, 195, 203–4, 234; as first women's dorm, 236
Sper, Norm, 42, 60
Spinal Tap, 228
Sports Illustrated, 10
sports medicine, 216
Springfest music festival, 71, 204–5. *See also* concerts
Springsteen, Bruce, 82, 144
Squirrel Nut Zippers, 56
Stacy, Inez Koonce, 234, 236
Stacy, Marvin Hendrix, 130, 183, 205
Stacy Residence Hall, 205
Stadium Drive, 14, 106, 217
St. Anthony Hall, 205
State, County, and Municipal Workers of America, 59
State Normal and Industrial School for Girls, 155
State University Railroad, 224
State v. Mann, 193
steam tunnels, 158, 163, 227
Steel, Emily, 156
Steele, Max, 73
Steele, Walter Leake, 205–6
Steele Building, 29, 132, 205–6; Book Exchange in, 77
Steinbrenner, George, 18, 30
Steinbrenner Family Courtyard, 18, 30
stewards, 88, 206

Steward's Hall, 84, 206
St. Joseph CME Church, 59
St. Mary's College, 236
Stockard, Sallie Walker, 236
Stone, Sonya Haynes, 206, 207
Stone Center. *See* Sonja Haynes Stone Center for Black Culture and History
stone walls, 159, 172, 203, *203*, 207–8, *208*
streaking, 209
S&T's Soda Shop, 188
student activities, 112–14
student affairs, 42, 44, 52
Student and Academic Services Building, 163, 226
Student Body (sculpture), 64, 209
Student Educational Broadcasting, 238
student fees, 75, 77, 112, 210
student government, 65, 84, 132, 167, 195, 209–10, 219; African Americans and, 26; Board of Trustees and, 28; elections for, 41; president of, 45, 93, 202, 237; reunions for, 123; women and, 236
student groups and organizations, 101–3, *102*, 159–60; African American, 27; for cheerleading, 60; debating societies, 44; early, 44; of gays and lesbians, 28, 195–96; German Club, 106–7; Glee Club, 110; of Hispanic students, 158, *159*; intramural sports teams and, 136; Jewish, 120–21; Monogram Club, 159–60; offices for, 112; oldest, 83–84; Order of Gimghoul, 109–10; Order of Golden Fleece, 110–11; religious, 41, 162, 190; Sangam, 194; secret societies, 109–11; sports boosters, 42; Student Recreation Center and, 210; Town Girls Association,

219–20; women's, 52. *See also* clubs; fraternities and sororities; *and names of specific groups and organizations*

student health services, 216

student life, 66, 101–3, *102*; beer, 188, 204–5; cable television, 211; check cashing, 78; chaperones, 234–35; coed-living, 122, 161; complaints about food, 2, 57, 206; dances, 67, 106–7; debating societies, 84; dining and dining out, 57, 67–68, 78, 84–85, 194, 206; e-mail, 134; flowers, 97; formal banquets, 153; fund raising, 152–53; health and sickness, 130; heating and cooling, 167–68; infirmary, 216; intramural sports, 135–36; Invisible University classes, 136; jokes and pranks, 70, 123; laundry service, 58; library hours, 128; mail, 59; marijuana, 120; married students, 171; private dorms, 114–15; religious exercises, 107; represented in *Student Body* sculpture, 209; residence selection, 73; residential communities, 119; soda fountains, 41, 46, 63, *63*, 137, 159–60, 188, 212; streaking, 209; student center, 64; student union, 112, 113; suits for men, 139; Sutton's Drug Store and, 212–13; swim test, 214; water retrieval and, 173, *174*; women's, 44, 235–36; YMCA, 41, *41*. *See also* dining; dormitories and residence halls

Student Recreation Center, 210

student services, 77, 128, 179–80

Student Stores, 78, 113, 128, 180, 194

Student Television, 210–11

Study Abroad, 211, 219, 233

Suh, Do Ho, 224

Sullivan, Ed, Show, 110

Summer Normal School, 89, 90, 177, 212

Summer Reading Program, 211–12

summer school, 99, 131, 169, 195, 212; African Americans admitted to, 132; women in, 236

SunSITE, 238

Superchunk, 56

Supremes, 43

Surgery, Department of, 35

Surhoff, B. J., 17

surveillance, electronic, 77

Sutton and Alderman's, 212

Sutton's Drug Store, 100, 212–13

Swain, David Lowry, 63–64, 65, 183, 189, 190, 206; as president, 157–58, 169, 213

Swain Hall, 67, 85, 148–49, 153, 186, 194, 213; Communication Center in, 222, 238

swimming, 12, 13, 36, 146; pools and, 30, 144–45; test for, 124, 214

Swing Building, 216

symbols, 81, 129, 166, 174, 188, 194, 220, 232

Symposium on Public Affairs, 42

tar and turpentine, 215

Tar Babies, 215

Tar Heel, 6, 36, 75, 106; on *Carolina Buccaneer*, 45; editors of, 236; on field hockey, 95; as first student newspaper, 215; on infirmary, 130; letters to, 17; origins of, 98; on Phillips Hall, 178; on School of Commerce, 141; on soccer, 197

Tar Heel Bus Tour, 45–46

Tar Heelettes, 19

Tar Heels, 215–16, 231; foot trademarked, 220

Tar Heel Tim, 187

Tarnation, 50

Tarrson, E. B. "Bud," 216

Tarrson Hall, 4, 216

Tarzan, 66

Task Force on Women at Carolina, 52

Tate, Jack, 216
Tate-Turner-Kuralt Building, 199, 216
Tau Epsilon Phi, 102
Tavern House, 88
taverns and hotels, 88–89, 89
Taylor, Dick, 89
Taylor, Isaac M., 216–17
Taylor, James (singer-songwriter), 217
Taylor, James A., 216
Taylor, John "Buck," 88
Taylor, Nelson Ferebee, 55, 217, 234
Taylor Campus Health Services Building, 216
Taylor Hall, 216–17
T. C. Thompson and Brothers, general contractors, 8
teaching, teachers, 45; training of, 89–90, 177, 212
teaching hospital, 126, 156
teach-ins, 3, 136
Teague, Claude Edward, 218
Teague Residence Hall, 14, 86, 217–18
technology, 22, 26, 32, 35, 99, 125, 146, 169, 196. See also computers
television, 99, 104, 132, 171, 186; public, 221–22; students on, 2, 110, 210–11
Tennessee, 2, 34, 107; escheated land in, 92, 164
tennis, 12, 13, 69–70, 136
Texas, 82, 186
textbooks, 29, 77, 78, 135, 161–62, 205
textile industry, 53, 69, 146, 201, 206, 224
theatre, theatres, 1, 50, 51, 99–100, 100, 108, 181
This Is Spinal Tap (1984 movie), 228
Thornton, Mary Lindsay, 169
Thorp, H. Holden, 55
Thorp Faculty Engaged Scholars, 46
Thurston, D. Jones "Doc," Jr., 218
Thurston-Bowles Building, 218

Tin Can, 95, 218
Title IX: women's sports and, 12, 218–19; women's student government and, 235
Tobacco Growers Association, 116
Toronto Exchange, 219
Town and Campus, 139
Town Girls Association, 219–20
town-gown relations, 33, 50, 227, 235
track and field, 12, 13, 89, 90–91, 95, 175
trademarks. See licensing and trademarks
tradition, traditions: Bibles for seniors, 190; Class Day ceremonies, 81; football and, 98; Homecoming, 123–24, 217; last day of class streak, 209; legends and, 122; oldest, 84; "Old Well Sing," 1; of public service, 45; of secret societies, 110; senior class gifts, 64–65, 195, 209, 225; senior bell tower climb, 24; Senior Walk, 195; at sporting events, 60; Springfest, 204–5; Sutton's Drug Store student photos, 212–13; Teague Hall and, 217; University Day, 6, 8, 43, 158, 197, 222, 223, 223
trees, 21; cherries in McCorkle Place, 62; in Coker Arboretum, 65–66; in Coker Pinetum, 157; Davie Poplar, 79–81, 80, 154; Hamilton Hall oak, 117; hedges and, 120; pitch pine, 215; as senior class gifts, 64; shade, 180; sugar maples along Cameron Avenue, 40; Trysting Poplar, 21; tulip poplar, 79. See also North Carolina Botanical Garden
Triangle University Computation Center, 134
Trinity College. See Duke University
Troll's (bar), 119
trustees. See Board of Trustees
Tufnel, Nigel, 228
tuition, 24, 220

Tulane University, 5
Turner, John, 216
Turner, Tina, 82

UNC Exchange Program, 211
UNC-Greensboro, 15, 29, 54, 72, 105, 137, 155, 211, 221, 222
UNC Health Care System, 127
UNC Hospitals, 127
UNC Latinx Center, 1
UNC System, 29; Board of Governors of, 29, 72, 148, 221; chancellors of, 54–55, 72; Consolidation and, 91, 128; governance of, 28–29; medical education and, 156; office of, 9, 55; officers of, 43; presidents of, 49, 72, 86, 103, 114, 203, 218, 221, 230; Sanders and, 145; UNC Press in, 223
UNC-TV, 104, 186, 221–22
undergraduates, 70, 160; African Americans as, 132, 205; archaeology and, 88–89; on Board of Trustees, 210; College of Arts and Sciences and, 66; Health Sciences Library and, 119; Honors Carolina and, 124; House Library and, 77, 127–28; personal computers and, 69; publications of, 45, 54; research by, 67; revised curriculum of, 99; in student government, 209; in study abroad programs, 211
Unheard Voices, 48
Union Carbide Company, 141, 160
Union troops, 213
United Daughters of the Confederacy (UDC), 70, 101
United Nations, 114
UNIVAC 1105, 68, 69
University Archives, 232
University Award for the Advancement of Women, 204
University Brass Band, 154
University Club of Chapel Hill, 12, 17

University Day Celebration, 6, 8, 43, 158, 197, 222; JFK at, 223, 223
University Inn, 88, 89
University Institute of Fisheries Research, 131
University Laundry, 34, 58–59, 59
University Library, 48, 150, 232
University Motel, 96
University of Georgia, 6, 96, 97, 143, 209
University of Lyon, 211
University of North Carolina Press, 8, 36, 115, 160, 222–23, 232; home of, 33, 121
University of Toronto, 219
University of Virginia, 5, 20, 231; as chief football rival, 98, 143
University Railroad, 224, 226
Unsung Founders Memorial, 64, 154, 197, 224, 225
Upendo Lounge, 224–25
U.S. Census Bureau, 68
U.S. Civil Aeronautics Agency, 125
U.S. Congress, 79, 150; alumni in, 73, 152, 206, 228
U.S. Constitution, 79; First Amendment of, 191, 212; Fifth Amendment of, 202
U.S. Department of Housing, Education, and Welfare, 103
U.S. government, Title IX and, 218–19
U.S. Green Building Council, 53
U.S. Naval Academy, 234
U.S. Navy: on campus during World War II, 30, 39, 115, 137, 139, 144–45, 158, 159, 165–66, 166, 184, 194, 214; ROTC and, 74, 192; secretary of, 78. See also Naval Armory; Navy, U.S., pre-flight school; Navy Field; Navy ROTC
U.S. News & World Report rankings, 131
U.S. senators, 113, 114, 161–62, 240; alumni as, 152, 228

U.S. Supreme Court, 2, 176
utilities, 226–27
Utley, Benton, 88
Utley, Martha, 88

valedictorians, 177
Vance, Zebulon Baird, 228
Vance Hall, 21, 86, 228
Vandermint Auditorium in *This Is Spinal Tap*, 228
Van Hecke, Maurice Taylor, 228
Van Hecke–Wettach Hall, 148, 153, 228–29
Varley's, 139
Varsity Theatre, 97, 100
Vaughn and Nancy Bryson Field, 30
Venable. *See* Carrboro
Venable, Francis Preston, 61–62, 70, 113, 183, 230
Venable and Murray Halls, 229–30
Venable Hall (first), 229, *229*
Venable Hall, 54, 62, 128
Venus de Milo, 64
Victory Bell, 230
Victory Gong, 73
Victory Village, 171, 230
Vietnam War, 192; protests against, 3, 42, 196, 217
Village Cemetery. *See* Old Chapel Hill Cemetery
Virginia, 149
Virginia Christian College, 18
volleyball, 12, 43
volunteerism, volunteers, 5, 221, 237

Wachovia Bank, 118
Wake Forest University, 13, 30, 86, 98
walkways and sidewalks, 31, *32*, 56, 65, 66, 126, 203, *203*
Wallace, Daniel, 74
Wallace, Patricia, 237
Walter Royal Davis Library, 81–82, 217
Washington, D.C., 105
Waters, Muddy, 139
Watkins, Lulie, 236

WCAR radio station, 238
Web and the Rock, The (Thomas Wolfe), 184
Weiss, Walt, 17
West Cameron Avenue, 111
West End. *See* Carrboro
West Rosemary Street, 59
Wettach, Robert H., 228
What to Expect When You're Expecting @ UNC, 52
White, Edward Higgins, II, *11*
White and Blue, 75
Whitehead, Richard Henry, 231
Whitehead Hall, 231
White House, students at, 1–2, 50
White Phantoms, 18, 215, 231
white supremacy, 15, 26, 46, 53, 70, 71, 78, 116, 118, 143, 159, 161, 204, 234
Wilburn, Frank, 8
Wilkinson, Frank, 121, 202–3, *203*
William and Ida Friday Center for Continuing Education. *See* Friday Center
William R. Kenan Jr. Professorships, 142
Williams, Cheryl, 9
Williams, Delmar, 123
Williams, Horace, 21, 110, 125, 184
Williams, Ken, 9
Williams, Robin, 176
Williams, Roy, 19, 82, 139–40, 147
Williams, Ted, 125, 165
Williams, William Carlos, 72
Williamsburg, Va., 31
Williams Field. *See* Anderson Stadium
Williamson, Harry, 175
Wilmington, 108, 122; 1898 coup in, 78, 143
Wilson, Henry Van Peters, 231–32
Wilson, John, 70
Wilson, Louis Round, 87, 131, 222, 232–33
Wilson, Woodrow, 78

Wilson Hall, 231–32

Wilson Library, 3, 23, 54, 58, 81, 87, 117, 120, 121, 131, 150, 169, 176, 182, 191, 233, 233; bookstore in, 34, 35; renovation of, 217, 227; slavery exhibit in, 197; Southern Historical Collection and, 118, 213; special collections in, 44, 232

Wilson Special Collections Library, 169, 201, 232

Wilson Street, 9, 46

Winston, George Tayloe, 183, 234

Winston, James Horner, 233

Winston House, 233

Winston Residence Hall, 71, 234

Winston-Salem, 25, 30, 118, 156

Wolfe, Thomas, 49, 50, 73; as *Daily Tar Heel* editor, 77; *Look Homeward Angel*, 184; *The Web and the Rock*, 115; as yearbook editor, 239

Womack, Dr. Nathan A., 35–36

Womack Surgical Society, 35–36

women, 1–2, 52, 84, 102, 109, 110, 155, 217; admittance of, 5, 218–19, 234–36; athletics and, 9, 12, 14, 19, 21, 43, 94, 95, 96, 135, 147, 175; on Board of Trustees, 29; as Chapel Hill residents, 219–20; as cheerleaders, 60; in coed dorms, 122, 161, 236; dean of, 234, 235, 236; as deans, 131; dormitories for, 5, 86, 115, 137, 142, 153, 155, 176, 192, 197, 203, 234, 236; empowerment of, 52; on faculty, 16, 90; first building named after, 197; in fraternities, 205; in Golden Fleece, 110; honors and awards for, 204; as lawyers, 229; as Morehead-Cain Scholarship recipients, 160; in Nursing School, 170; physical education and, 179; public education of, 204; rights of, 103; in sororities, 102, 102; as state supreme court chief justices, 148; in student government, 93, 210; in summer school, 212, 235; in Town Girls Association, 219–20; unequal rules for, 43–44, 235–36; violence against, 66, 70, 93; Women's Studies Department and, 39; YWCA and, 190

Women's and Gender Studies, Department of, 197

Women's Athletic Association, 12, 219

Women's Council, 235

Women's/Gender Week, 52

Women's Glee Club, 110

Women's Handbook, 235

Women's Hospital, 127

Women's Issue Network, 52

women's rules, 43–44, 235–36

women's sports, and Title IX, 218–19

Women's Studies, Department of, 39

Woodhouse, E. J., 50

Woodward, John, 212

Woollen, Charles T., 43, 236–37

Woollen Gym, 18, 36, 43, 192, 210, 218, 236–37; pool in, 30

World Cup soccer, 199

World Health Organization, 16

World War I, 68, 84, 118, 179, 197

World War II, 12, 85, 90, 98, 114, 128, 186, 191; expansion after, 51, 71, 86, 108, 113, 128, 137, 230; overcrowding during, 218; physical education and, 214; POWs during, 165, 184; ROTC and, 192; U.S. Navy on campus during, 30, 39, 115, 125, 137, 144, 158, 159, 163, 165–66, 194

Worthy, James, 19

WPA (Works Progress Administration), 95, 99, 145, 191

WRAL TV, 240

wrestling, 12, 13, 43

writers, writing, 72, 73–74, 134–35, 151, 204

Writing Center, 67

WUNC 91.5 FM Radio, 186, 237, 237–38

WUNC-TV, 221–22
WXYC radio station, 238
Wynn, Earl, 186, 222

Yackety Yack, 27, *38*, 60, 101, 112, 239
"Yackety Yack" (cheer), 60
Yacovelli v. Moeser, 191, 212
Yale University, 61, 109, 159, 178
Yankee Stadium, 99
Year at Lyons study abroad program, 211
yearbooks, 239; photos for, 212, 239
Yesulaitis, John, 154

YMCA (Young Men's Christian Association), 41–42, 179, 190
Young, Andrew, 161
YUVA (Youth for Unity, Virtues and Action), 122–23
YWCA (Young Women's Christian Association), 41–42, 190

Zeta Phi Beta Sorority, Inc., 164
Zoo, Carolina's, 38
zoo, UNC as, 240
Zoology, Department of, 66, 79, 231
Zoom Zoom Room, 79